AWA UPSHOT

PRESENTS

the Joneses

MICHAEL MORECI
WRITER

ALESSANDRO VITTI
ARTIST

IVE SVORCINA
COLORIST

SAL CIPRIANO
LETTERER

JOHN GALLAGHER
COVER ARTIST

MIKE DEODATO JR. AND LEE LOUGHRIDGE
COLLECTION COVER ARTISTS

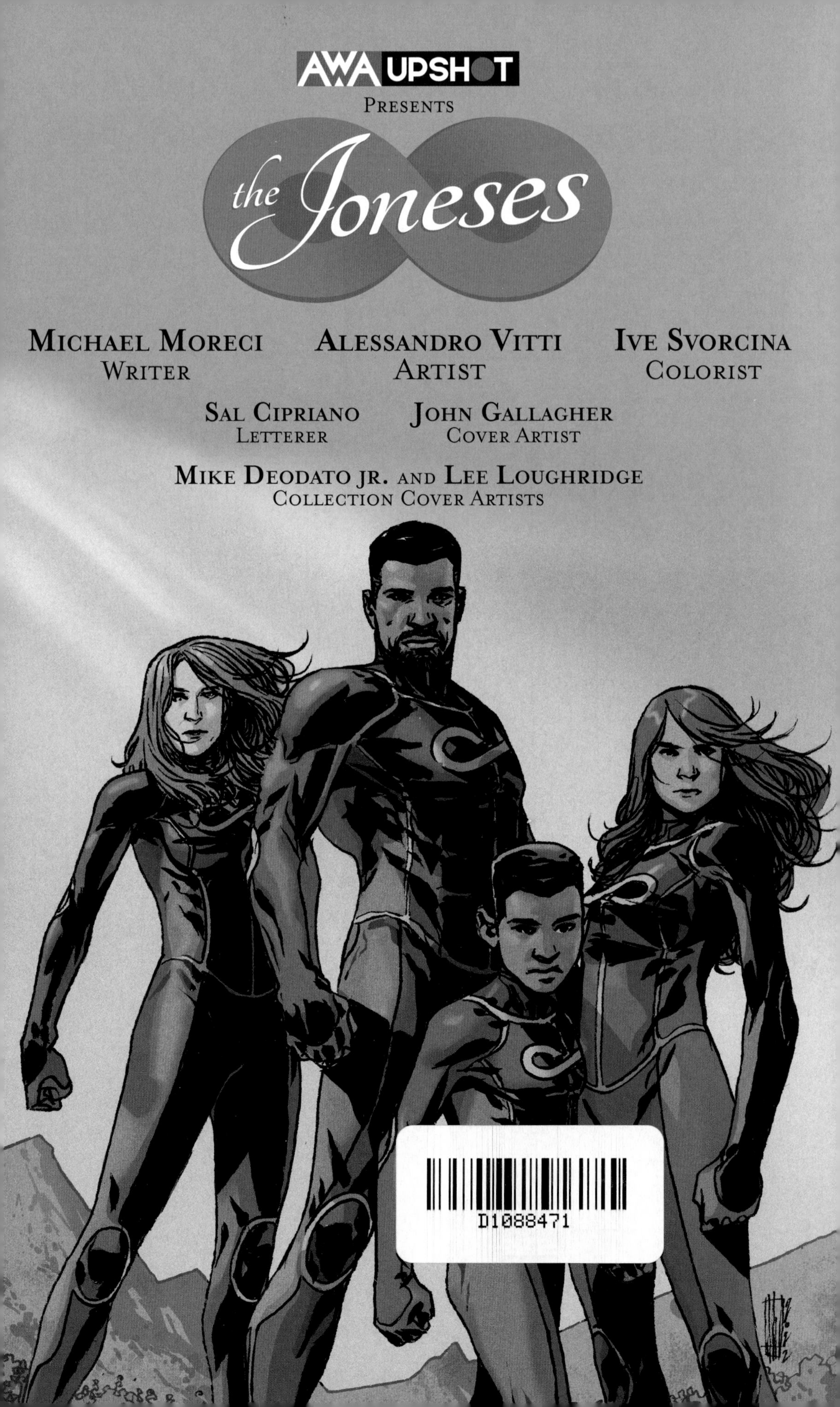

 UPSHOT   @AWA_studios   @awastudiosofficial    @awastudiosofficial   awastudios.net

Axel Alonso Chief Creative Officer
Matthew Anderson Co-Chair & President
Ariane Baya Financial Controller
Chris Burns Production Editor
Ramsee Chand AWA Studios Assistant
Thea Cheuk Assistant Editor
Michael Coast Senior Editor
Bob Cohen EVP, General Counsel
Michael Cotton Executive Editor

Chris Ferguson Art Director
Frank Fochetta Senior Consultant, Sales & Distribution
Jackie Liu Digital Marketing Manager
Dulce Montoya Associate Editor
Kevin Park Associate General Counsel
Andrew Serwin Managing Editor
Daphney Stephen Accounting Assistant
Zach Studin President, AWA Studios

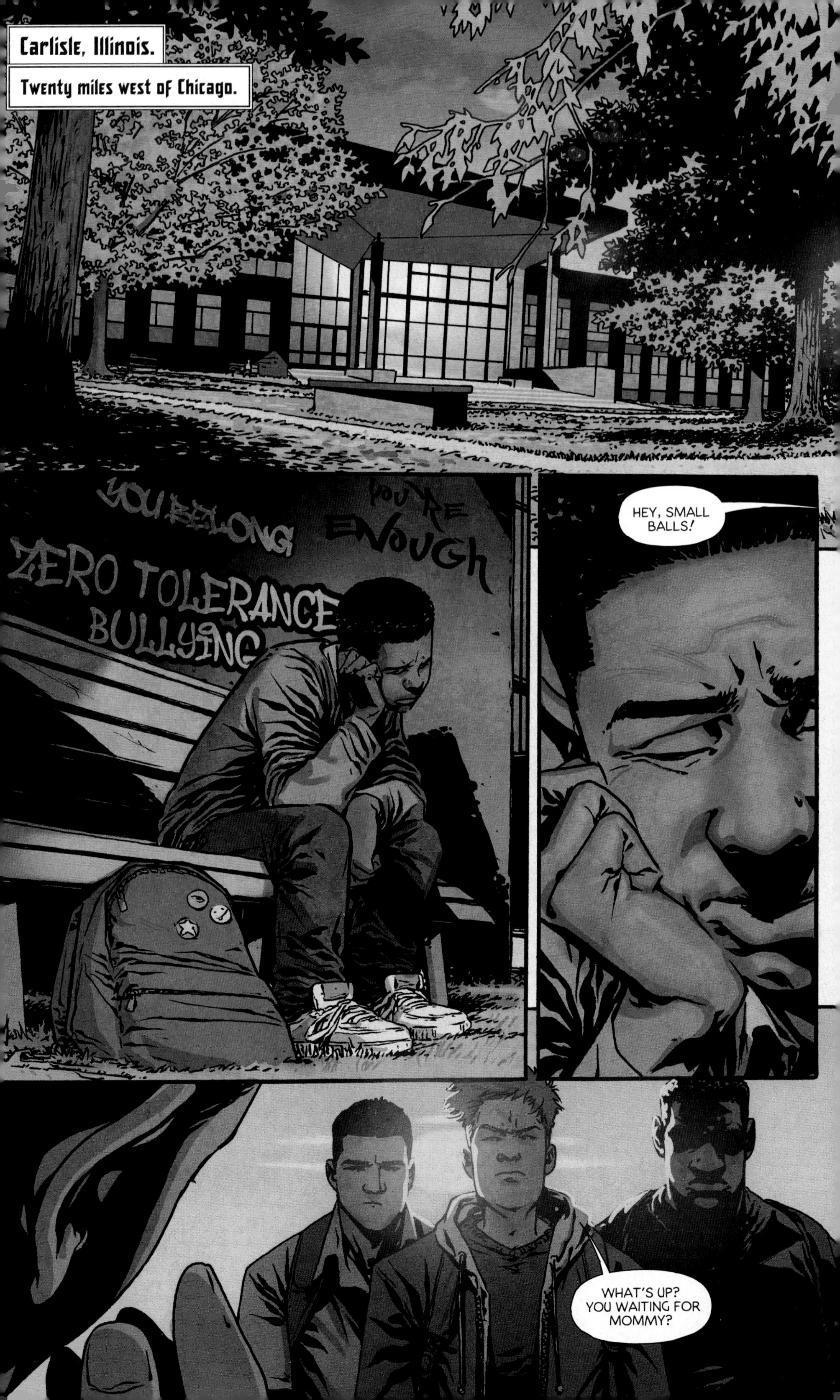

Carlisle, Illinois.
Twenty miles west of Chicago.
YOU BELONG
YOU'RE ENOUGH
ZERO TOLERANCE BULLYING
HEY, SMALL BALLS!
WHAT'S UP? YOU WAITING FOR MOMMY?

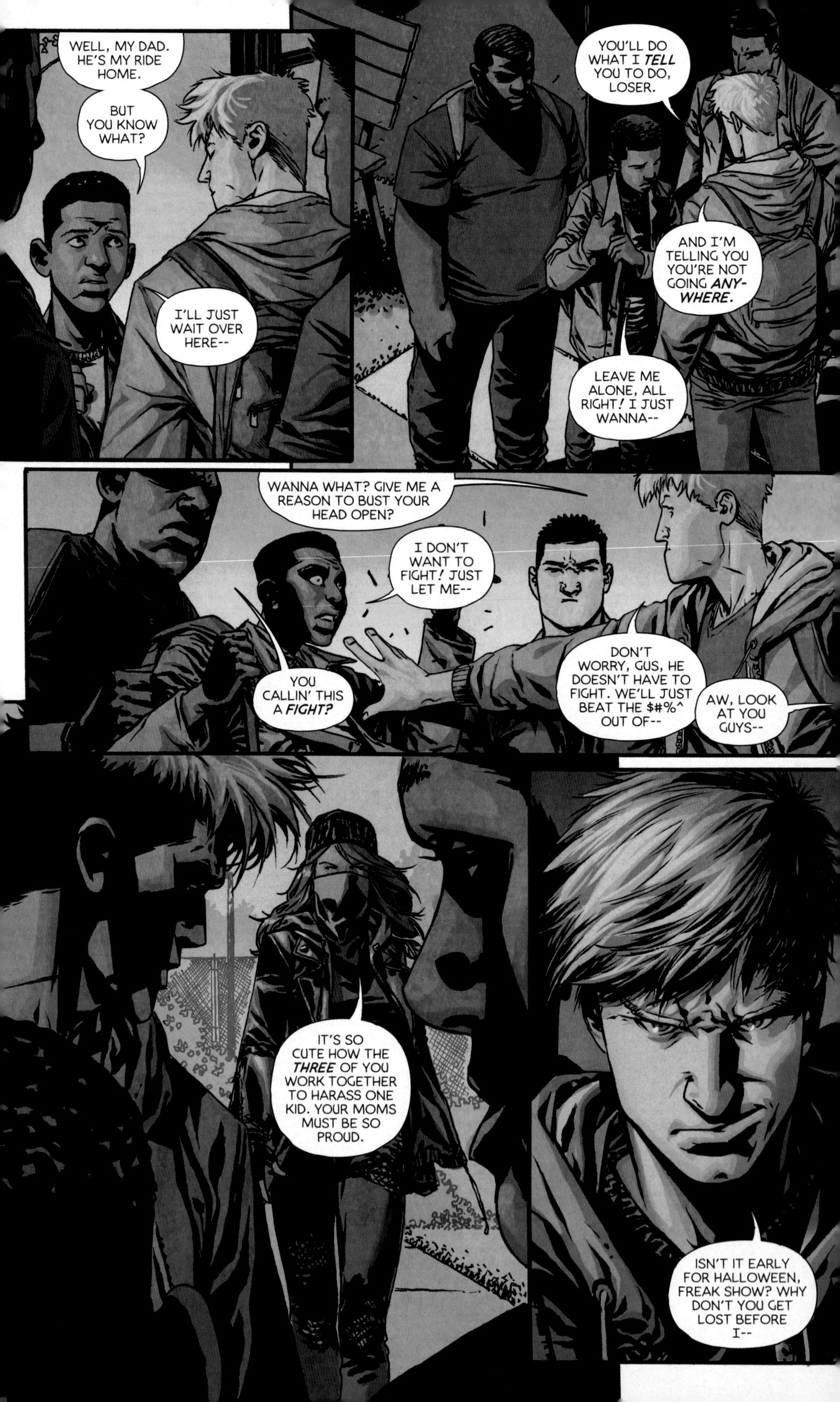
WELL, MY DAD. HE'S MY RIDE HOME.
BUT YOU KNOW WHAT?
I'LL JUST WAIT OVER HERE--
YOU'LL DO WHAT I *TELL* YOU TO DO, LOSER.
AND I'M TELLING YOU YOU'RE NOT GOING *ANYWHERE.*
LEAVE ME ALONE, ALL RIGHT! I JUST WANNA--
WANNA WHAT? GIVE ME A REASON TO BUST YOUR HEAD OPEN?
I DON'T WANT TO FIGHT! JUST LET ME--
YOU CALLIN' THIS A *FIGHT?*
DON'T WORRY, GUS, HE DOESN'T HAVE TO FIGHT. WE'LL JUST BEAT THE $#%^ OUT OF--
AW, LOOK AT YOU GUYS--
IT'S SO CUTE HOW THE *THREE* OF YOU WORK TOGETHER TO HARASS ONE KID. YOUR MOMS MUST BE SO PROUD.
ISN'T IT EARLY FOR HALLOWEEN, FREAK SHOW? WHY DON'T YOU GET LOST BEFORE I--

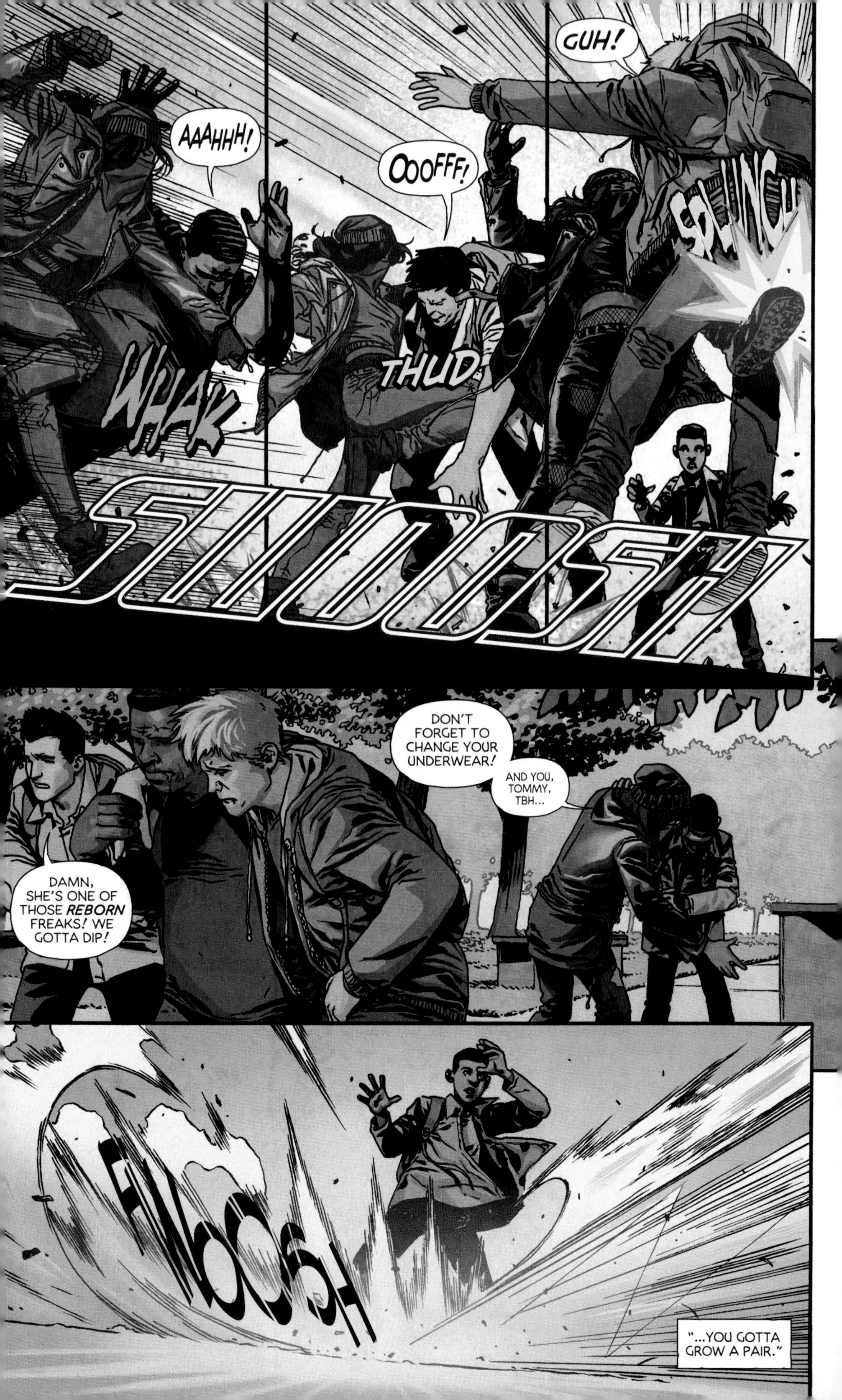
AAAHHH!
WHAK
OOOFFF!
THUD
GUH!
SHOOSH
DON'T FORGET TO CHANGE YOUR UNDERWEAR!
AND YOU, TOMMY, TBH...
DAMN, SHE'S ONE OF THOSE REBORN FREAKS! WE GOTTA DIP!
FWOOSH
"...YOU GOTTA GROW A PAIR."

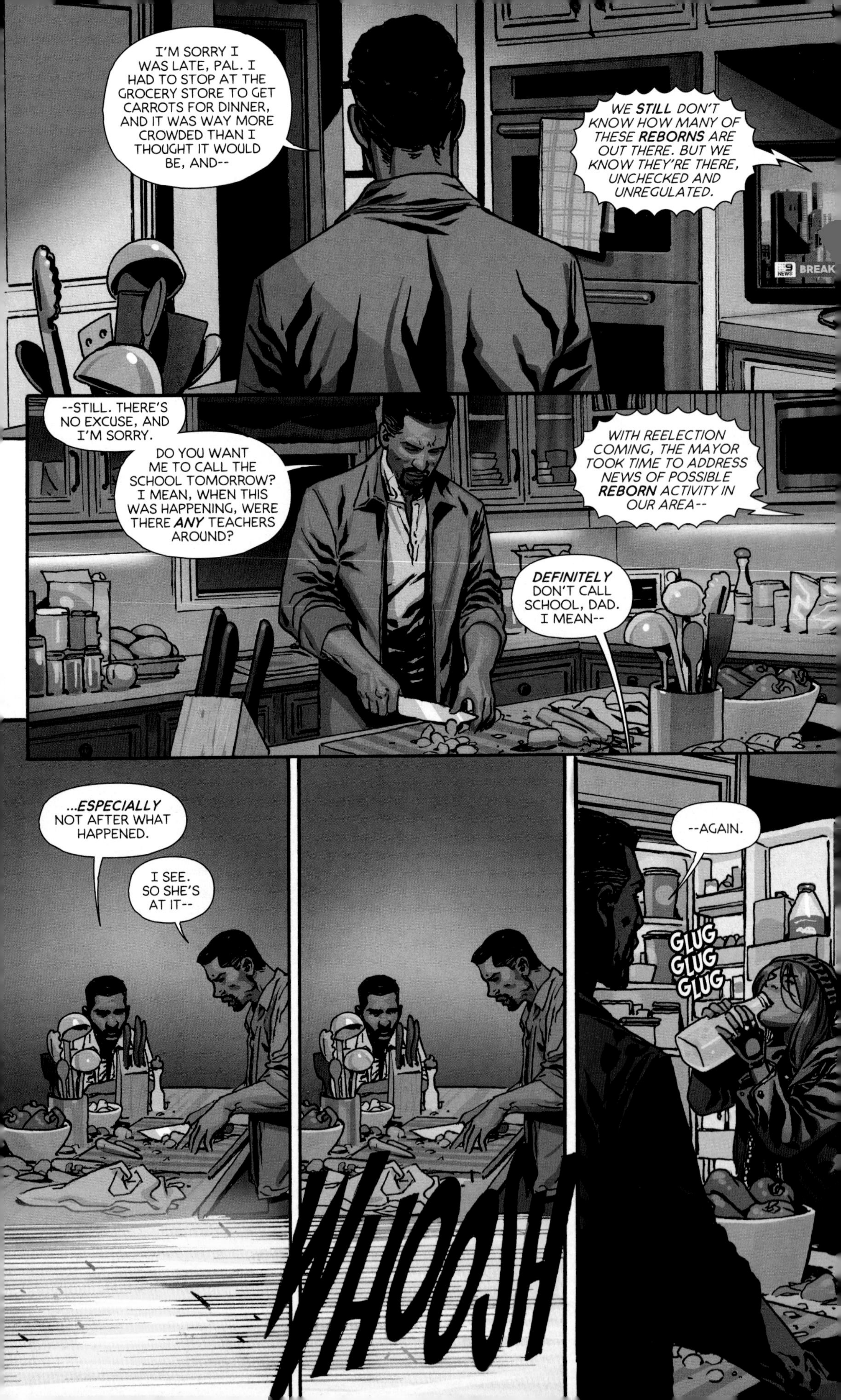
I'M SORRY I WAS LATE, PAL. I HAD TO STOP AT THE GROCERY STORE TO GET CARROTS FOR DINNER, AND IT WAS WAY MORE CROWDED THAN I THOUGHT IT WOULD BE, AND--
WE STILL DON'T KNOW HOW MANY OF THESE REBORNS ARE OUT THERE. BUT WE KNOW THEY'RE THERE, UNCHECKED AND UNREGULATED.
9 NEWS BREAK
--STILL. THERE'S NO EXCUSE, AND I'M SORRY.
DO YOU WANT ME TO CALL THE SCHOOL TOMORROW? I MEAN, WHEN THIS WAS HAPPENING, WERE THERE ANY TEACHERS AROUND?
WITH REELECTION COMING, THE MAYOR TOOK TIME TO ADDRESS NEWS OF POSSIBLE REBORN ACTIVITY IN OUR AREA--
DEFINITELY DON'T CALL SCHOOL, DAD. I MEAN--
...ESPECIALLY NOT AFTER WHAT HAPPENED.
I SEE. SO SHE'S AT IT--
WHOOSH
--AGAIN.
GLUG GLUG GLUG

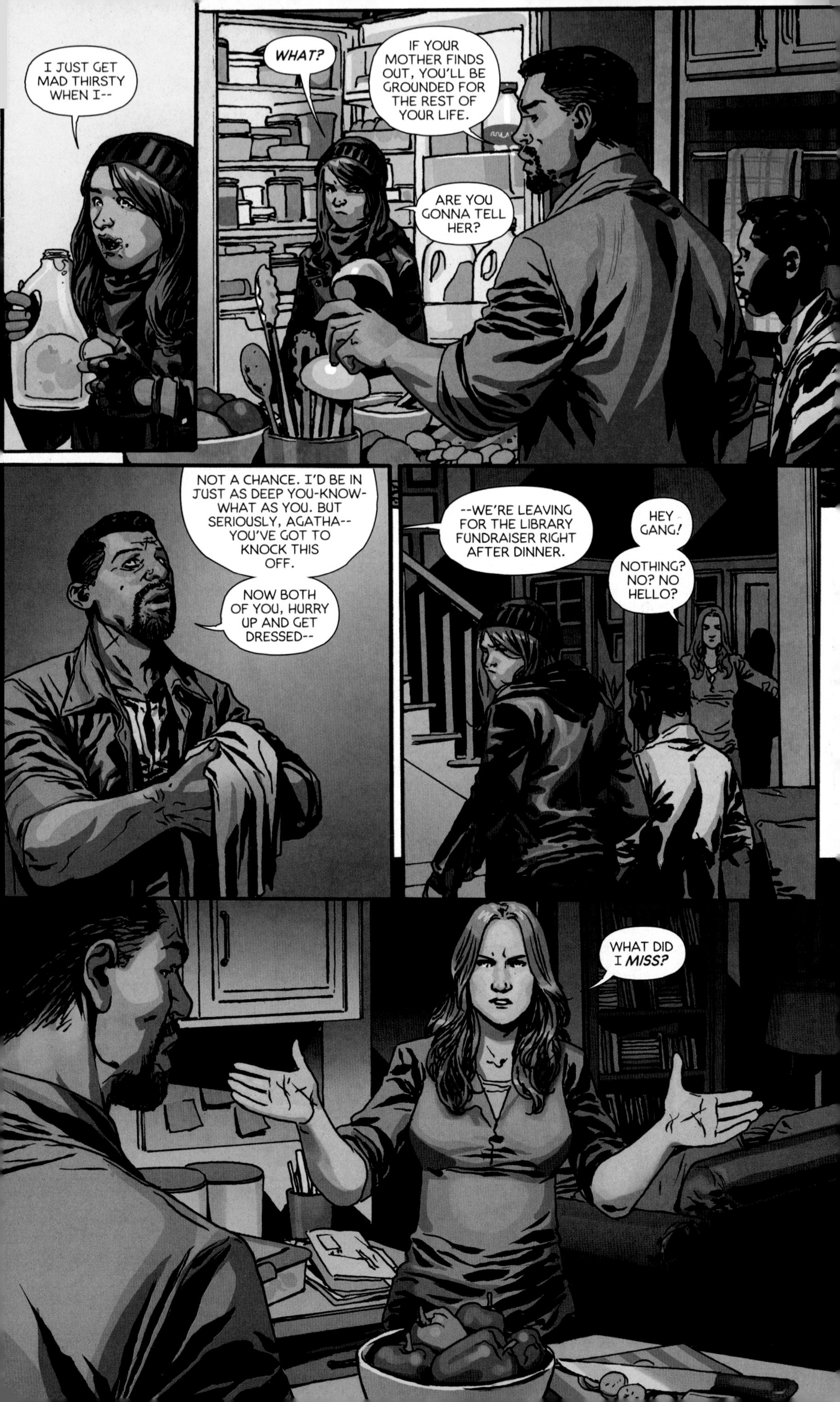
I JUST GET MAD THIRSTY WHEN I--
WHAT?
IF YOUR MOTHER FINDS OUT, YOU'LL BE GROUNDED FOR THE REST OF YOUR LIFE.
ARE YOU GONNA TELL HER?
NOT A CHANCE. I'D BE IN JUST AS DEEP YOU-KNOW-WHAT AS YOU. BUT SERIOUSLY, AGATHA-- YOU'VE GOT TO KNOCK THIS OFF.
NOW BOTH OF YOU, HURRY UP AND GET DRESSED--
--WE'RE LEAVING FOR THE LIBRARY FUNDRAISER RIGHT AFTER DINNER.
HEY GANG!
NOTHING? NO? NO HELLO?
WHAT DID I MISS?

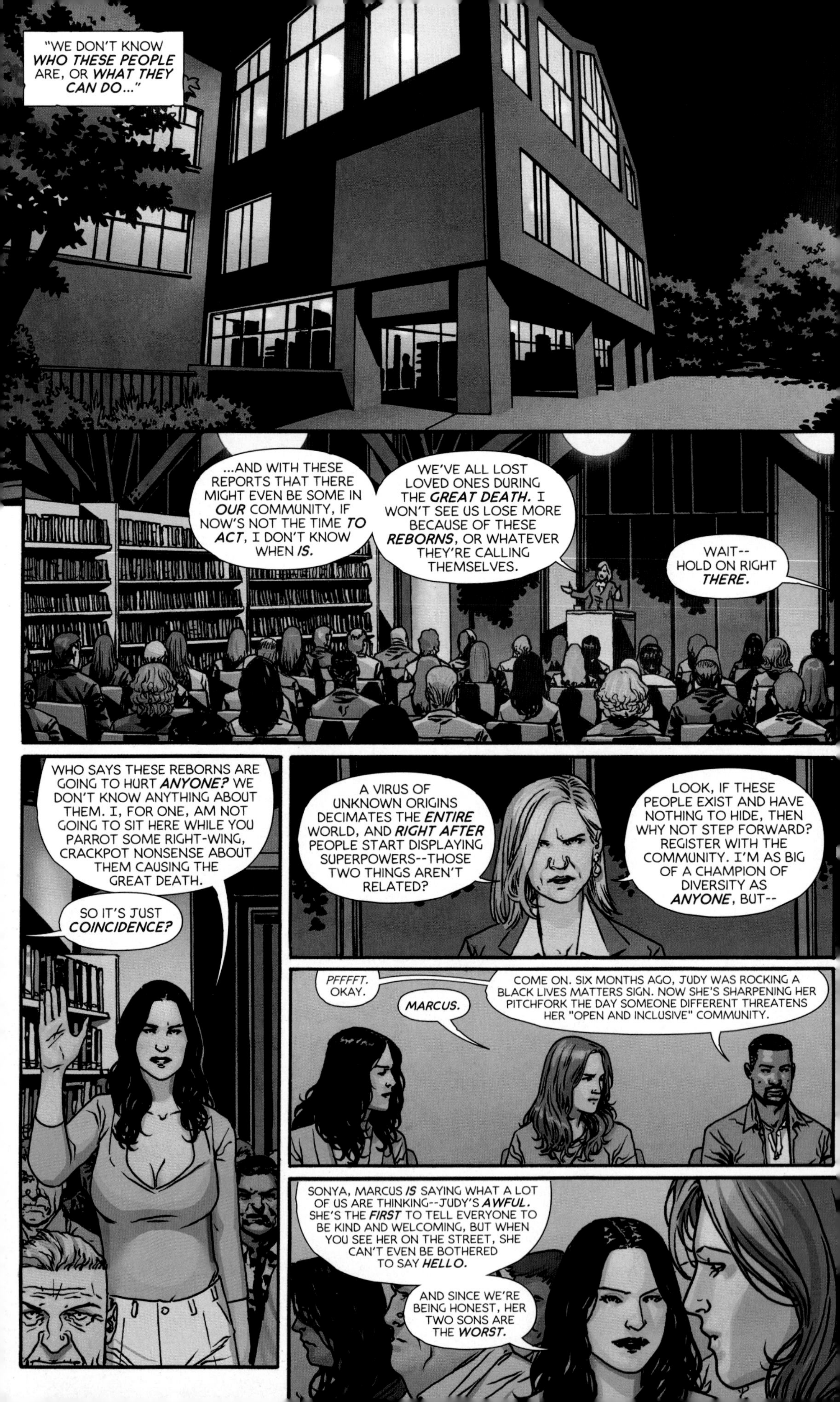
"WE DON'T KNOW *WHO THESE PEOPLE* ARE, OR *WHAT THEY CAN DO*..."
...AND WITH THESE REPORTS THAT THERE MIGHT EVEN BE SOME IN *OUR* COMMUNITY, IF NOW'S NOT THE TIME *TO ACT*, I DON'T KNOW WHEN *IS.*
WE'VE ALL LOST LOVED ONES DURING THE *GREAT DEATH.* I WON'T SEE US LOSE MORE BECAUSE OF THESE *REBORNS*, OR WHATEVER THEY'RE CALLING THEMSELVES.
WAIT-- HOLD ON RIGHT *THERE.*
WHO SAYS THESE REBORNS ARE GOING TO HURT *ANYONE?* WE DON'T KNOW ANYTHING ABOUT THEM. I, FOR ONE, AM NOT GOING TO SIT HERE WHILE YOU PARROT SOME RIGHT-WING, CRACKPOT NONSENSE ABOUT THEM CAUSING THE GREAT DEATH.
SO IT'S JUST *COINCIDENCE?*
A VIRUS OF UNKNOWN ORIGINS DECIMATES THE *ENTIRE* WORLD, AND *RIGHT AFTER* PEOPLE START DISPLAYING SUPERPOWERS--THOSE TWO THINGS AREN'T RELATED?
LOOK, IF THESE PEOPLE EXIST AND HAVE NOTHING TO HIDE, THEN WHY NOT STEP FORWARD? REGISTER WITH THE COMMUNITY. I'M AS BIG OF A CHAMPION OF DIVERSITY AS *ANYONE*, BUT--
PFFFFT. OKAY.
COME ON. SIX MONTHS AGO, JUDY WAS ROCKING A BLACK LIVES MATTERS SIGN. NOW SHE'S SHARPENING HER PITCHFORK THE DAY SOMEONE DIFFERENT THREATENS HER "OPEN AND INCLUSIVE" COMMUNITY.
MARCUS.
SONYA, MARCUS *IS* SAYING WHAT A LOT OF US ARE THINKING--JUDY'S *AWFUL.* SHE'S THE *FIRST* TO TELL EVERYONE TO BE KIND AND WELCOMING, BUT WHEN YOU SEE HER ON THE STREET, SHE CAN'T EVEN BE BOTHERED TO SAY *HELLO.*
AND SINCE WE'RE BEING HONEST, HER TWO SONS ARE THE *WORST.*

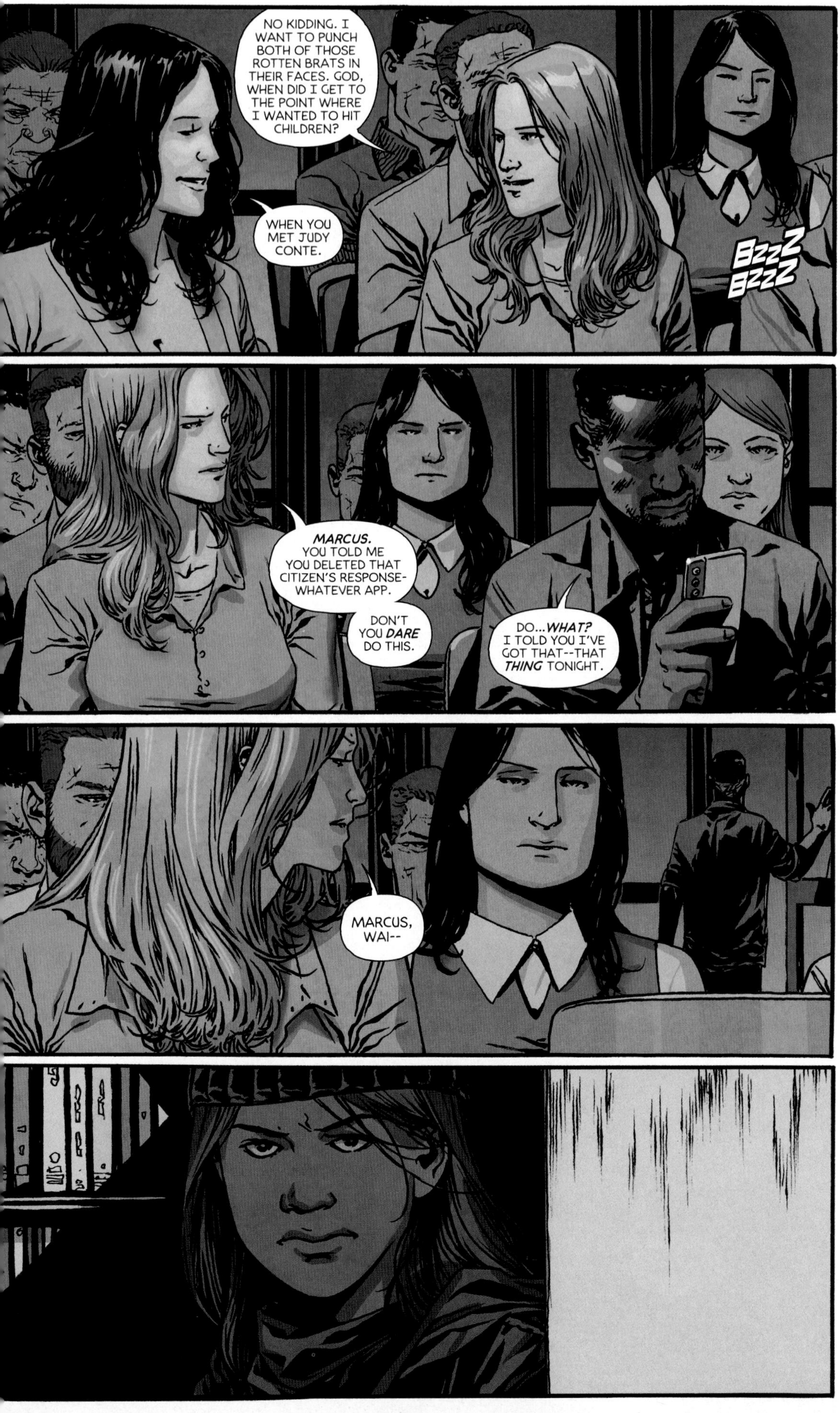
NO KIDDING. I WANT TO PUNCH BOTH OF THOSE ROTTEN BRATS IN THEIR FACES. GOD, WHEN DID I GET TO THE POINT WHERE I WANTED TO HIT CHILDREN?
WHEN YOU MET JUDY CONTE.
BzzZ BzzZ
MARCUS. YOU TOLD ME YOU DELETED THAT CITIZEN'S RESPONSE-WHATEVER APP.
DON'T YOU DARE DO THIS.
DO...WHAT? I TOLD YOU I'VE GOT THAT--THAT THING TONIGHT.
MARCUS, WAI--

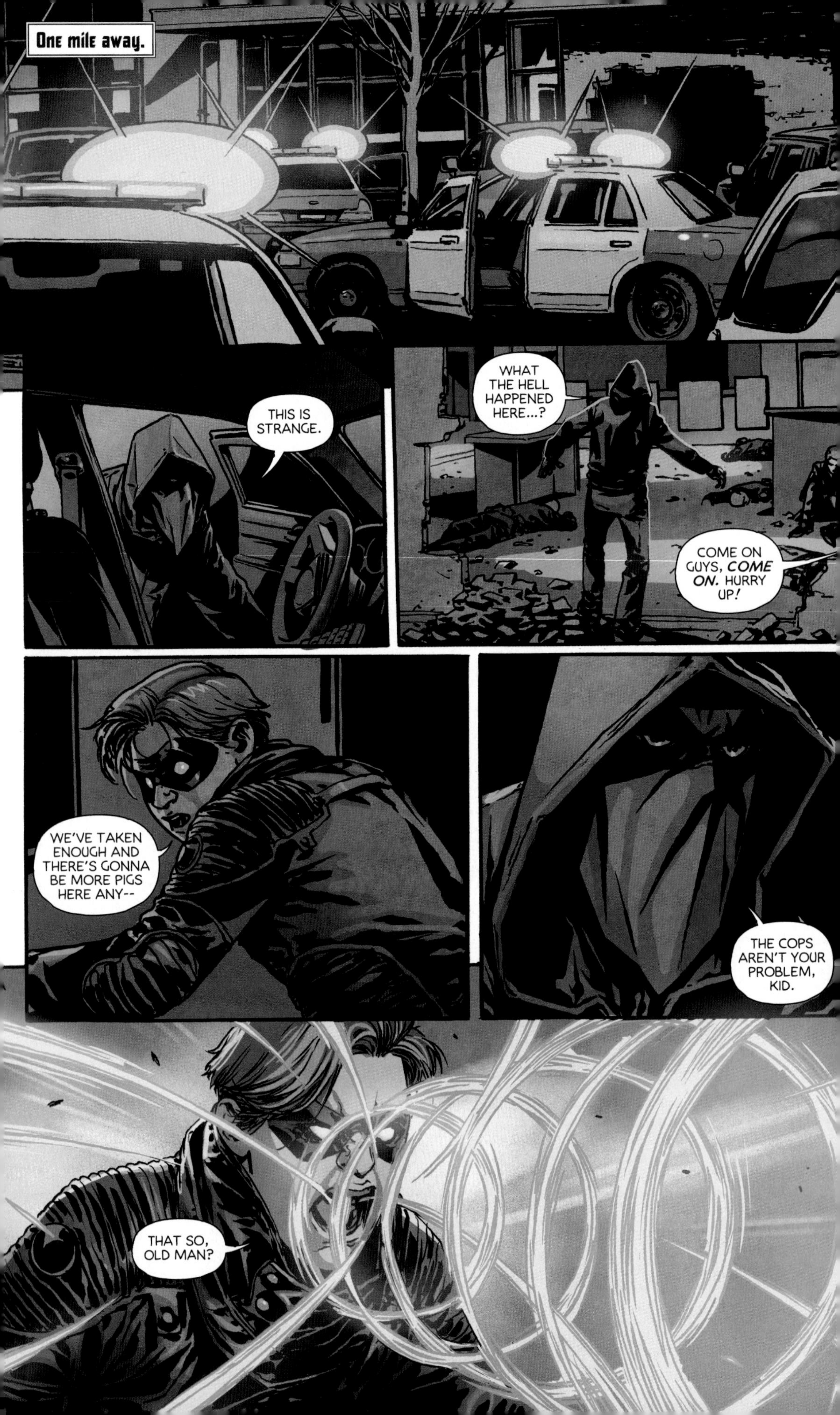
One mile away.
THIS IS STRANGE.
WHAT THE HELL HAPPENED HERE...?
COME ON GUYS, *COME ON.* HURRY UP*!*
WE'VE TAKEN ENOUGH AND THERE'S GONNA BE MORE PIGS HERE ANY--
THE COPS AREN'T YOUR PROBLEM, KID.
THAT SO, OLD MAN?

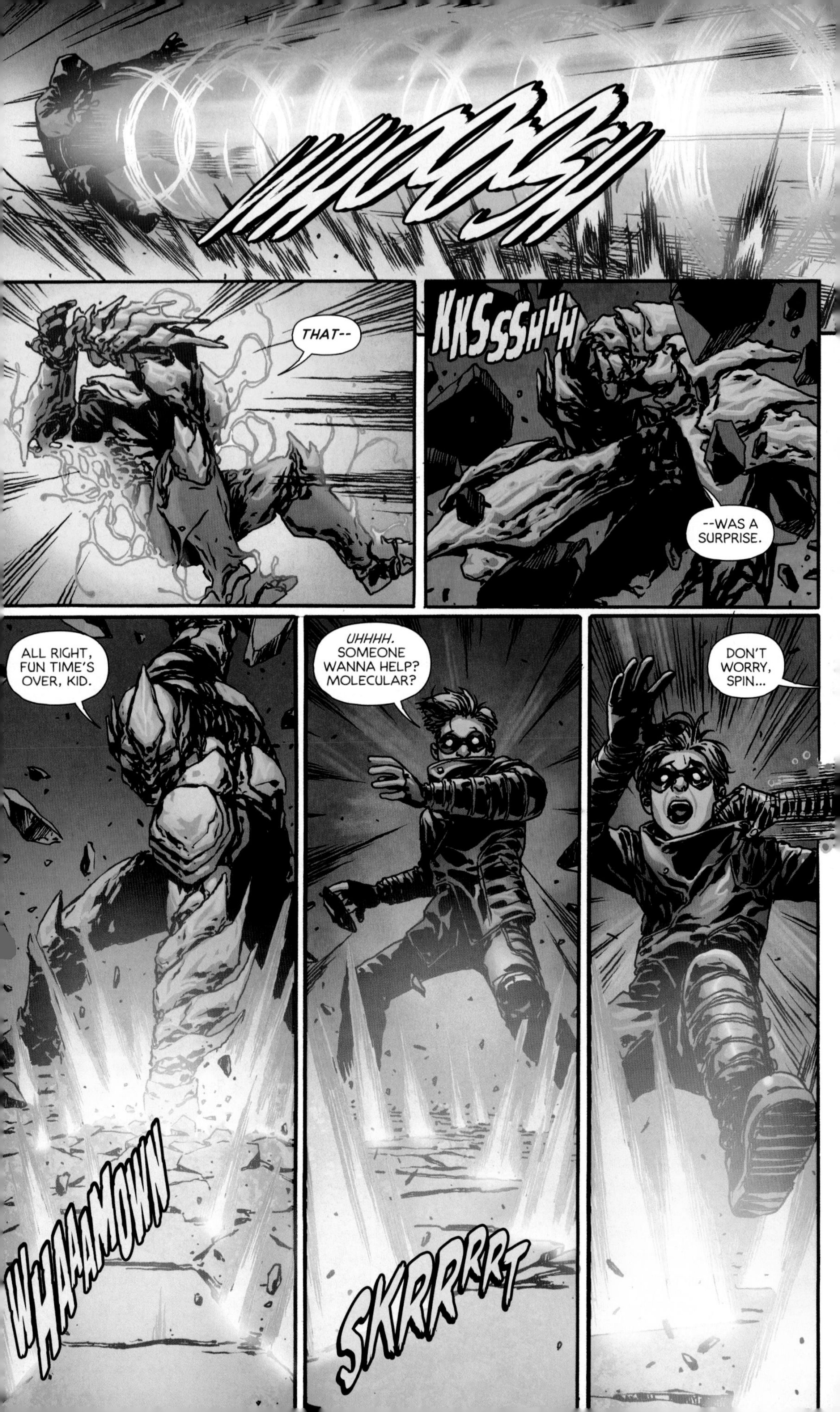
WHOOSH
THAT--
KKSSSHHH
--WAS A SURPRISE.
ALL RIGHT, FUN TIME'S OVER, KID.
WHAAAMOWN
UHHHH. SOMEONE WANNA HELP? MOLECULAR?
SKRRRRT
DON'T WORRY, SPIN...

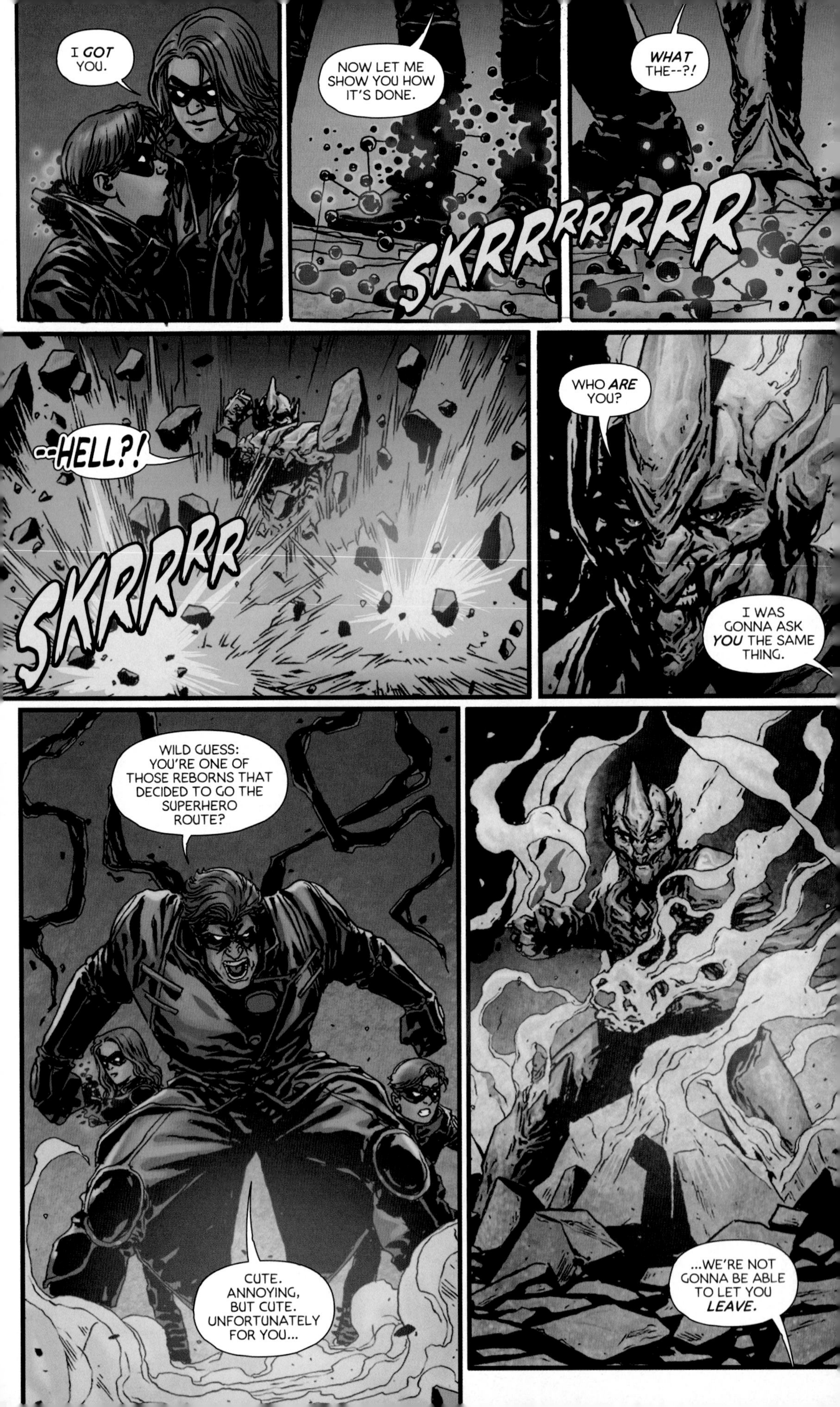
I *GOT* YOU.
NOW LET ME SHOW YOU HOW IT'S DONE.
WHAT THE--?!
SKRRRRRRRR
--HELL?!
SKRRRRR
WHO *ARE* YOU?
I WAS GONNA ASK *YOU* THE SAME THING.
WILD GUESS: YOU'RE ONE OF THOSE REBORNS THAT DECIDED TO GO THE SUPERHERO ROUTE?
CUTE. ANNOYING, BUT CUTE. UNFORTUNATELY FOR YOU...
...WE'RE NOT GONNA BE ABLE TO LET YOU *LEAVE.*

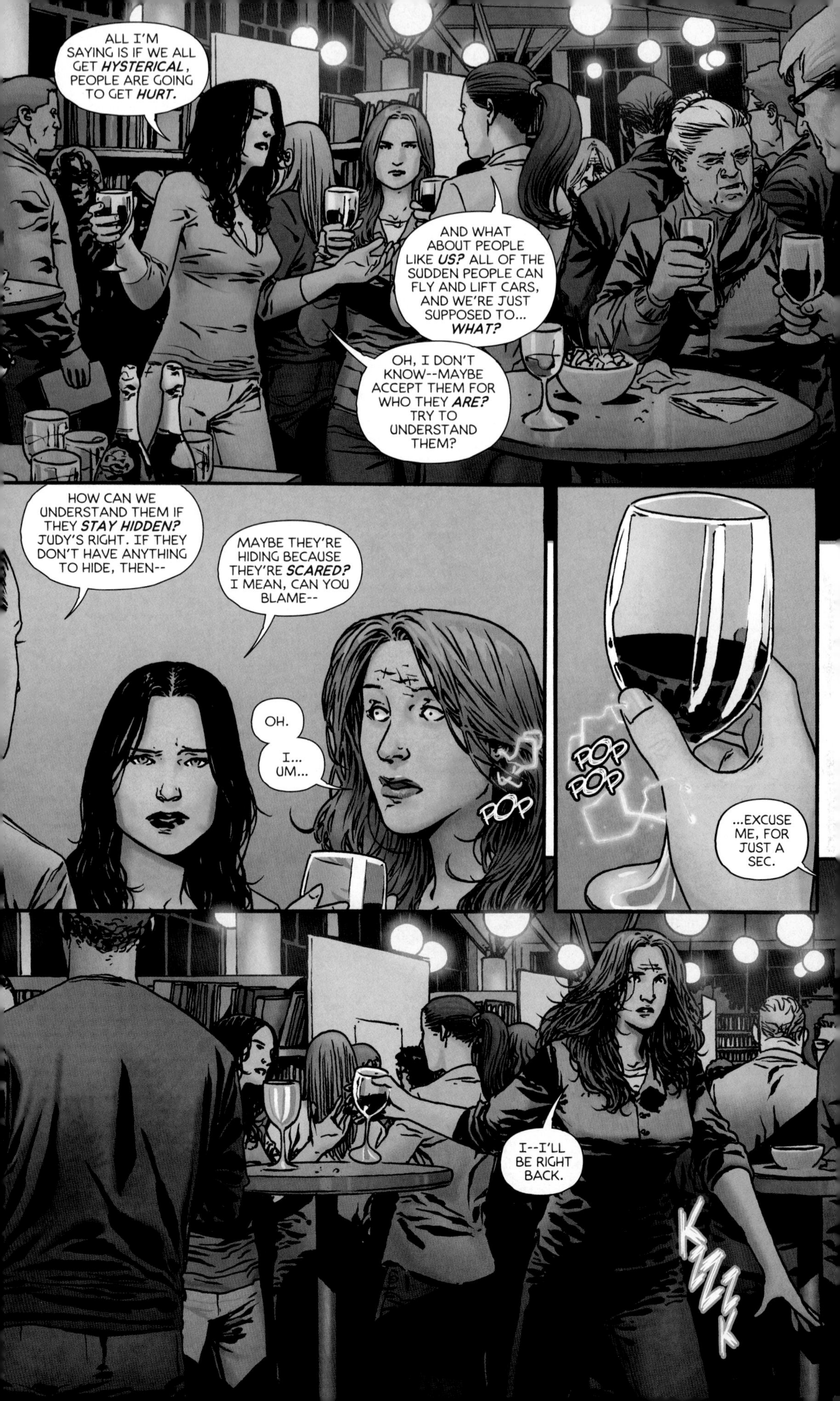

ALL I'M SAYING IS IF WE ALL GET HYSTERICAL, PEOPLE ARE GOING TO GET HURT.
AND WHAT ABOUT PEOPLE LIKE US? ALL OF THE SUDDEN PEOPLE CAN FLY AND LIFT CARS, AND WE'RE JUST SUPPOSED TO... WHAT?
OH, I DON'T KNOW--MAYBE ACCEPT THEM FOR WHO THEY ARE? TRY TO UNDERSTAND THEM?
HOW CAN WE UNDERSTAND THEM IF THEY STAY HIDDEN? JUDY'S RIGHT. IF THEY DON'T HAVE ANYTHING TO HIDE, THEN--
MAYBE THEY'RE HIDING BECAUSE THEY'RE SCARED? I MEAN, CAN YOU BLAME--
OH.
I... UM...
POP
POP POP
...EXCUSE ME, FOR JUST A SEC.
I--I'LL BE RIGHT BACK.
KZZZK

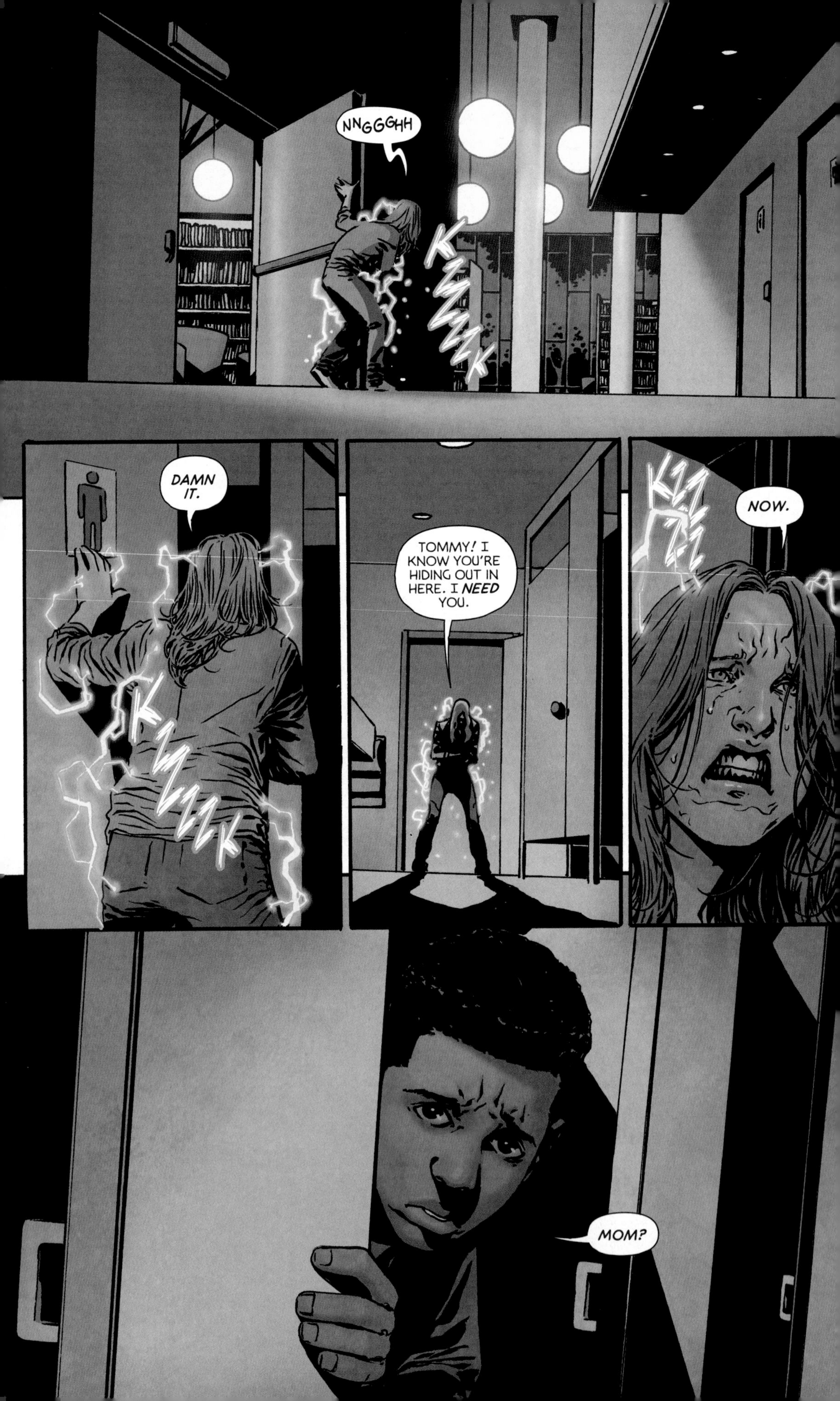

NNGGGHH
KZZZZZK
DAMN IT.
KZZZZZK
TOMMY! I KNOW YOU'RE HIDING OUT IN HERE. I *NEED* YOU.
KZZZ
NOW.
MOM?

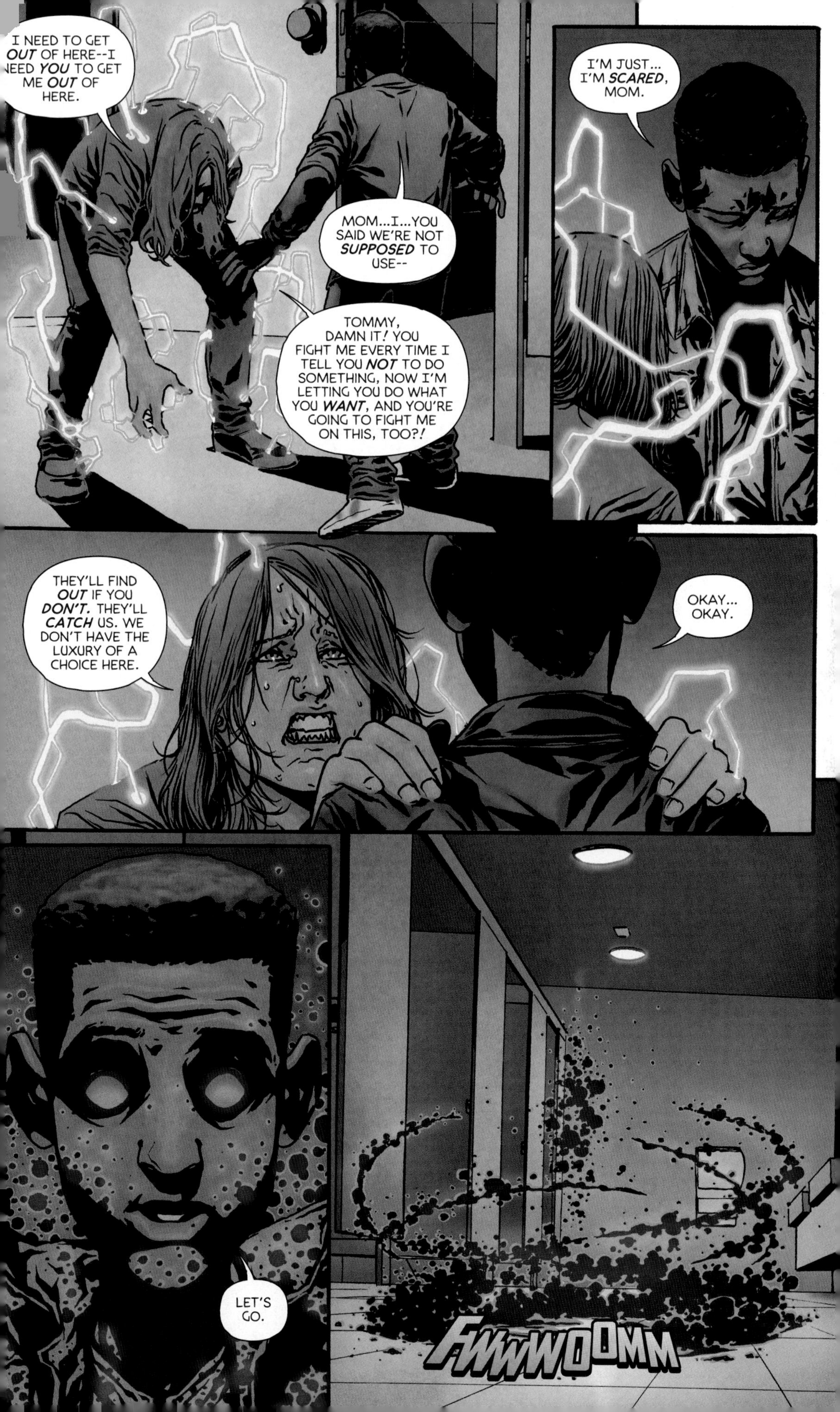
I NEED TO GET OUT OF HERE--I NEED YOU TO GET ME OUT OF HERE.
MOM...I...YOU SAID WE'RE NOT SUPPOSED TO USE--
TOMMY, DAMN IT! YOU FIGHT ME EVERY TIME I TELL YOU NOT TO DO SOMETHING, NOW I'M LETTING YOU DO WHAT YOU WANT, AND YOU'RE GOING TO FIGHT ME ON THIS, TOO?!
I'M JUST... I'M SCARED, MOM.
THEY'LL FIND OUT IF YOU DON'T. THEY'LL CATCH US. WE DON'T HAVE THE LUXURY OF A CHOICE HERE.
OKAY... OKAY.
LET'S GO.
FWWWOOMM

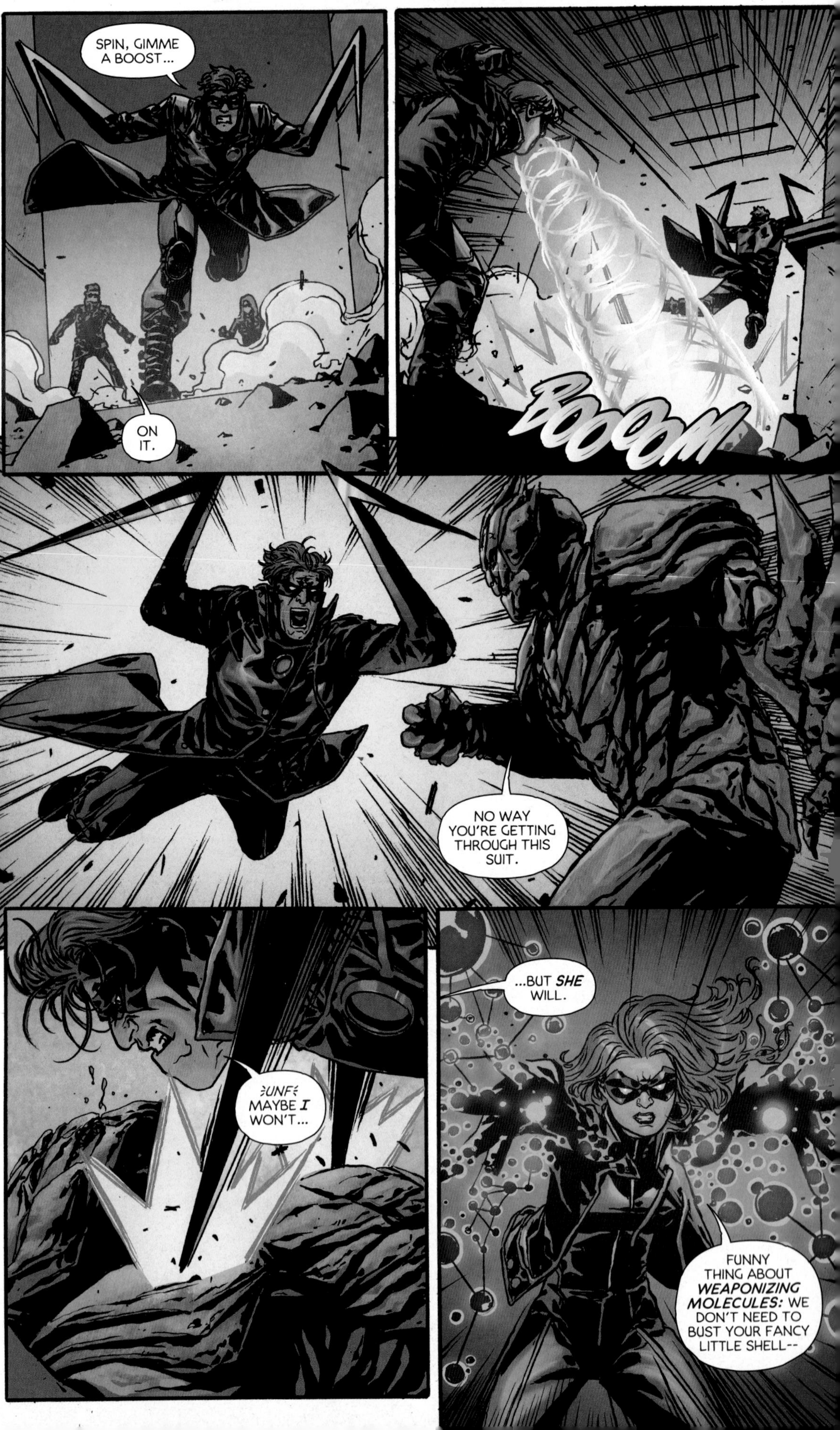
SPIN, GIMME A BOOST...
ON IT.
BOOOOM
NO WAY YOU'RE GETTING THROUGH THIS SUIT.
UNF MAYBE I WON'T...
...BUT SHE WILL.
FUNNY THING ABOUT WEAPONIZING MOLECULES: WE DON'T NEED TO BUST YOUR FANCY LITTLE SHELL--

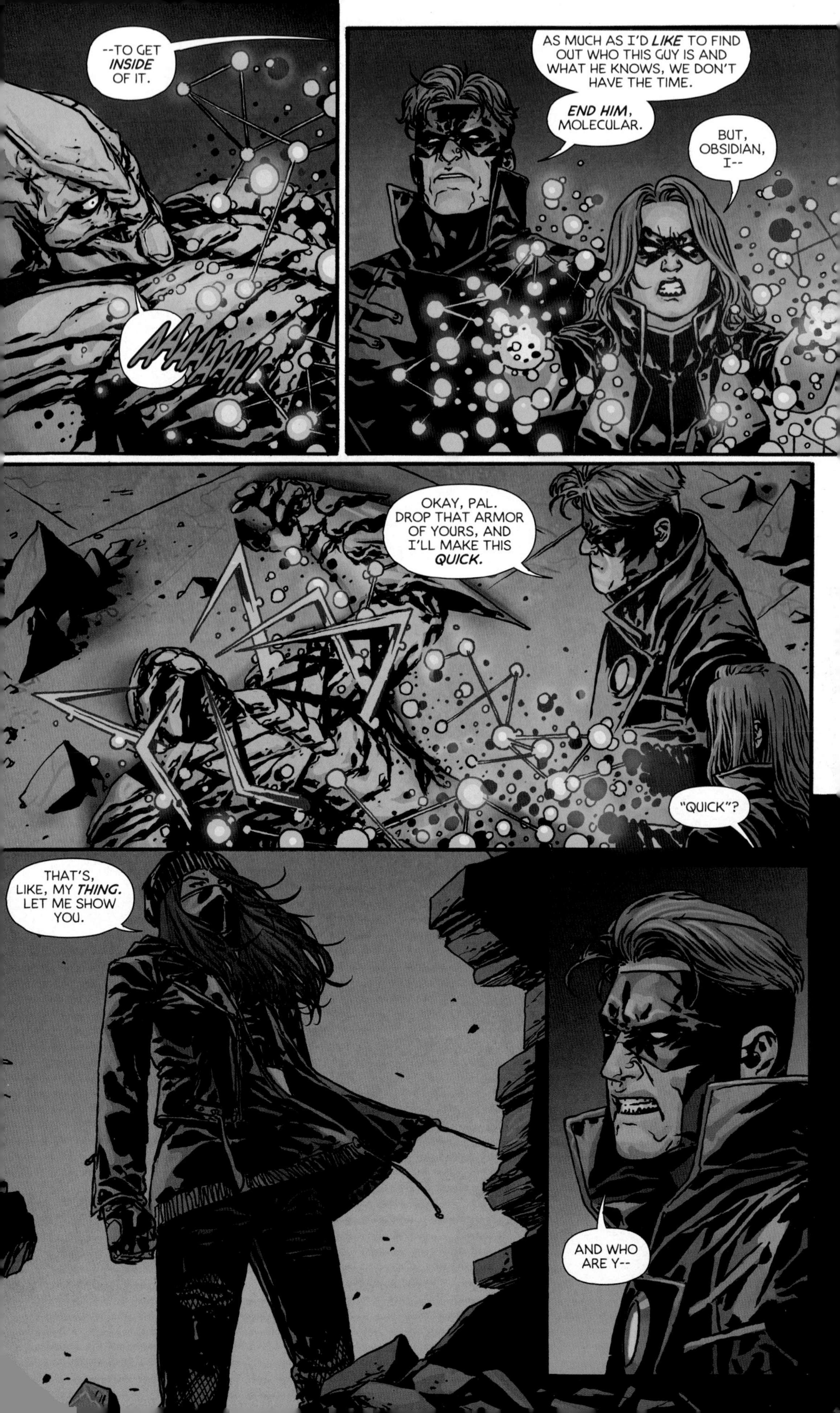
--TO GET INSIDE OF IT.
AAAAAAH!
AS MUCH AS I'D LIKE TO FIND OUT WHO THIS GUY IS AND WHAT HE KNOWS, WE DON'T HAVE THE TIME.
END HIM, MOLECULAR.
BUT, OBSIDIAN, I--
OKAY, PAL. DROP THAT ARMOR OF YOURS, AND I'LL MAKE THIS QUICK.
"QUICK"?
THAT'S, LIKE, MY THING. LET ME SHOW YOU.
AND WHO ARE Y--

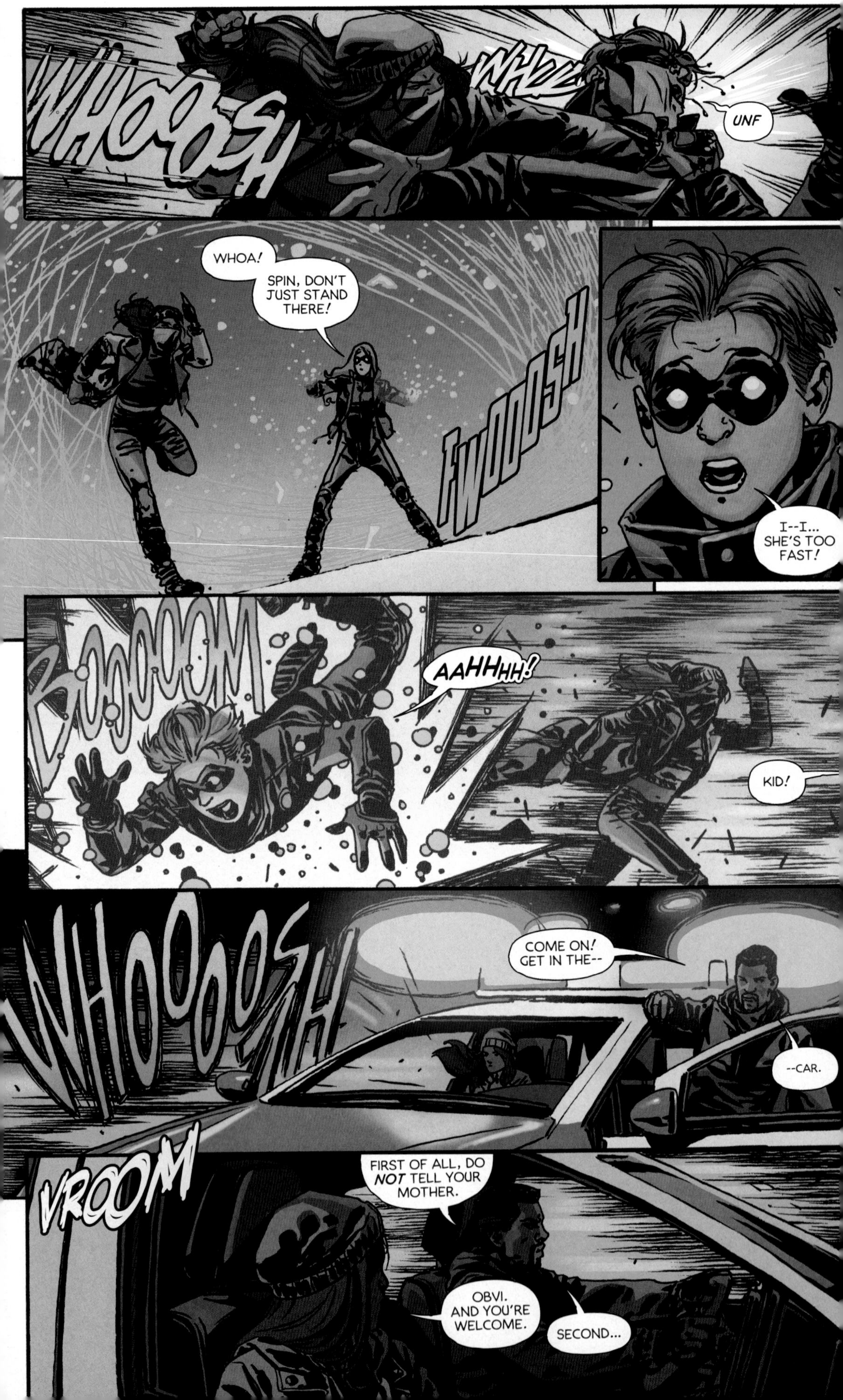
WHOOOSH
WHUMP
UNF
WHOA!
SPIN, DON'T JUST STAND THERE!
FWOOOSH
I--I... SHE'S TOO FAST!
BOOOOOM
AAHHhh!
KID!
WHOOOOSH
COME ON! GET IN THE--
--CAR.
VROOM
FIRST OF ALL, DO *NOT* TELL YOUR MOTHER.
OBVI. AND YOU'RE WELCOME.
SECOND...

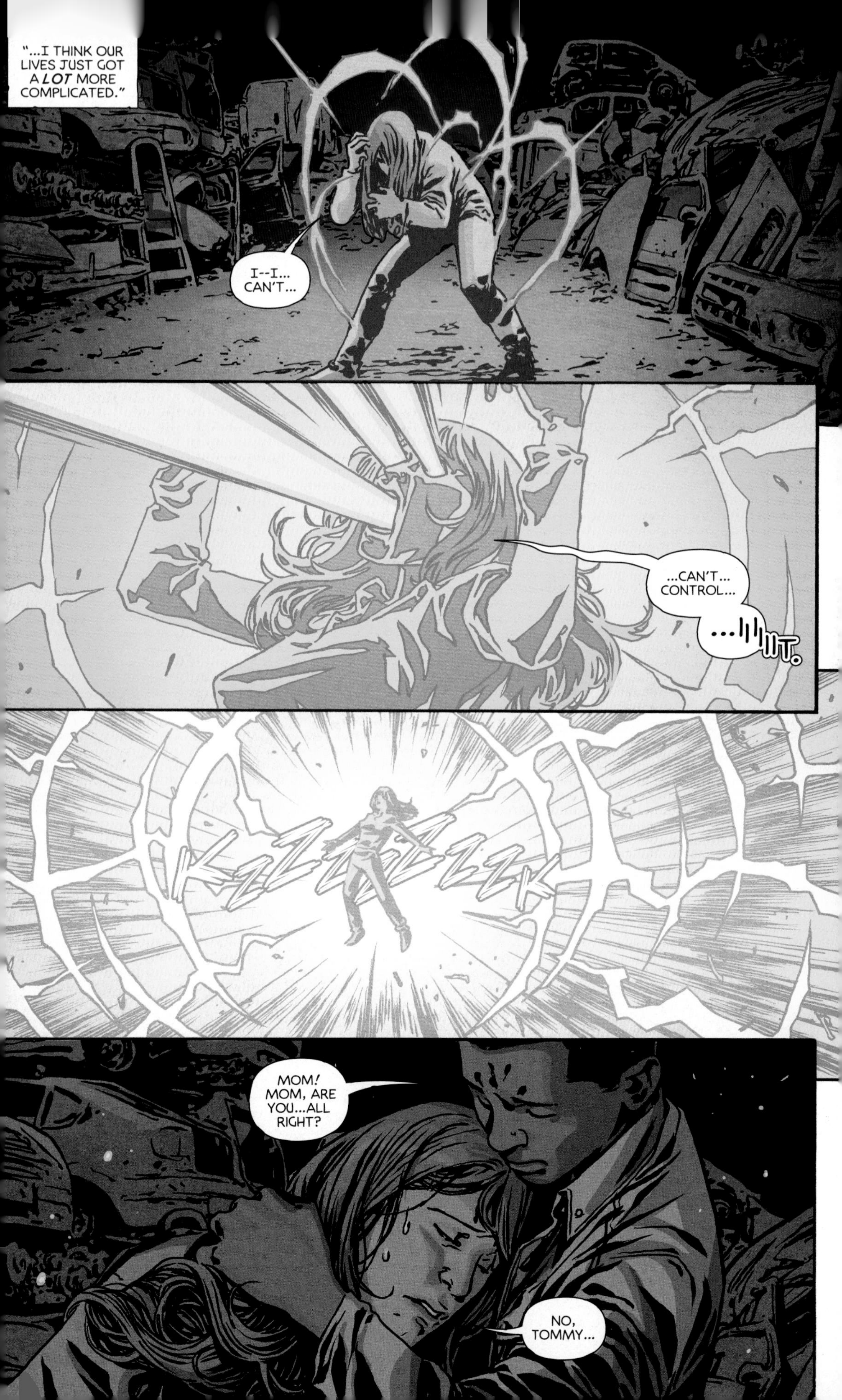
"...I THINK OUR LIVES JUST GOT A LOT MORE COMPLICATED."
I--I... CAN'T...
...CAN'T... CONTROL...
...IIIIIT.
KZZZZZZZZK
MOM! MOM, ARE YOU...ALL RIGHT?
NO, TOMMY...

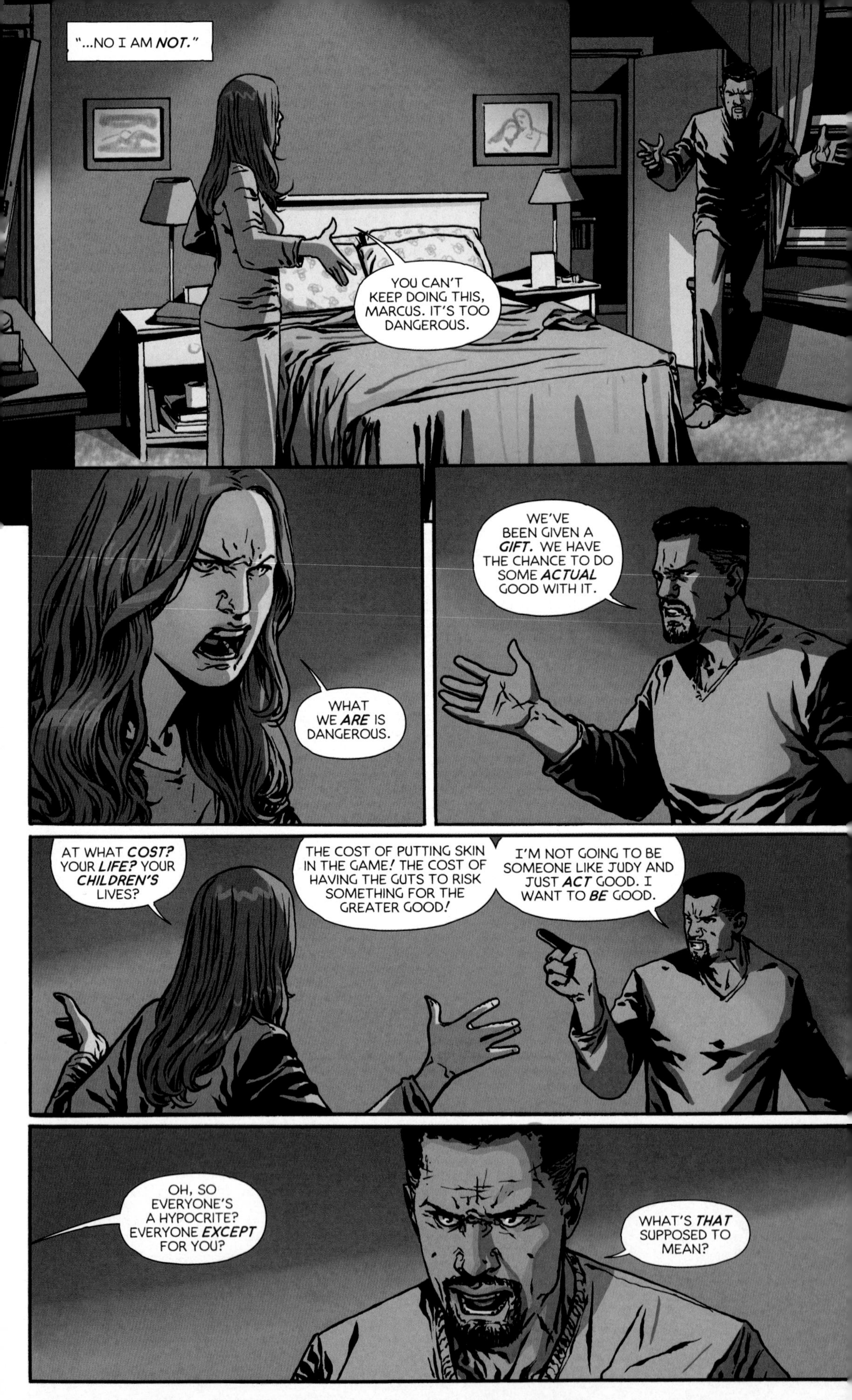
"...NO I AM *NOT.*"
YOU CAN'T KEEP DOING THIS, MARCUS. IT'S TOO DANGEROUS.
WE'VE BEEN GIVEN A *GIFT.* WE HAVE THE CHANCE TO DO SOME *ACTUAL* GOOD WITH IT.
WHAT WE *ARE* IS DANGEROUS.
AT WHAT *COST?* YOUR *LIFE?* YOUR *CHILDREN'S* LIVES?
THE COST OF PUTTING SKIN IN THE GAME! THE COST OF HAVING THE GUTS TO RISK SOMETHING FOR THE GREATER GOOD!
I'M NOT GOING TO BE SOMEONE LIKE JUDY AND JUST *ACT* GOOD. I WANT TO *BE* GOOD.
OH, SO EVERYONE'S A HYPOCRITE? EVERYONE *EXCEPT* FOR YOU?
WHAT'S *THAT* SUPPOSED TO MEAN?

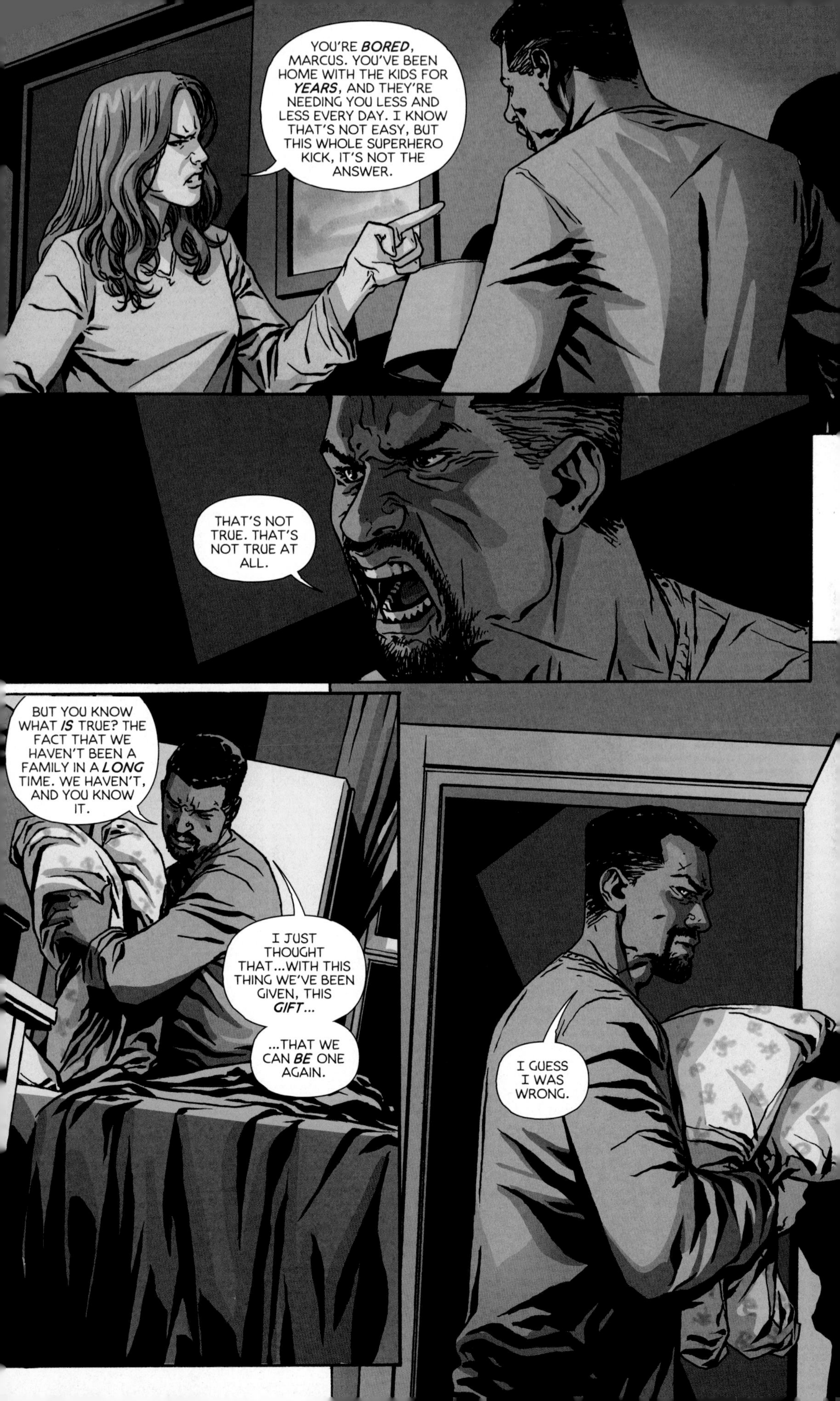
YOU'RE BORED, MARCUS. YOU'VE BEEN HOME WITH THE KIDS FOR YEARS, AND THEY'RE NEEDING YOU LESS AND LESS EVERY DAY. I KNOW THAT'S NOT EASY, BUT THIS WHOLE SUPERHERO KICK, IT'S NOT THE ANSWER.
THAT'S NOT TRUE. THAT'S NOT TRUE AT ALL.
BUT YOU KNOW WHAT IS TRUE? THE FACT THAT WE HAVEN'T BEEN A FAMILY IN A LONG TIME. WE HAVEN'T, AND YOU KNOW IT.
I JUST THOUGHT THAT...WITH THIS THING WE'VE BEEN GIVEN, THIS GIFT...
...THAT WE CAN BE ONE AGAIN.
I GUESS I WAS WRONG.

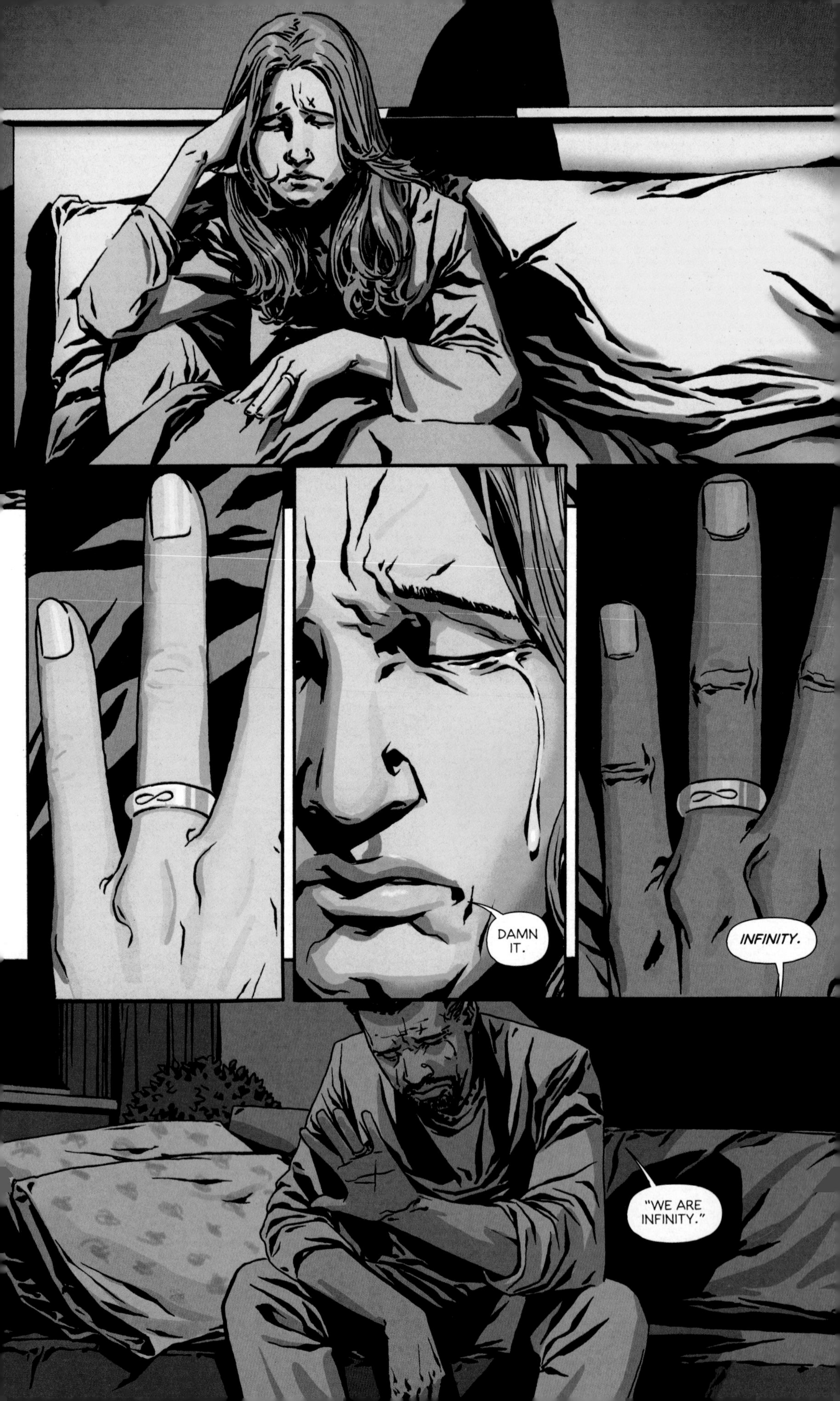
DAMN IT.
INFINITY.
"WE ARE INFINITY."

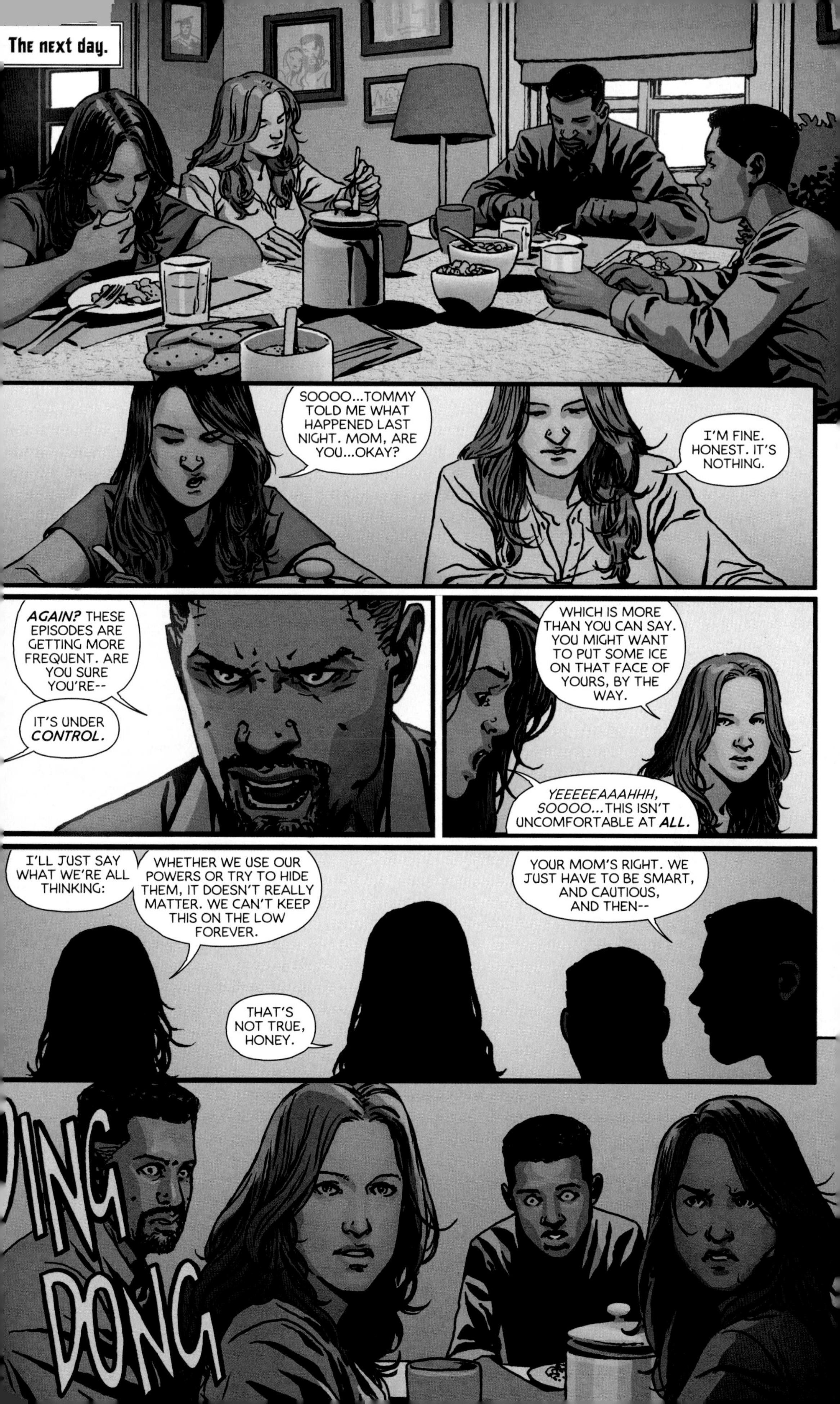
The next day.
SOOOO...TOMMY TOLD ME WHAT HAPPENED LAST NIGHT. MOM, ARE YOU...OKAY?
I'M FINE. HONEST. IT'S NOTHING.
AGAIN? THESE EPISODES ARE GETTING MORE FREQUENT. ARE YOU SURE YOU'RE--
IT'S UNDER CONTROL.
WHICH IS MORE THAN YOU CAN SAY. YOU MIGHT WANT TO PUT SOME ICE ON THAT FACE OF YOURS, BY THE WAY.
YEEEEEAAAHHH, SOOOO...THIS ISN'T UNCOMFORTABLE AT ALL.
I'LL JUST SAY WHAT WE'RE ALL THINKING:
WHETHER WE USE OUR POWERS OR TRY TO HIDE THEM, IT DOESN'T REALLY MATTER. WE CAN'T KEEP THIS ON THE LOW FOREVER.
THAT'S NOT TRUE, HONEY.
YOUR MOM'S RIGHT. WE JUST HAVE TO BE SMART, AND CAUTIOUS, AND THEN--
DONG

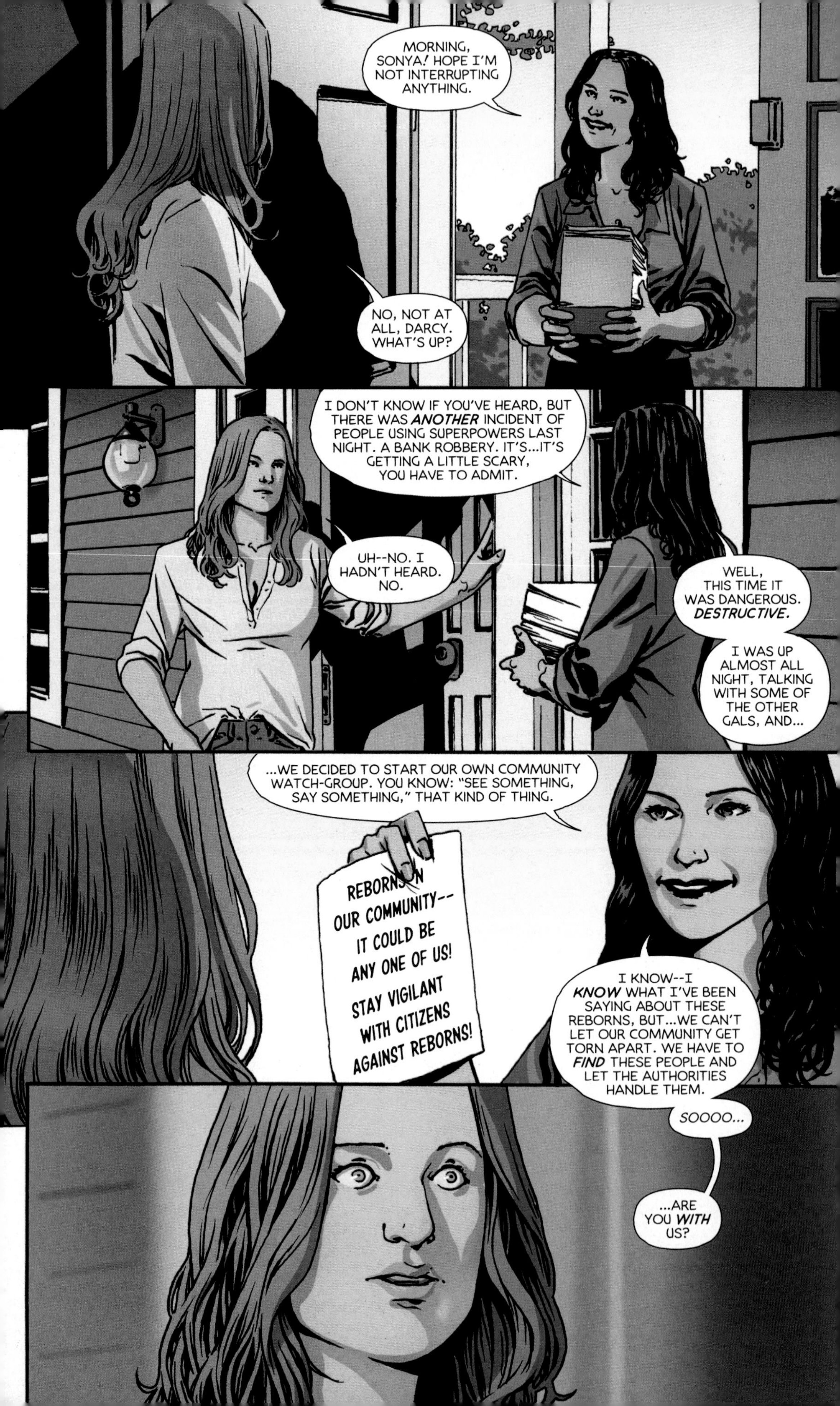
MORNING, SONYA! HOPE I'M NOT INTERRUPTING ANYTHING.
NO, NOT AT ALL, DARCY. WHAT'S UP?
I DON'T KNOW IF YOU'VE HEARD, BUT THERE WAS ANOTHER INCIDENT OF PEOPLE USING SUPERPOWERS LAST NIGHT. A BANK ROBBERY. IT'S...IT'S GETTING A LITTLE SCARY, YOU HAVE TO ADMIT.
UH--NO. I HADN'T HEARD. NO.
WELL, THIS TIME IT WAS DANGEROUS. DESTRUCTIVE.
I WAS UP ALMOST ALL NIGHT, TALKING WITH SOME OF THE OTHER GALS, AND...
...WE DECIDED TO START OUR OWN COMMUNITY WATCH-GROUP. YOU KNOW: "SEE SOMETHING, SAY SOMETHING," THAT KIND OF THING.
REBORNS IN OUR COMMUNITY-- IT COULD BE ANY ONE OF US! STAY VIGILANT WITH CITIZENS AGAINST REBORNS!
I KNOW--I KNOW WHAT I'VE BEEN SAYING ABOUT THESE REBORNS, BUT...WE CAN'T LET OUR COMMUNITY GET TORN APART. WE HAVE TO FIND THESE PEOPLE AND LET THE AUTHORITIES HANDLE THEM.
SOOOO...
...ARE YOU WITH US?

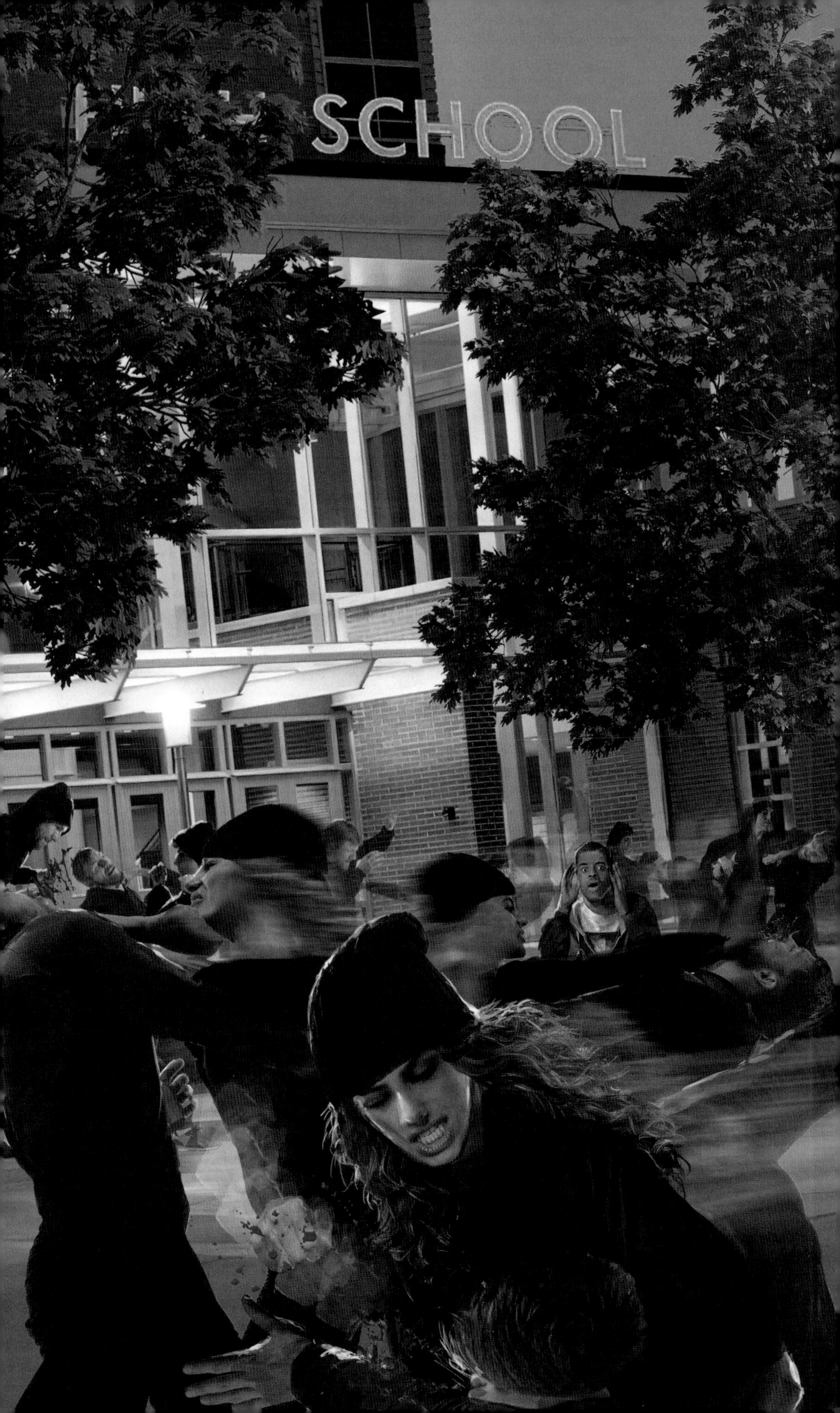
SCHOOL

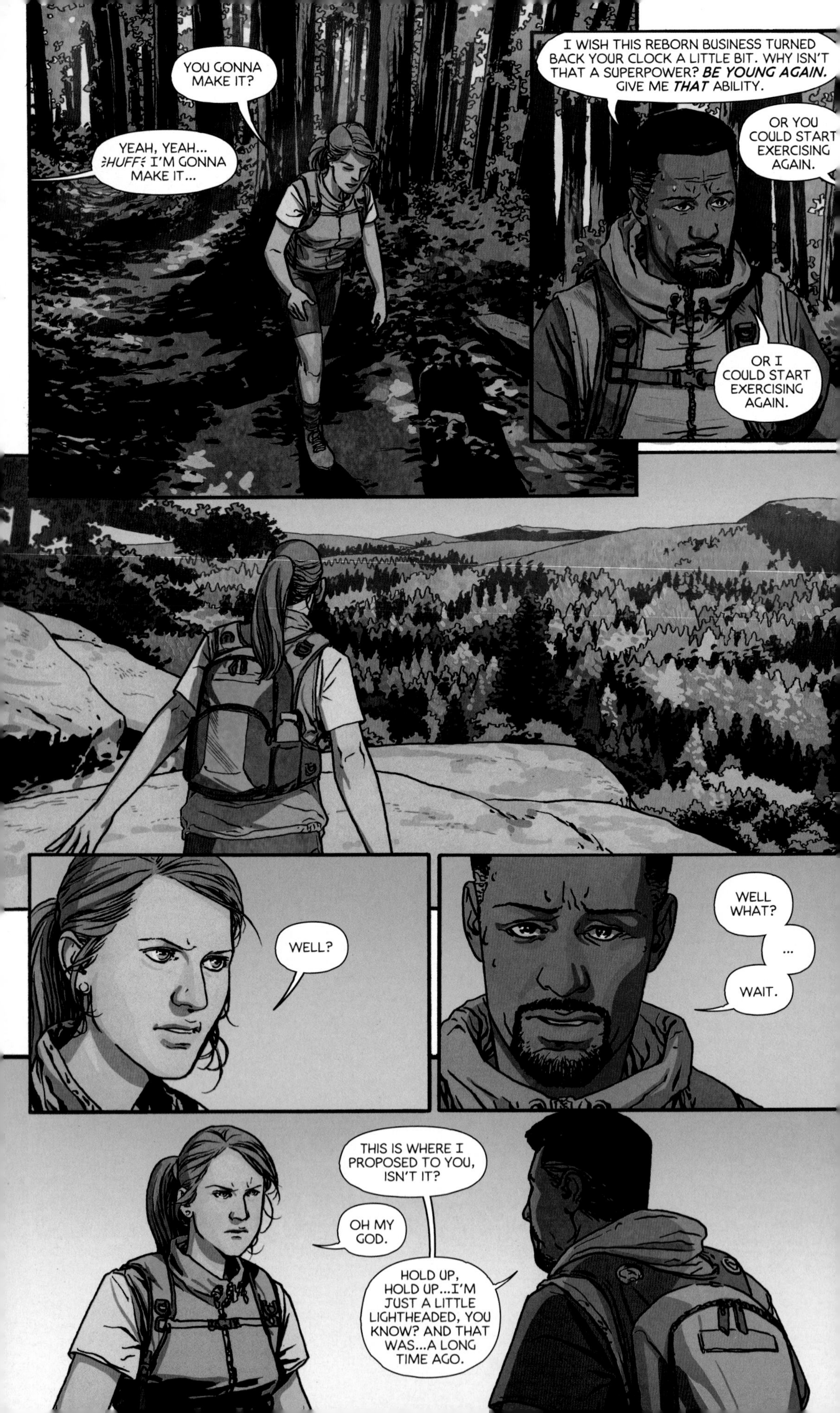
YOU GONNA MAKE IT?
YEAH, YEAH... *HUFF* I'M GONNA MAKE IT...
I WISH THIS REBORN BUSINESS TURNED BACK YOUR CLOCK A LITTLE BIT. WHY ISN'T THAT A SUPERPOWER? ***BE YOUNG AGAIN.*** GIVE ME ***THAT*** ABILITY.
OR YOU COULD START EXERCISING AGAIN.
OR I COULD START EXERCISING AGAIN.
WELL?
WELL WHAT?
...
WAIT.
THIS IS WHERE I PROPOSED TO YOU, ISN'T IT?
OH MY GOD.
HOLD UP, HOLD UP...I'M JUST A LITTLE LIGHTHEADED, YOU KNOW? AND THAT WAS...A LONG TIME AGO.

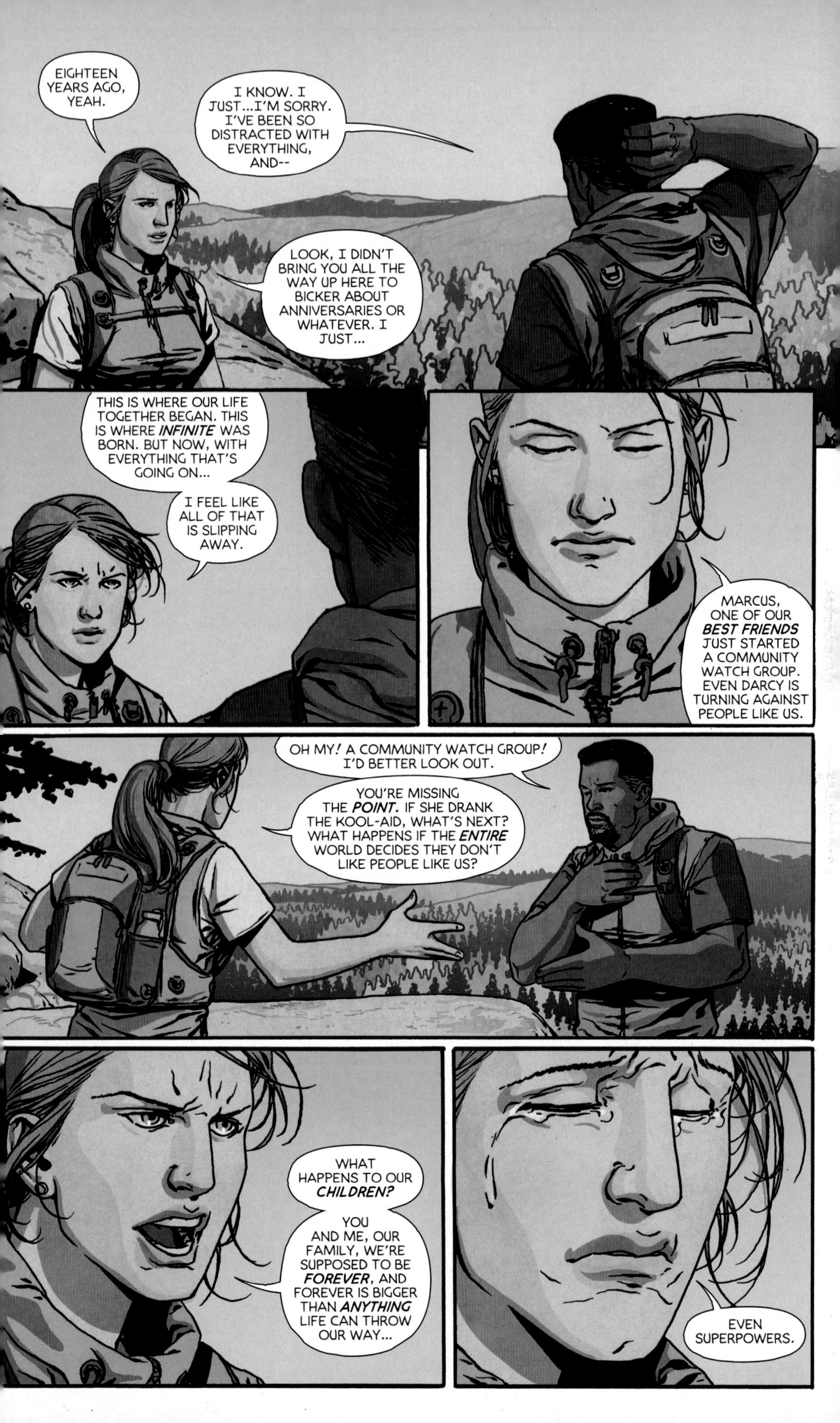
EIGHTEEN YEARS AGO, YEAH.
I KNOW. I JUST...I'M SORRY. I'VE BEEN SO DISTRACTED WITH EVERYTHING, AND--
LOOK, I DIDN'T BRING YOU ALL THE WAY UP HERE TO BICKER ABOUT ANNIVERSARIES OR WHATEVER. I JUST...
THIS IS WHERE OUR LIFE TOGETHER BEGAN. THIS IS WHERE *INFINITE* WAS BORN. BUT NOW, WITH EVERYTHING THAT'S GOING ON...
I FEEL LIKE ALL OF THAT IS SLIPPING AWAY.
MARCUS, ONE OF OUR ***BEST FRIENDS*** JUST STARTED A COMMUNITY WATCH GROUP. EVEN DARCY IS TURNING AGAINST PEOPLE LIKE US.
OH MY*!* A COMMUNITY WATCH GROUP*!* I'D BETTER LOOK OUT.
YOU'RE MISSING THE ***POINT.*** IF SHE DRANK THE KOOL-AID, WHAT'S NEXT? WHAT HAPPENS IF THE ***ENTIRE*** WORLD DECIDES THEY DON'T LIKE PEOPLE LIKE US?
WHAT HAPPENS TO OUR ***CHILDREN?***
YOU AND ME, OUR FAMILY, WE'RE SUPPOSED TO BE ***FOREVER***, AND FOREVER IS BIGGER THAN ***ANYTHING*** LIFE CAN THROW OUR WAY...
EVEN SUPERPOWERS.

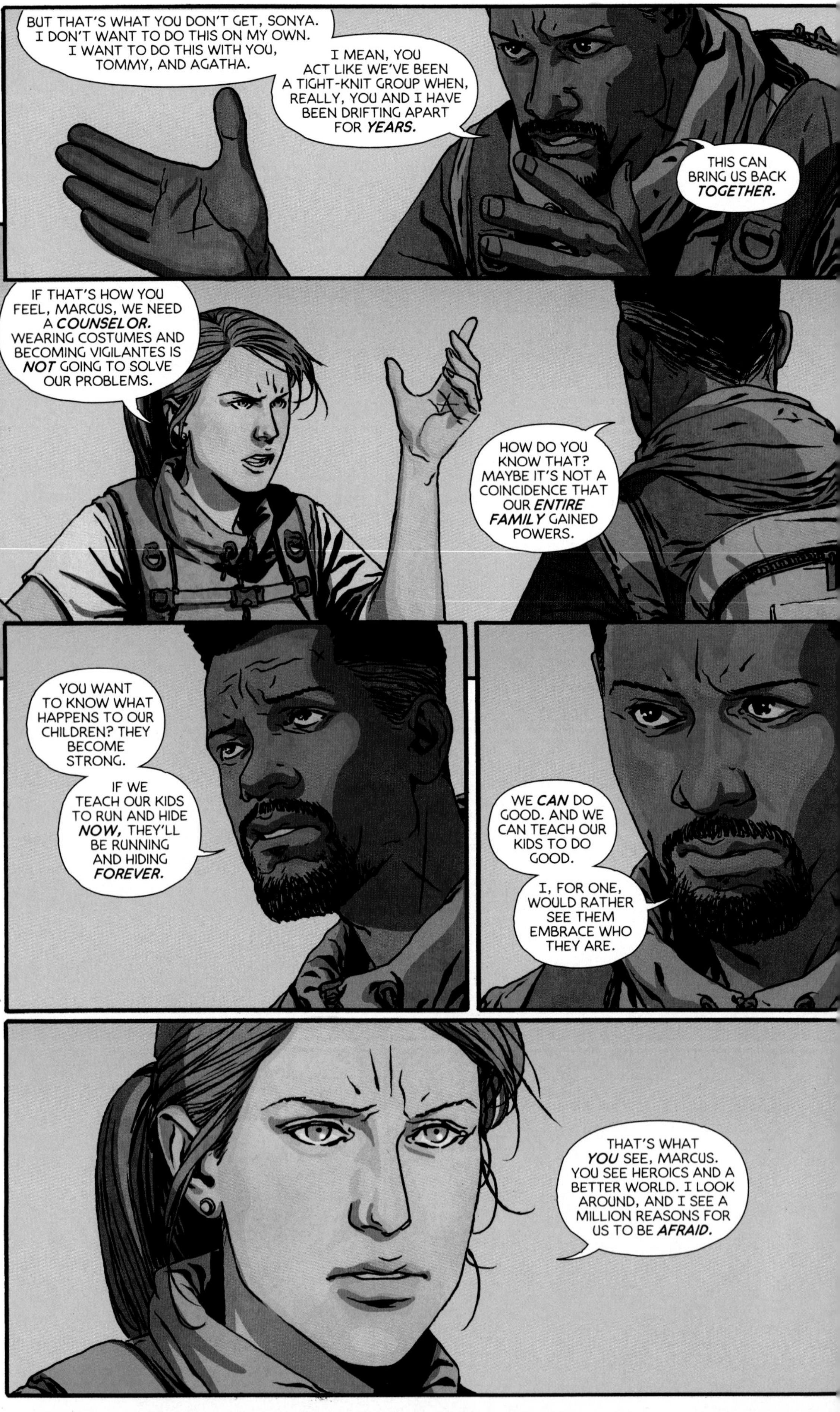
BUT THAT'S WHAT YOU DON'T GET, SONYA. I DON'T WANT TO DO THIS ON MY OWN. I WANT TO DO THIS WITH YOU, TOMMY, AND AGATHA.
I MEAN, YOU ACT LIKE WE'VE BEEN A TIGHT-KNIT GROUP WHEN, REALLY, YOU AND I HAVE BEEN DRIFTING APART FOR *YEARS.*
THIS CAN BRING US BACK *TOGETHER.*
IF THAT'S HOW YOU FEEL, MARCUS, WE NEED A *COUNSELOR.* WEARING COSTUMES AND BECOMING VIGILANTES IS *NOT* GOING TO SOLVE OUR PROBLEMS.
HOW DO YOU KNOW THAT? MAYBE IT'S NOT A COINCIDENCE THAT OUR *ENTIRE FAMILY* GAINED POWERS.
YOU WANT TO KNOW WHAT HAPPENS TO OUR CHILDREN? THEY BECOME STRONG.
IF WE TEACH OUR KIDS TO RUN AND HIDE *NOW,* THEY'LL BE RUNNING AND HIDING *FOREVER.*
WE *CAN* DO GOOD. AND WE CAN TEACH OUR KIDS TO DO GOOD.
I, FOR ONE, WOULD RATHER SEE THEM EMBRACE WHO THEY ARE.
THAT'S WHAT *YOU* SEE, MARCUS. YOU SEE HEROICS AND A BETTER WORLD. I LOOK AROUND, AND I SEE A MILLION REASONS FOR US TO BE *AFRAID.*

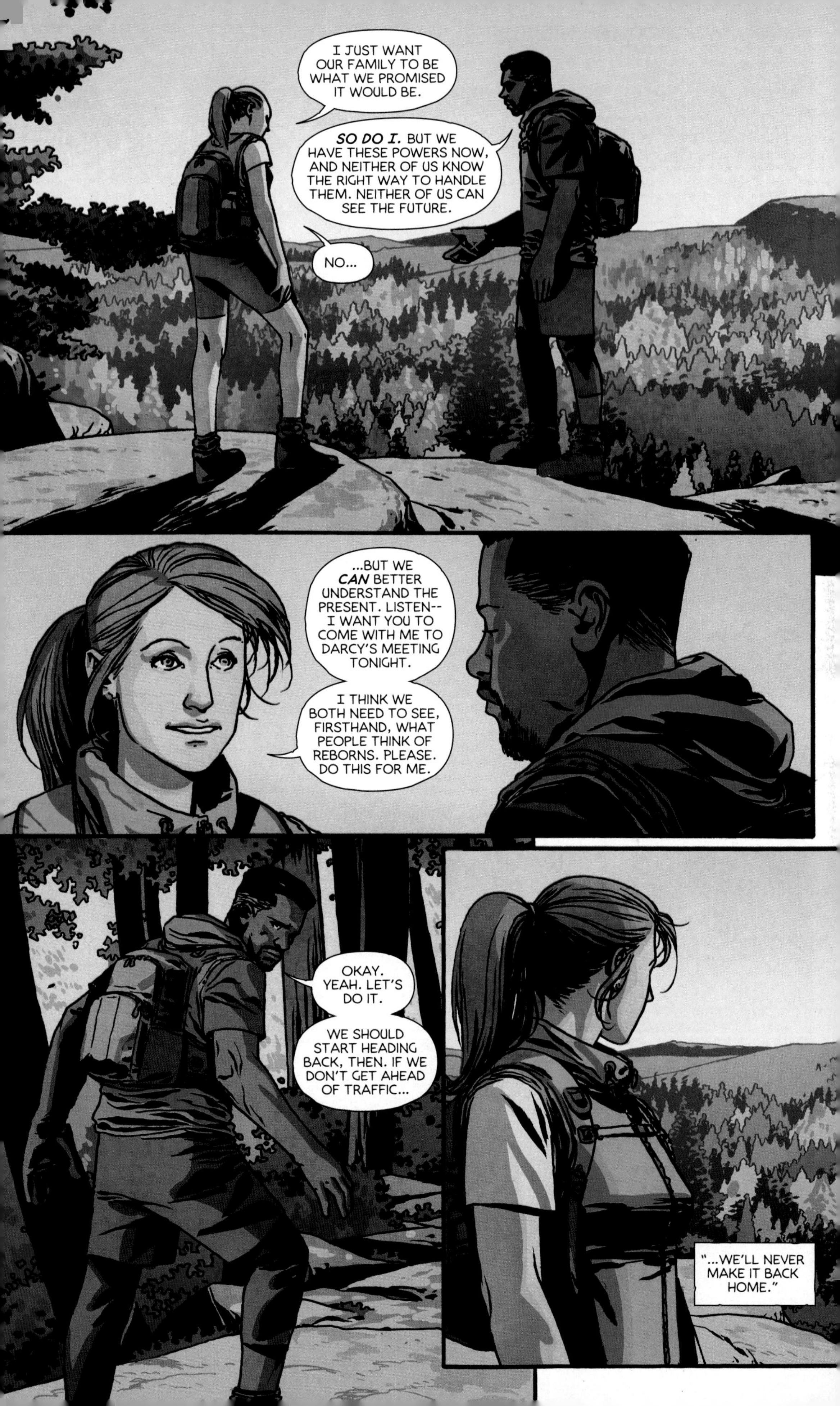
I JUST WANT OUR FAMILY TO BE WHAT WE PROMISED IT WOULD BE.
SO DO I. BUT WE HAVE THESE POWERS NOW, AND NEITHER OF US KNOW THE RIGHT WAY TO HANDLE THEM. NEITHER OF US CAN SEE THE FUTURE.
NO...
...BUT WE CAN BETTER UNDERSTAND THE PRESENT. LISTEN-- I WANT YOU TO COME WITH ME TO DARCY'S MEETING TONIGHT.
I THINK WE BOTH NEED TO SEE, FIRSTHAND, WHAT PEOPLE THINK OF REBORNS. PLEASE. DO THIS FOR ME.
OKAY. YEAH. LET'S DO IT.
WE SHOULD START HEADING BACK, THEN. IF WE DON'T GET AHEAD OF TRAFFIC...
"...WE'LL NEVER MAKE IT BACK HOME."

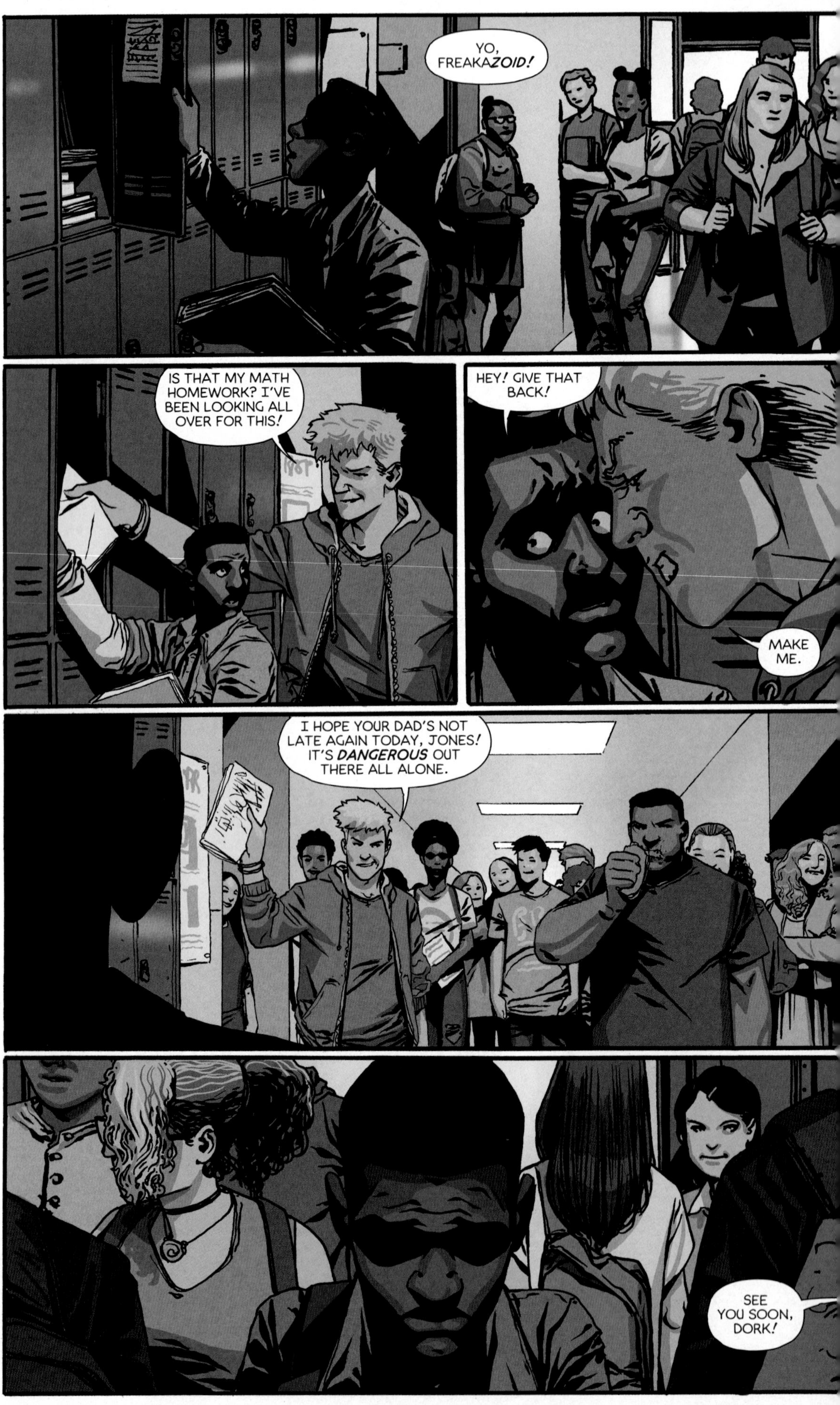
YO, FREAKAZOID!
IS THAT MY MATH HOMEWORK? I'VE BEEN LOOKING ALL OVER FOR THIS!
HEY! GIVE THAT BACK!
MAKE ME.
I HOPE YOUR DAD'S NOT LATE AGAIN TODAY, JONES! IT'S DANGEROUS OUT THERE ALL ALONE.
SEE YOU SOON, DORK!

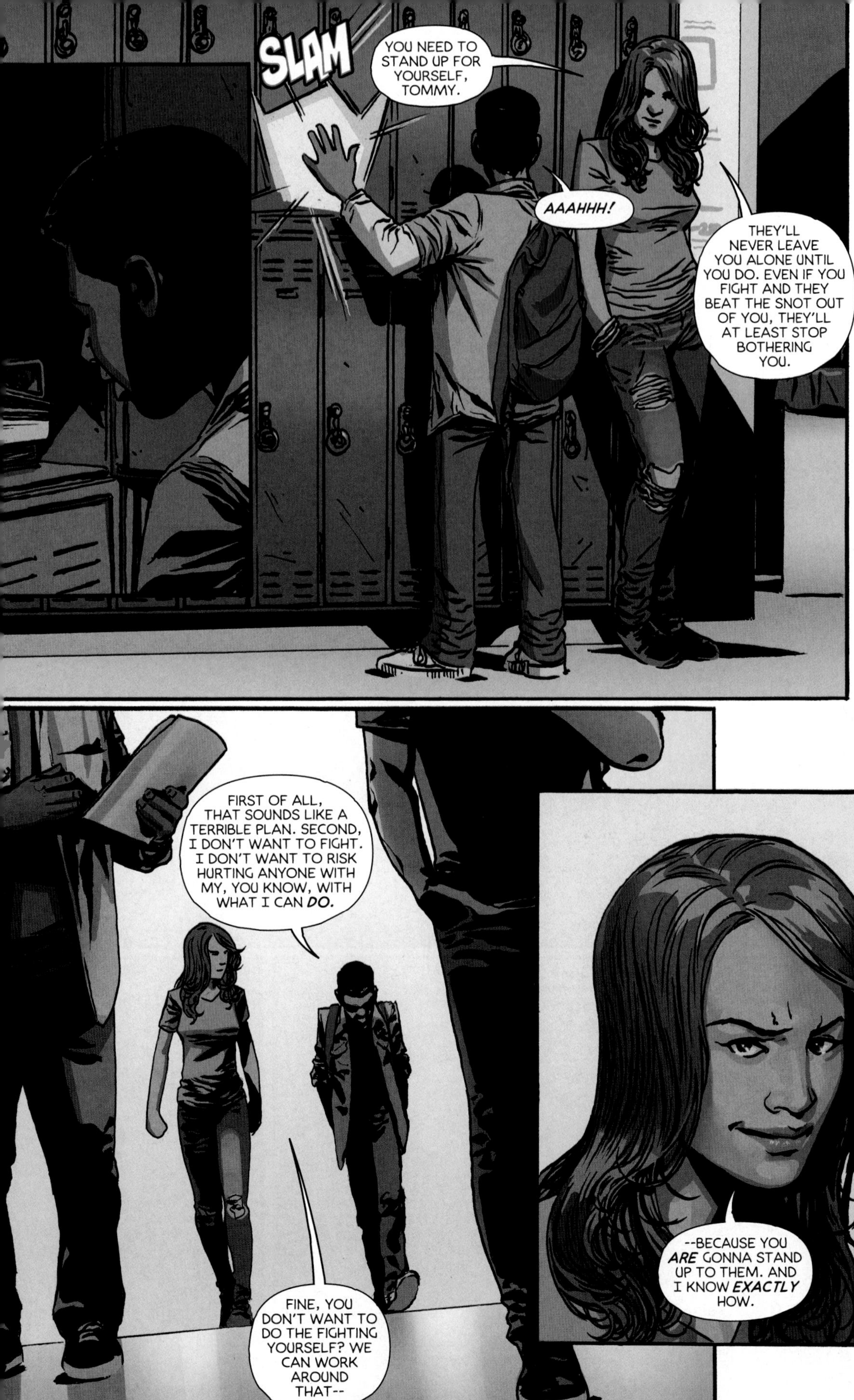
SLAM
YOU NEED TO STAND UP FOR YOURSELF, TOMMY.
AAAHHH!
THEY'LL NEVER LEAVE YOU ALONE UNTIL YOU DO. EVEN IF YOU FIGHT AND THEY BEAT THE SNOT OUT OF YOU, THEY'LL AT LEAST STOP BOTHERING YOU.
FIRST OF ALL, THAT SOUNDS LIKE A TERRIBLE PLAN. SECOND, I DON'T WANT TO FIGHT. I DON'T WANT TO RISK HURTING ANYONE WITH MY, YOU KNOW, WITH WHAT I CAN *DO.*
FINE, YOU DON'T WANT TO DO THE FIGHTING YOURSELF? WE CAN WORK AROUND THAT--
--BECAUSE YOU *ARE* GONNA STAND UP TO THEM. AND I KNOW *EXACTLY* HOW.

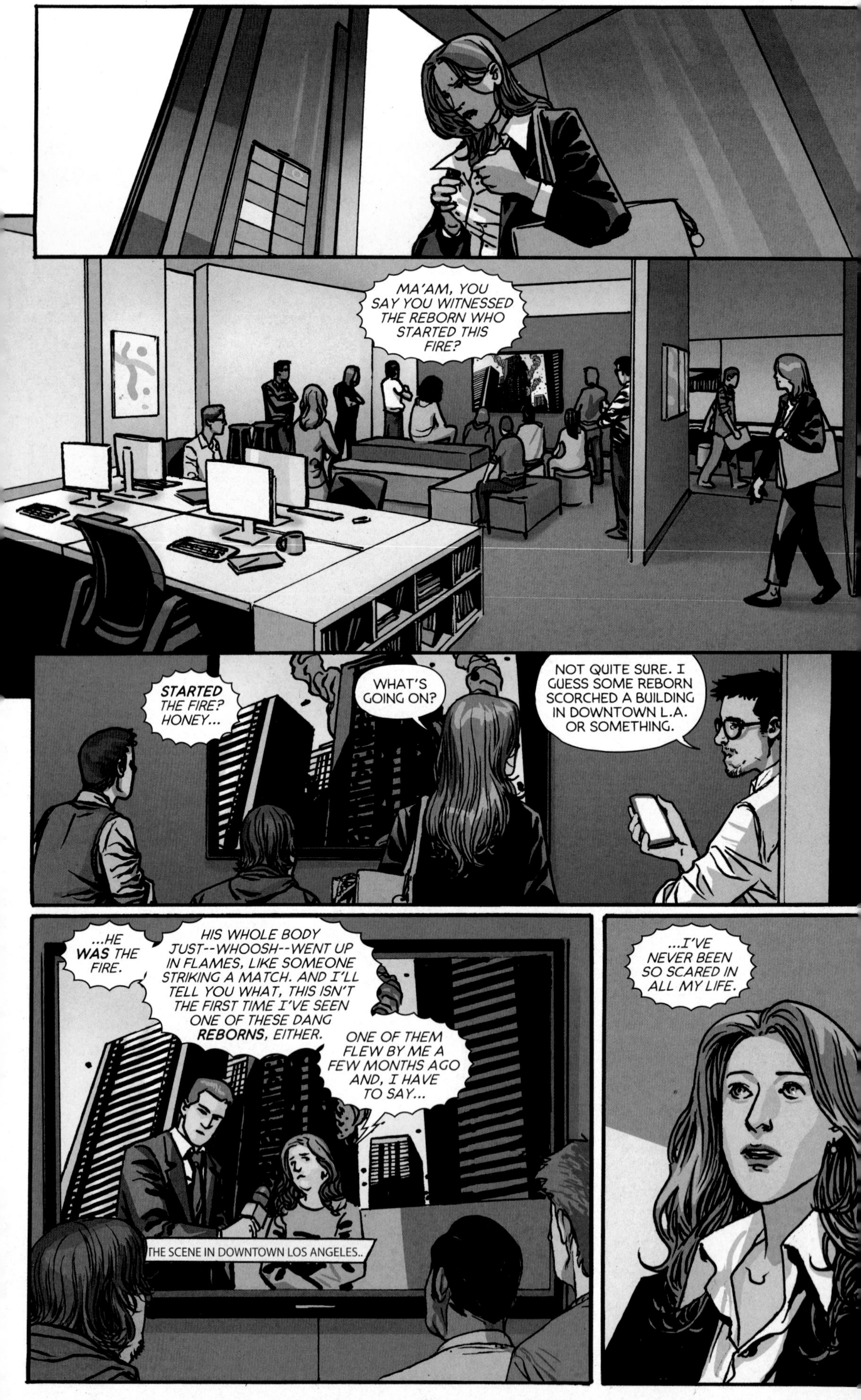

MA'AM, YOU SAY YOU WITNESSED THE REBORN WHO STARTED THIS FIRE?
STARTED THE FIRE? HONEY...
WHAT'S GOING ON?
NOT QUITE SURE. I GUESS SOME REBORN SCORCHED A BUILDING IN DOWNTOWN L.A. OR SOMETHING.
...HE WAS THE FIRE.
HIS WHOLE BODY JUST--WHOOSH--WENT UP IN FLAMES, LIKE SOMEONE STRIKING A MATCH. AND I'LL TELL YOU WHAT, THIS ISN'T THE FIRST TIME I'VE SEEN ONE OF THESE DANG REBORNS, EITHER.
ONE OF THEM FLEW BY ME A FEW MONTHS AGO AND, I HAVE TO SAY...
THE SCENE IN DOWNTOWN LOS ANGELES..
...I'VE NEVER BEEN SO SCARED IN ALL MY LIFE.

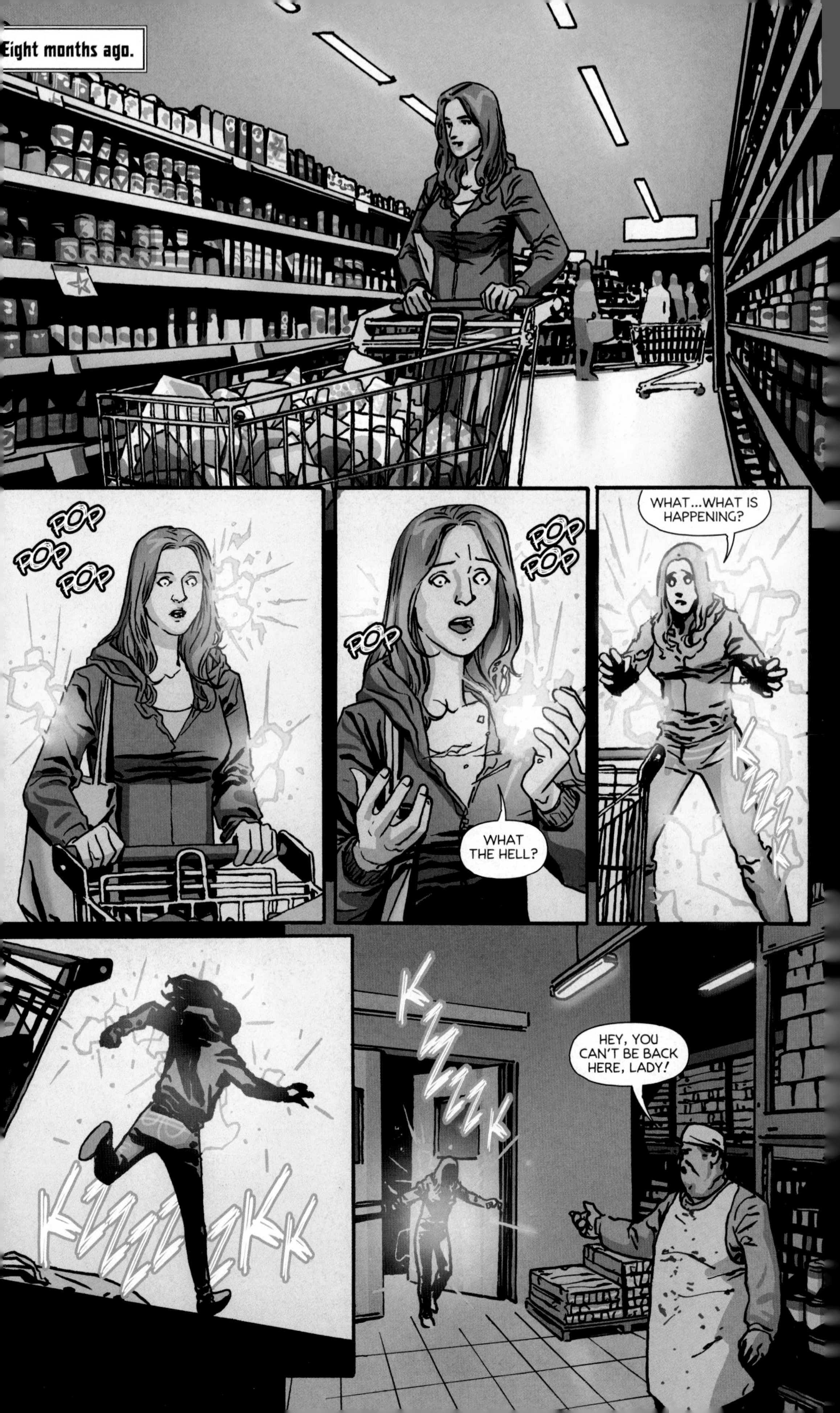
Eight months ago.
POP
POP
POP
POP
POP
POP
WHAT THE HELL?
WHAT...WHAT IS HAPPENING?
KZZZZK
KZZZZZZKK
KZZZZZK
HEY, YOU CAN'T BE BACK HERE, LADY!

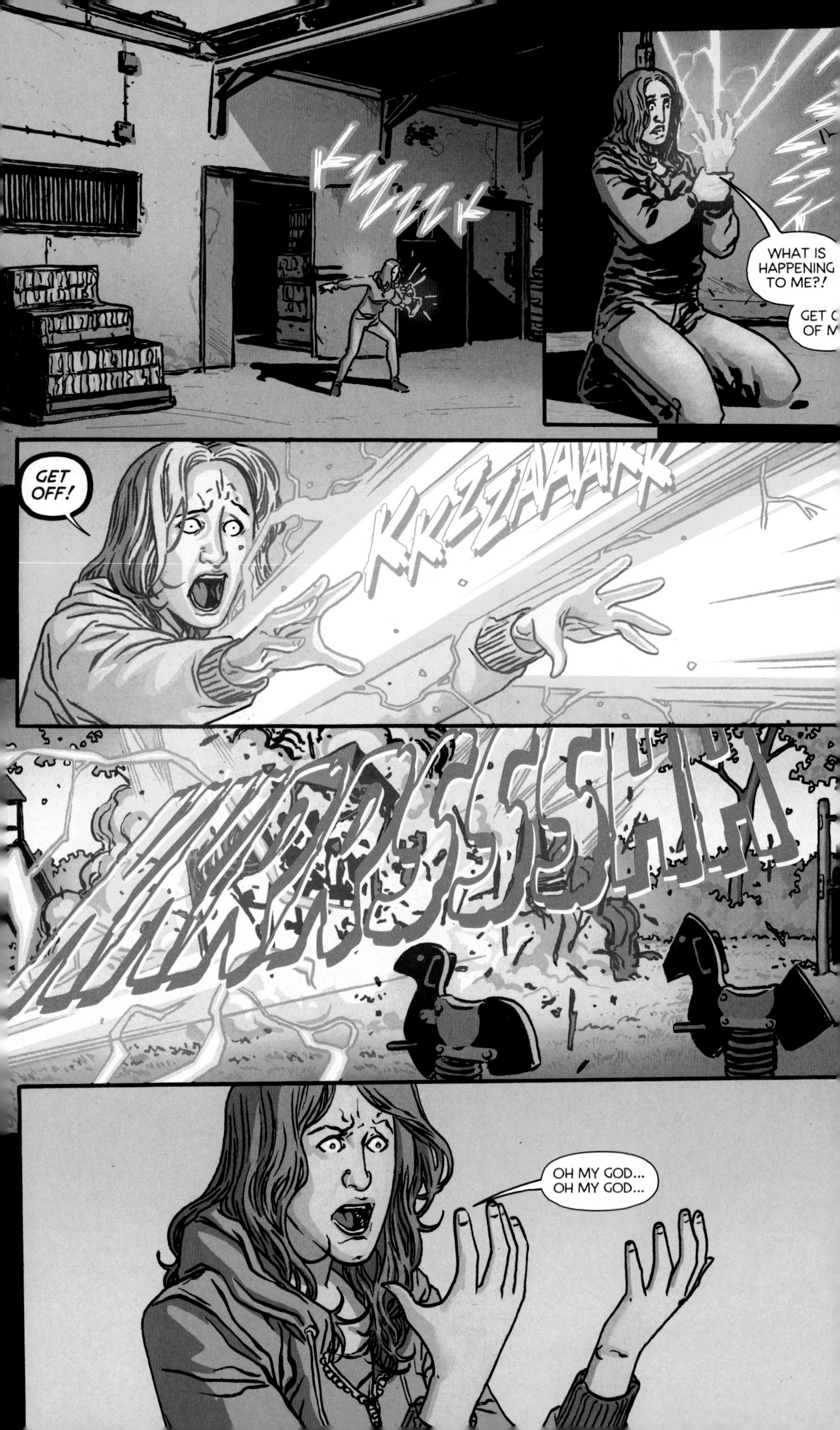
KZZZZZK
WHAT IS HAPPENING TO ME?!
GET O
OF M
GET OFF!
KKZZAAARK
OH MY GOD... OH MY GOD...

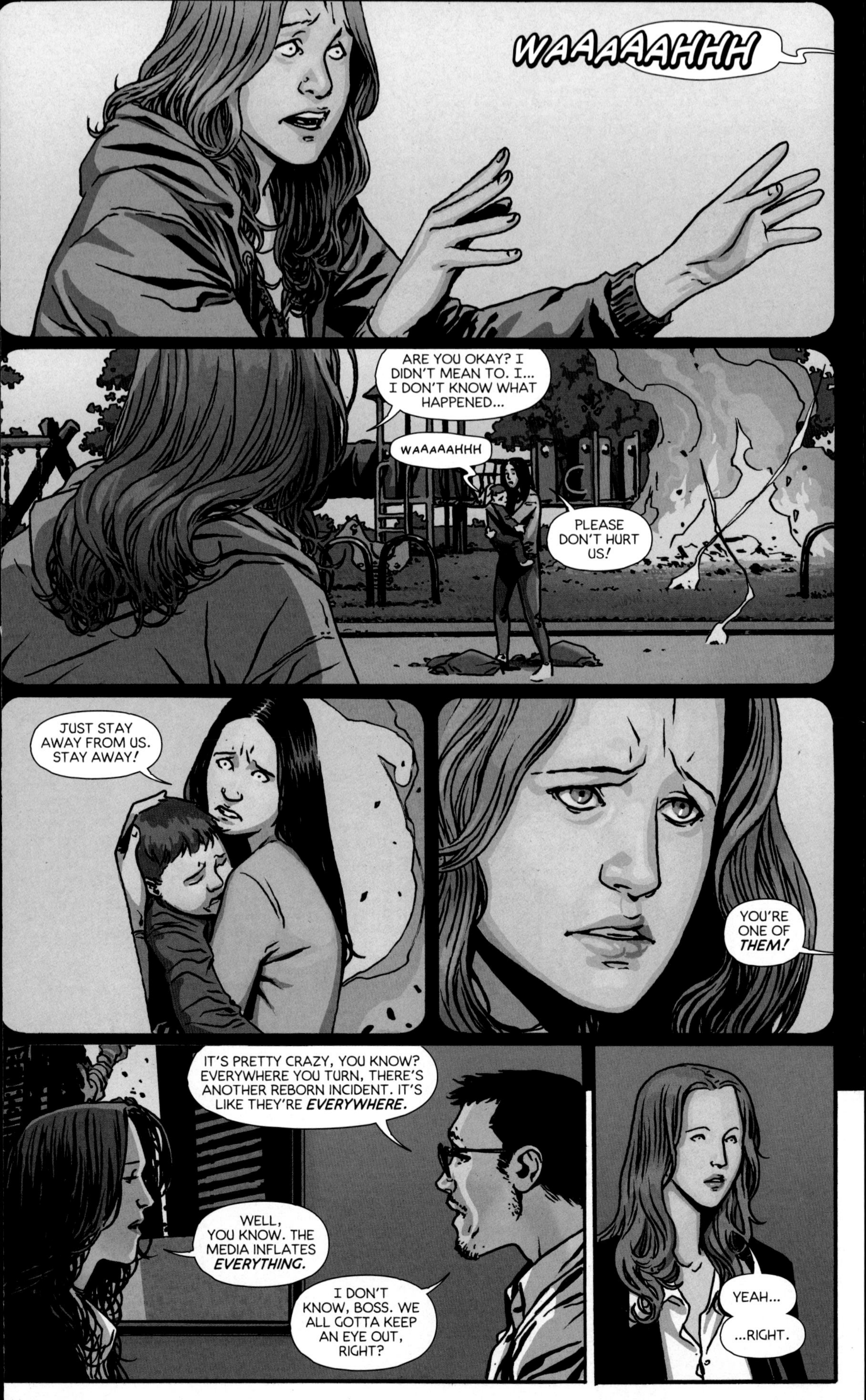
WAAAAAHHH
ARE YOU OKAY? I DIDN'T MEAN TO. I... I DON'T KNOW WHAT HAPPENED...
WAAAAAHHH
PLEASE DON'T HURT US!
JUST STAY AWAY FROM US. STAY AWAY!
YOU'RE ONE OF THEM!
IT'S PRETTY CRAZY, YOU KNOW? EVERYWHERE YOU TURN, THERE'S ANOTHER REBORN INCIDENT. IT'S LIKE THEY'RE EVERYWHERE.
WELL, YOU KNOW. THE MEDIA INFLATES EVERYTHING.
I DON'T KNOW, BOSS. WE ALL GOTTA KEEP AN EYE OUT, RIGHT?
YEAH...
...RIGHT.

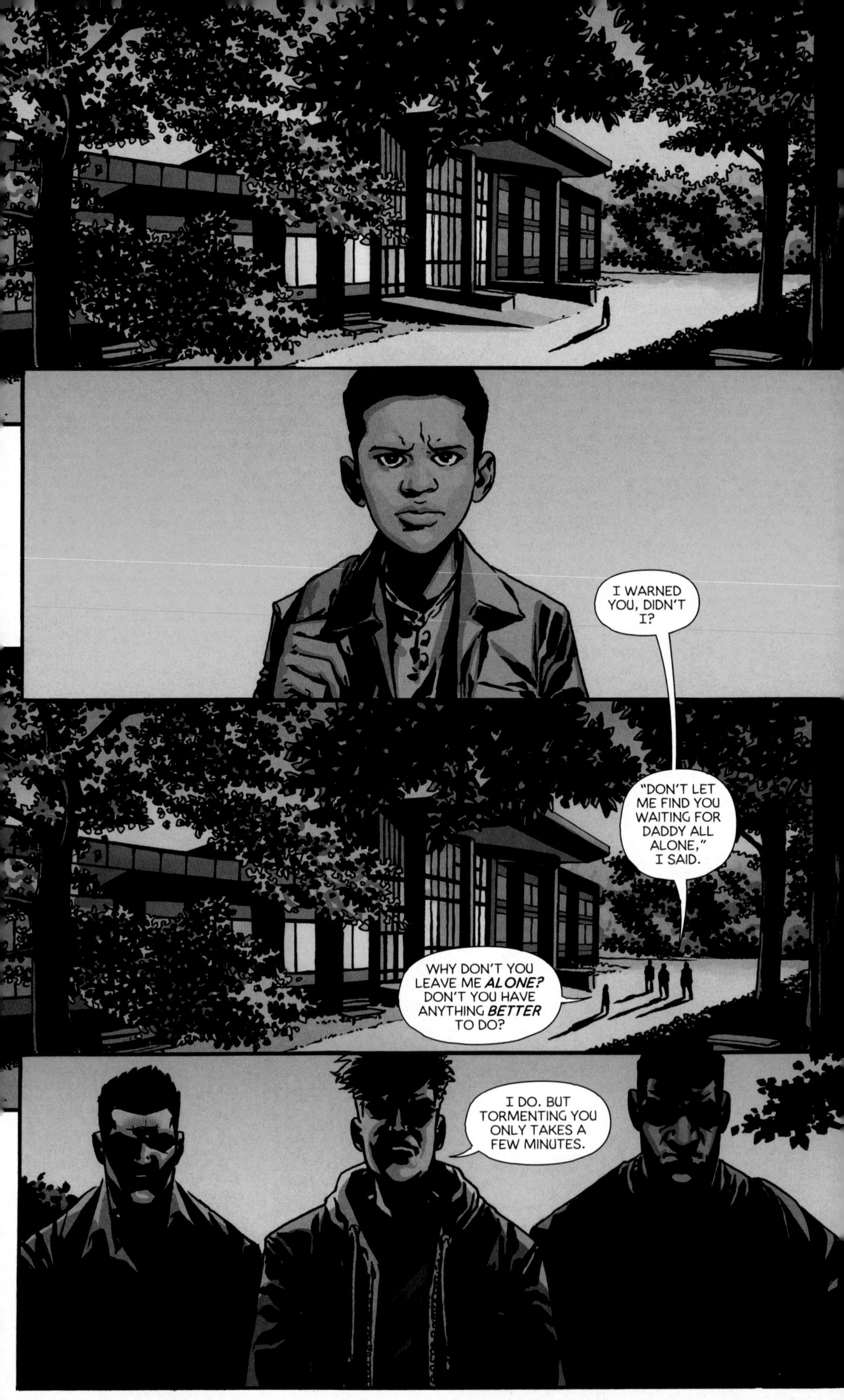
I WARNED YOU, DIDN'T I?
"DON'T LET ME FIND YOU WAITING FOR DADDY ALL ALONE," I SAID.
WHY DON'T YOU LEAVE ME ALONE? DON'T YOU HAVE ANYTHING BETTER TO DO?
I DO. BUT TORMENTING YOU ONLY TAKES A FEW MINUTES.

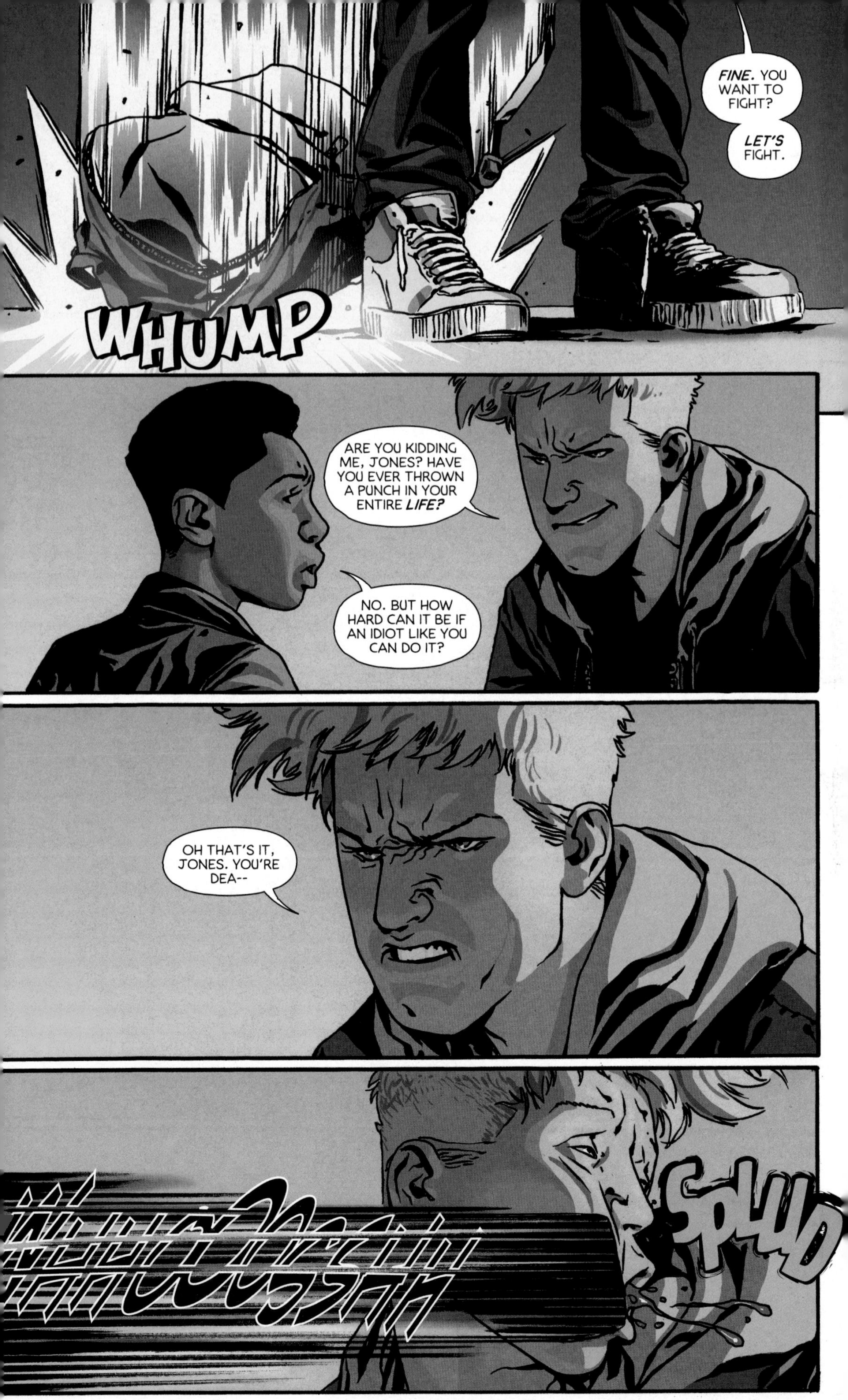
FINE. YOU WANT TO FIGHT?
LET'S FIGHT.
WHUMP
ARE YOU KIDDING ME, JONES? HAVE YOU EVER THROWN A PUNCH IN YOUR ENTIRE LIFE?
NO. BUT HOW HARD CAN IT BE IF AN IDIOT LIKE YOU CAN DO IT?
OH THAT'S IT, JONES. YOU'RE DEA--
SPLUD

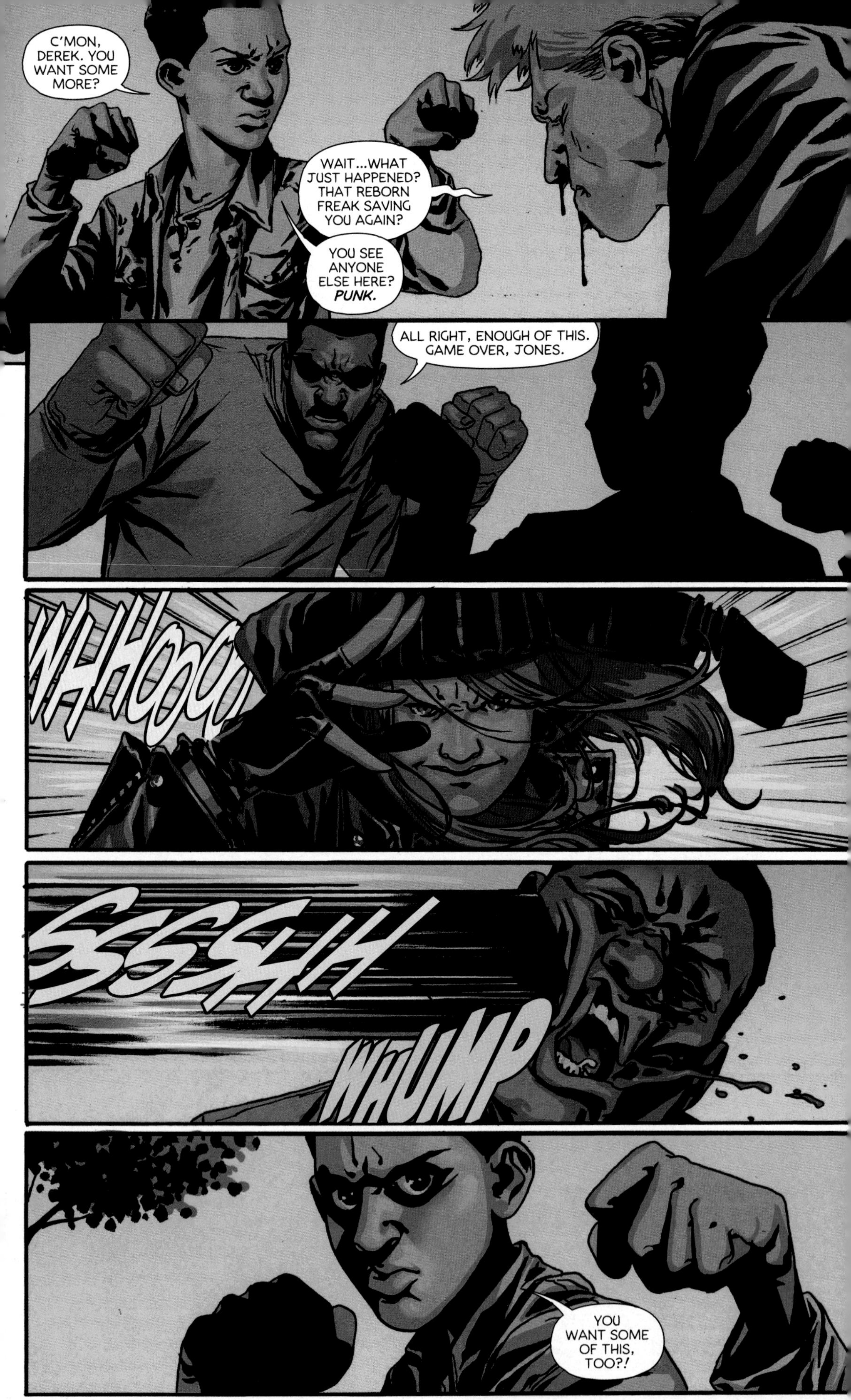

C'MON, DEREK. YOU WANT SOME MORE?
WAIT...WHAT JUST HAPPENED? THAT REBORN FREAK SAVING YOU AGAIN?
YOU SEE ANYONE ELSE HERE? *PUNK.*
ALL RIGHT, ENOUGH OF THIS. GAME OVER, JONES.
WHHOOO
SSSSH
WHUMP
YOU WANT SOME OF THIS, TOO?!

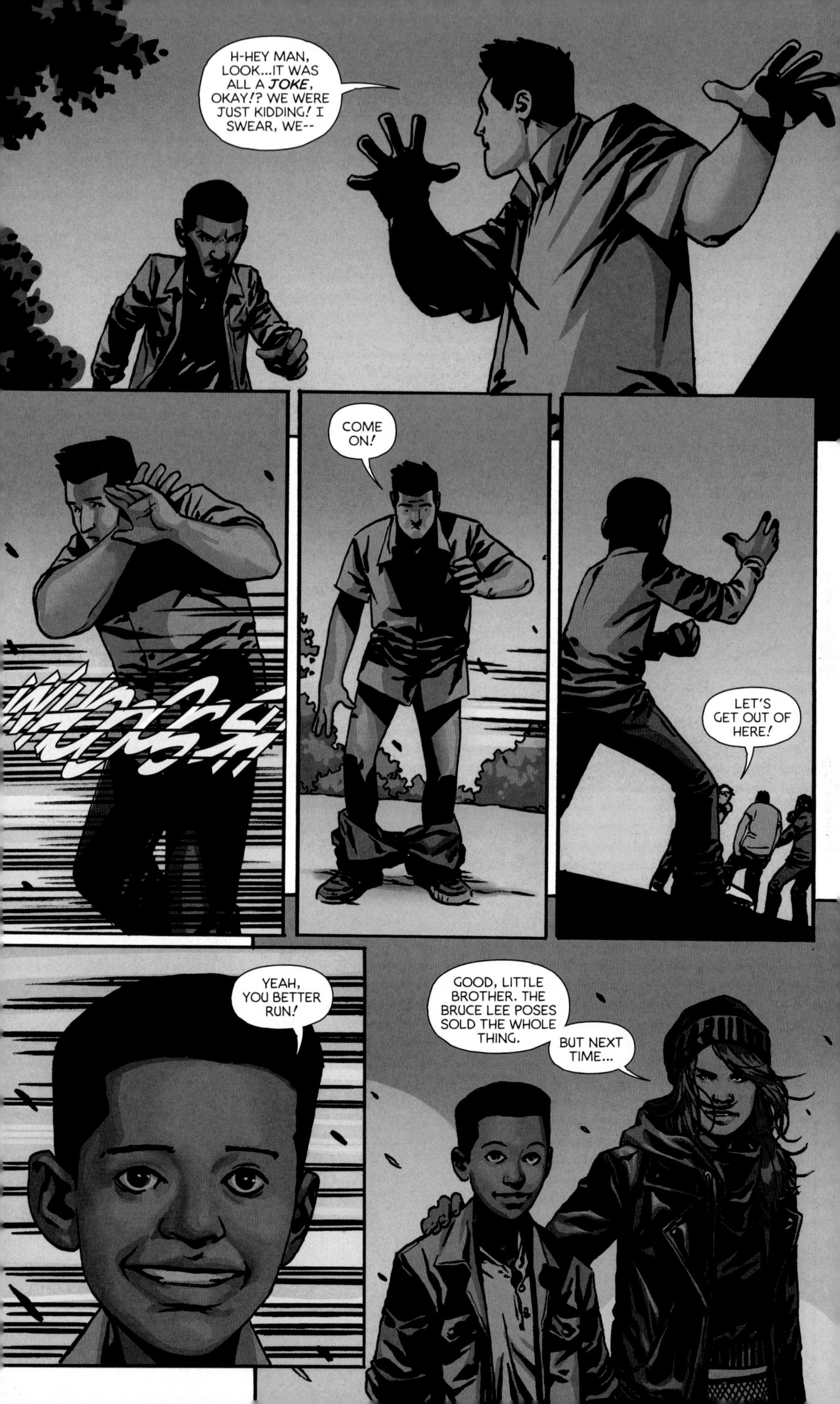
H-HEY MAN, LOOK...IT WAS ALL A *JOKE*, OKAY!? WE WERE JUST KIDDING! I SWEAR, WE--
COME ON!
LET'S GET OUT OF HERE!
YEAH, YOU BETTER RUN!
GOOD, LITTLE BROTHER. THE BRUCE LEE POSES SOLD THE WHOLE THING.
BUT NEXT TIME...

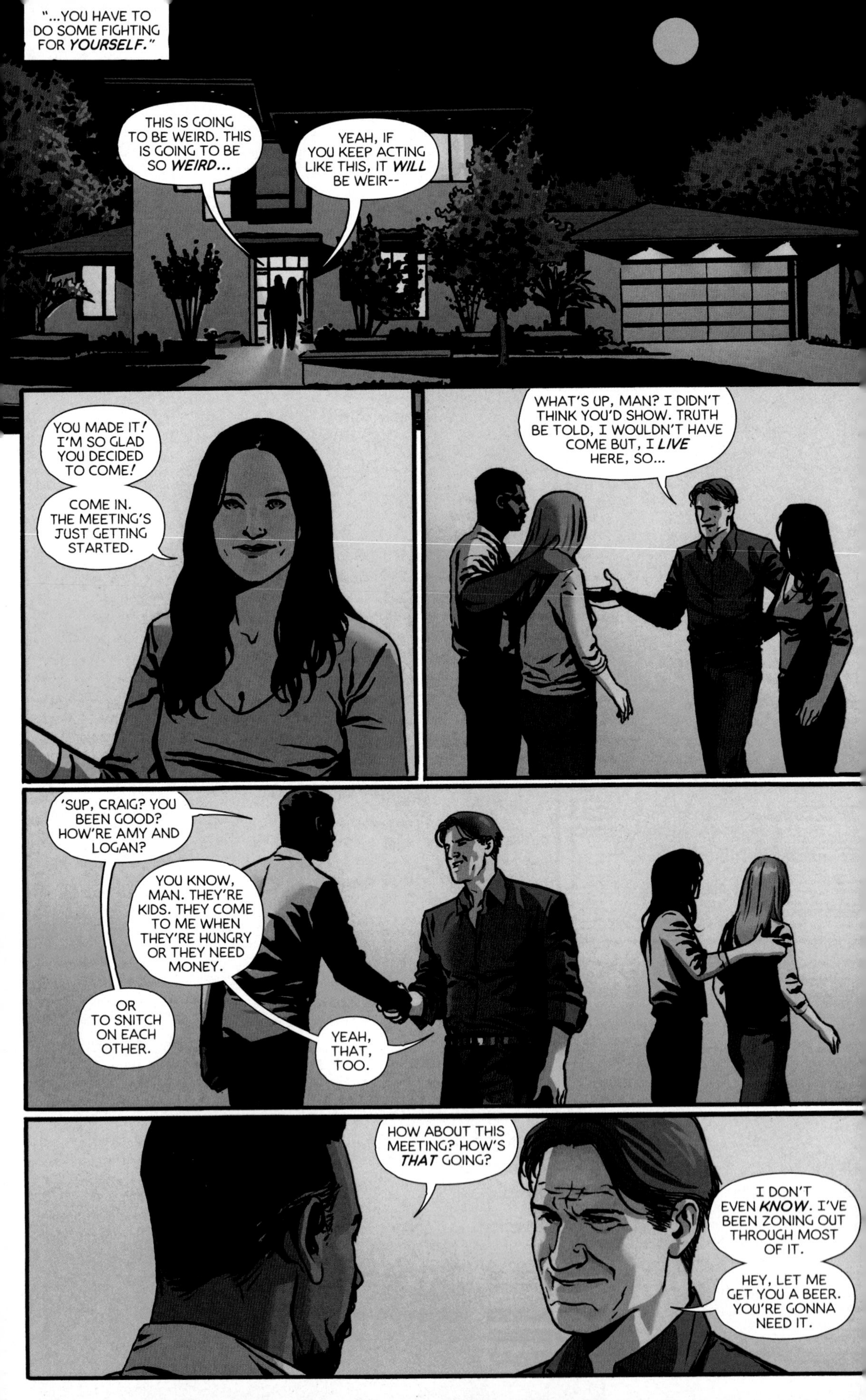
"...YOU HAVE TO DO SOME FIGHTING FOR *YOURSELF.*"
THIS IS GOING TO BE WEIRD. THIS IS GOING TO BE SO *WEIRD...*
YEAH, IF YOU KEEP ACTING LIKE THIS, IT *WILL* BE WEIR--
YOU MADE IT! I'M SO GLAD YOU DECIDED TO COME!
COME IN. THE MEETING'S JUST GETTING STARTED.
WHAT'S UP, MAN? I DIDN'T THINK YOU'D SHOW. TRUTH BE TOLD, I WOULDN'T HAVE COME BUT, I *LIVE* HERE, SO...
'SUP, CRAIG? YOU BEEN GOOD? HOW'RE AMY AND LOGAN?
YOU KNOW, MAN. THEY'RE KIDS. THEY COME TO ME WHEN THEY'RE HUNGRY OR THEY NEED MONEY.
OR TO SNITCH ON EACH OTHER.
YEAH, THAT, TOO.
HOW ABOUT THIS MEETING? HOW'S *THAT* GOING?
I DON'T EVEN ***KNOW***. I'VE BEEN ZONING OUT THROUGH MOST OF IT.
HEY, LET ME GET YOU A BEER. YOU'RE GONNA NEED IT.

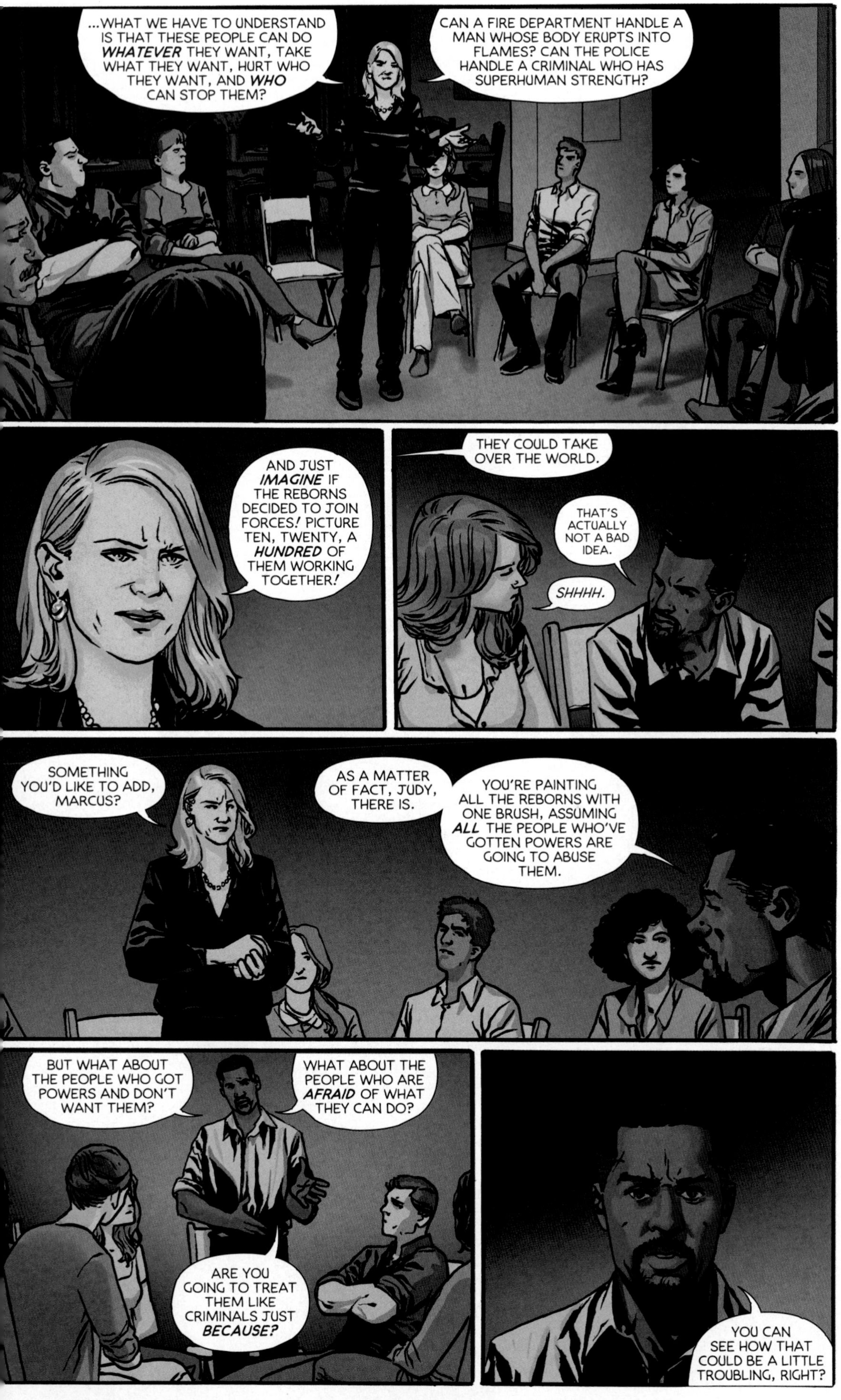
...WHAT WE HAVE TO UNDERSTAND IS THAT THESE PEOPLE CAN DO WHATEVER THEY WANT, TAKE WHAT THEY WANT, HURT WHO THEY WANT, AND WHO CAN STOP THEM?
CAN A FIRE DEPARTMENT HANDLE A MAN WHOSE BODY ERUPTS INTO FLAMES? CAN THE POLICE HANDLE A CRIMINAL WHO HAS SUPERHUMAN STRENGTH?
AND JUST IMAGINE IF THE REBORNS DECIDED TO JOIN FORCES! PICTURE TEN, TWENTY, A HUNDRED OF THEM WORKING TOGETHER!
THEY COULD TAKE OVER THE WORLD.
THAT'S ACTUALLY NOT A BAD IDEA.
SHHHH.
SOMETHING YOU'D LIKE TO ADD, MARCUS?
AS A MATTER OF FACT, JUDY, THERE IS.
YOU'RE PAINTING ALL THE REBORNS WITH ONE BRUSH, ASSUMING ALL THE PEOPLE WHO'VE GOTTEN POWERS ARE GOING TO ABUSE THEM.
BUT WHAT ABOUT THE PEOPLE WHO GOT POWERS AND DON'T WANT THEM?
WHAT ABOUT THE PEOPLE WHO ARE AFRAID OF WHAT THEY CAN DO?
ARE YOU GOING TO TREAT THEM LIKE CRIMINALS JUST BECAUSE?
YOU CAN SEE HOW THAT COULD BE A LITTLE TROUBLING, RIGHT?

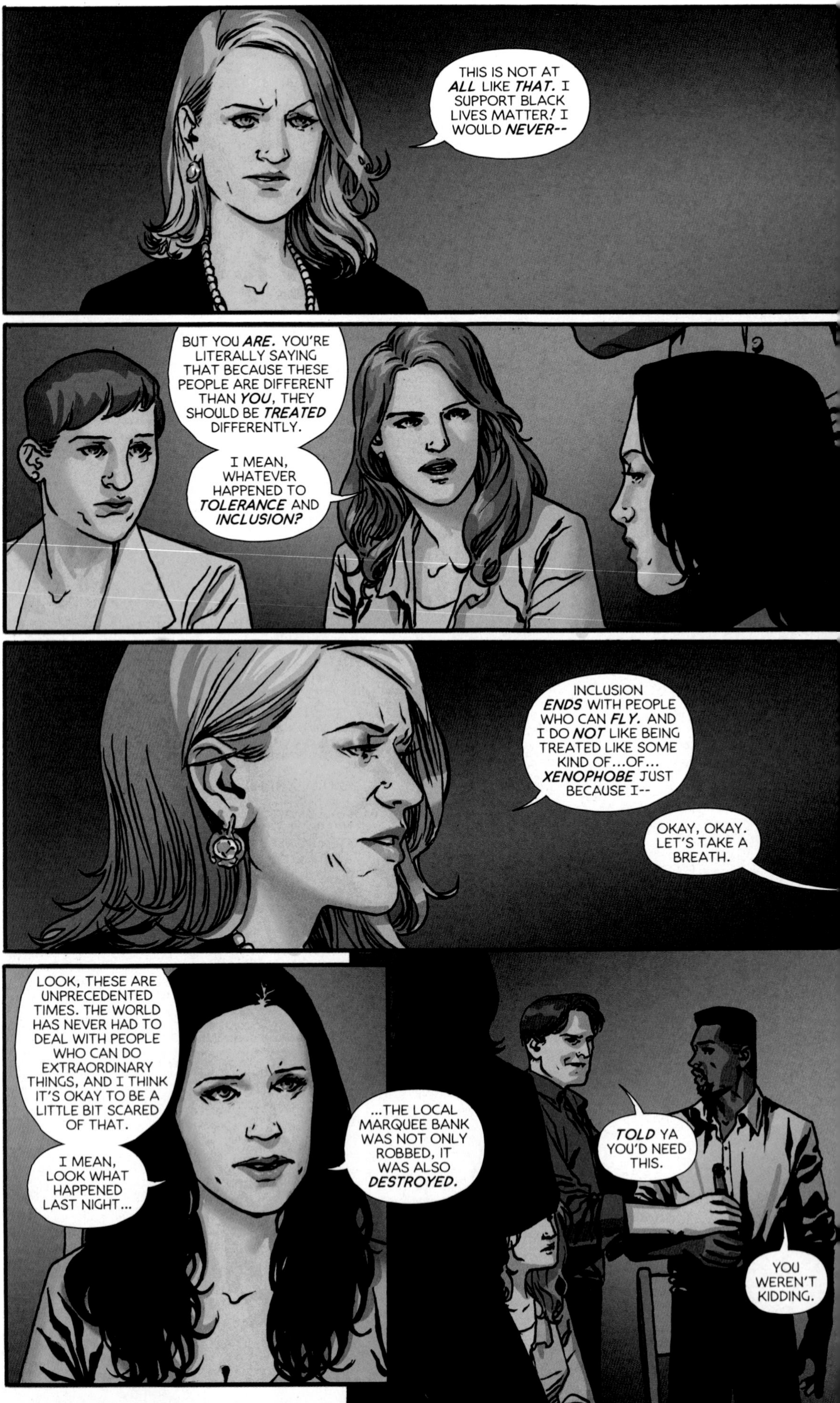

THIS IS NOT AT ALL LIKE THAT. I SUPPORT BLACK LIVES MATTER! I WOULD NEVER--
BUT YOU ARE. YOU'RE LITERALLY SAYING THAT BECAUSE THESE PEOPLE ARE DIFFERENT THAN YOU, THEY SHOULD BE TREATED DIFFERENTLY.
I MEAN, WHATEVER HAPPENED TO TOLERANCE AND INCLUSION?
INCLUSION ENDS WITH PEOPLE WHO CAN FLY. AND I DO NOT LIKE BEING TREATED LIKE SOME KIND OF...OF... XENOPHOBE JUST BECAUSE I--
OKAY, OKAY. LET'S TAKE A BREATH.
LOOK, THESE ARE UNPRECEDENTED TIMES. THE WORLD HAS NEVER HAD TO DEAL WITH PEOPLE WHO CAN DO EXTRAORDINARY THINGS, AND I THINK IT'S OKAY TO BE A LITTLE BIT SCARED OF THAT.
I MEAN, LOOK WHAT HAPPENED LAST NIGHT...
...THE LOCAL MARQUEE BANK WAS NOT ONLY ROBBED, IT WAS ALSO DESTROYED.
TOLD YA YOU'D NEED THIS.
YOU WEREN'T KIDDING.

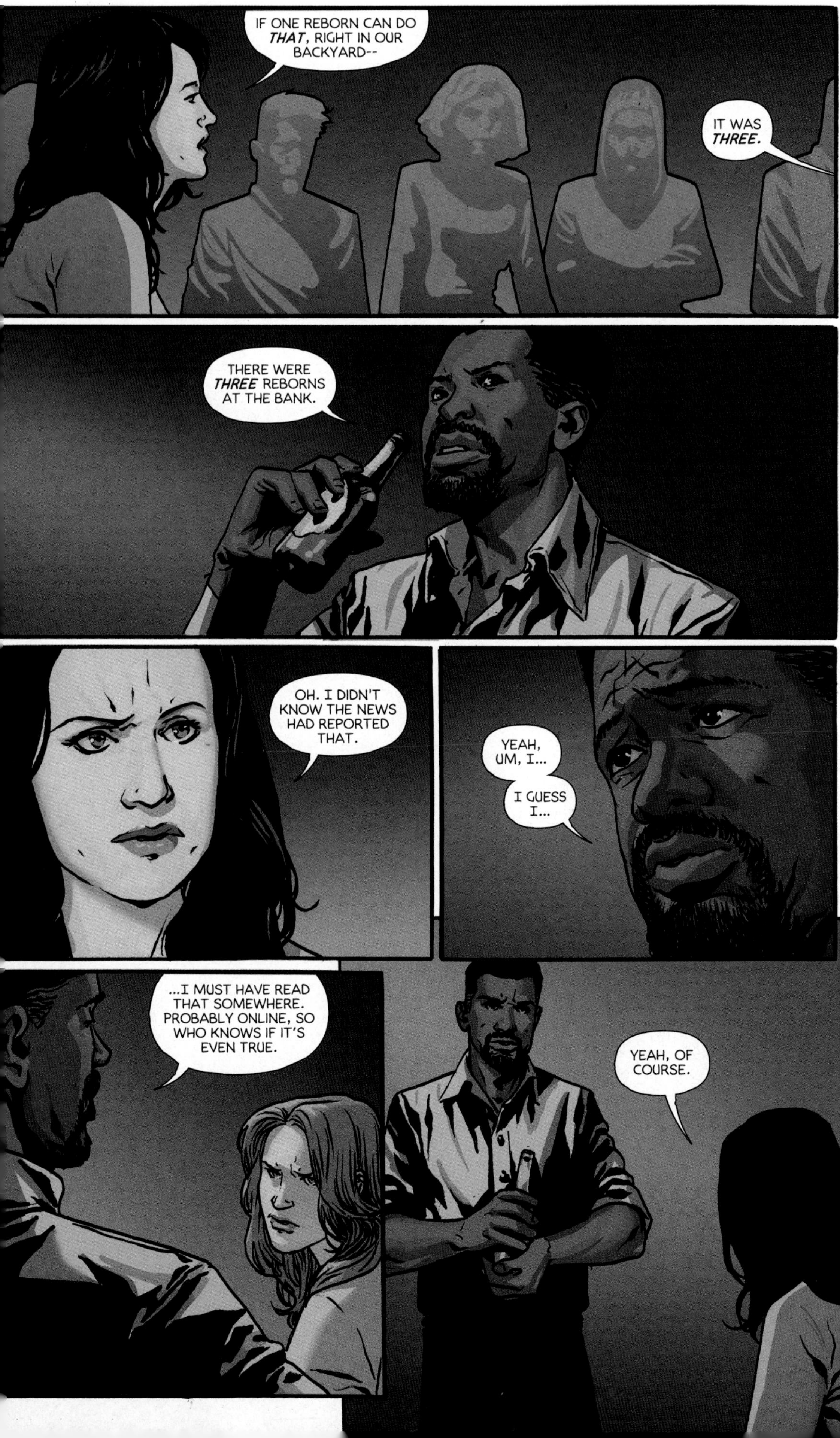
IF ONE REBORN CAN DO *THAT*, RIGHT IN OUR BACKYARD--
IT WAS *THREE.*
THERE WERE *THREE* REBORNS AT THE BANK.
OH. I DIDN'T KNOW THE NEWS HAD REPORTED THAT.
YEAH, UM, I...
I GUESS I...
...I MUST HAVE READ THAT SOMEWHERE. PROBABLY ONLINE, SO WHO KNOWS IF IT'S EVEN TRUE.
YEAH, OF COURSE.

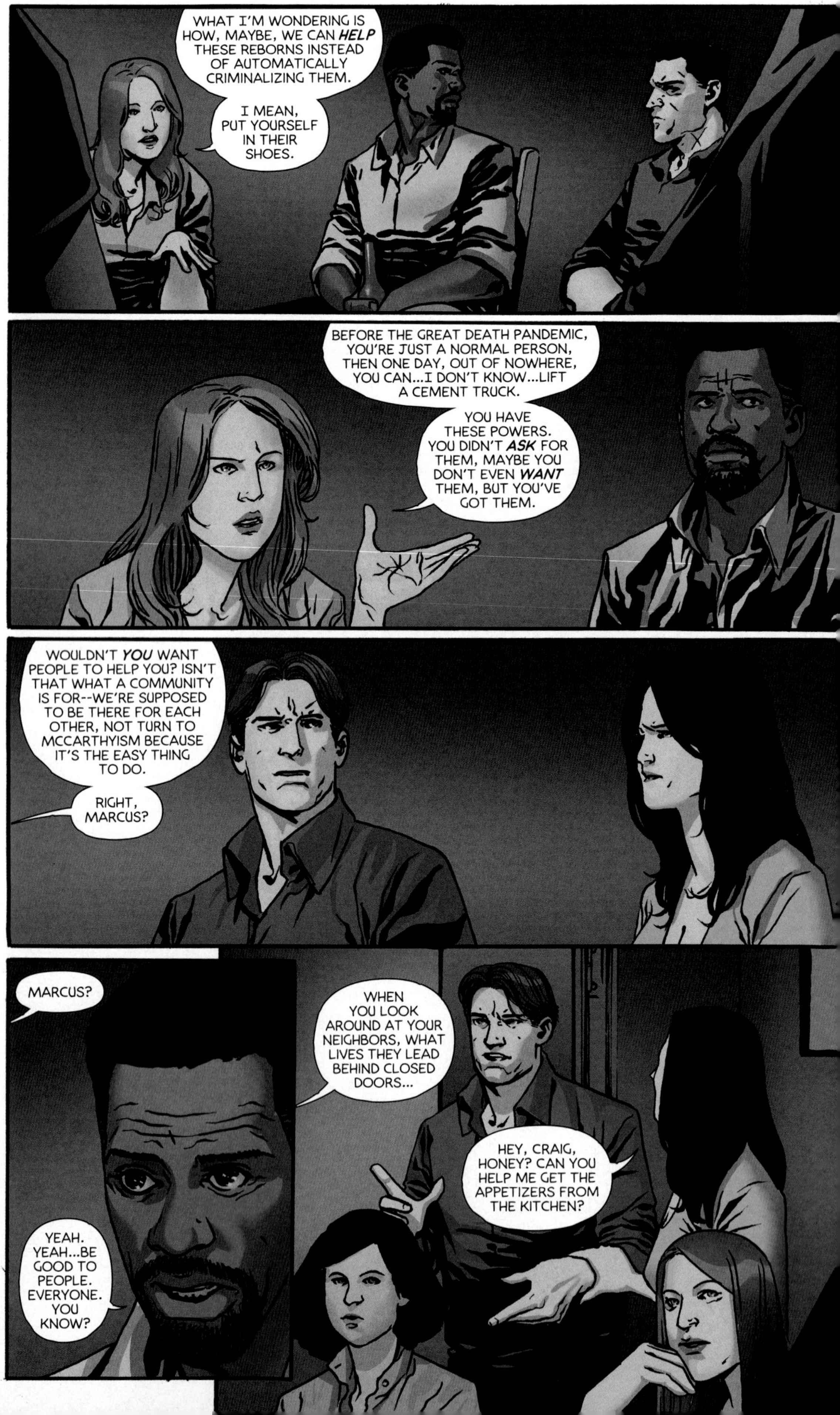
WHAT I'M WONDERING IS HOW, MAYBE, WE CAN HELP THESE REBORNS INSTEAD OF AUTOMATICALLY CRIMINALIZING THEM.
I MEAN, PUT YOURSELF IN THEIR SHOES.
BEFORE THE GREAT DEATH PANDEMIC, YOU'RE JUST A NORMAL PERSON, THEN ONE DAY, OUT OF NOWHERE, YOU CAN...I DON'T KNOW...LIFT A CEMENT TRUCK.
YOU HAVE THESE POWERS. YOU DIDN'T ASK FOR THEM, MAYBE YOU DON'T EVEN WANT THEM, BUT YOU'VE GOT THEM.
WOULDN'T YOU WANT PEOPLE TO HELP YOU? ISN'T THAT WHAT A COMMUNITY IS FOR--WE'RE SUPPOSED TO BE THERE FOR EACH OTHER, NOT TURN TO MCCARTHYISM BECAUSE IT'S THE EASY THING TO DO.
RIGHT, MARCUS?
MARCUS?
WHEN YOU LOOK AROUND AT YOUR NEIGHBORS, WHAT LIVES THEY LEAD BEHIND CLOSED DOORS...
HEY, CRAIG, HONEY? CAN YOU HELP ME GET THE APPETIZERS FROM THE KITCHEN?
YEAH. YEAH...BE GOOD TO PEOPLE. EVERYONE. YOU KNOW?

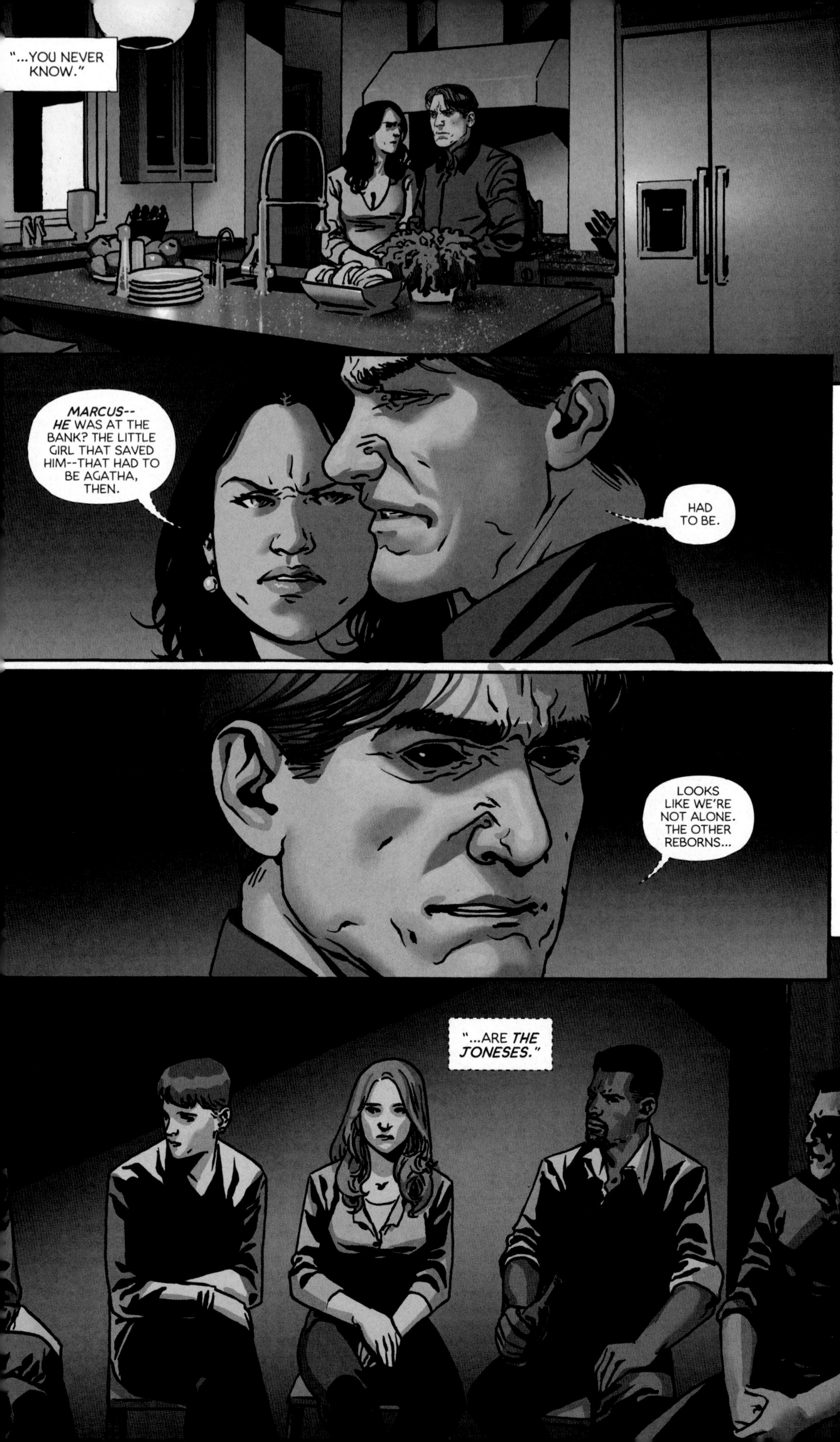
"...YOU NEVER KNOW."
MARCUS-- *HE* WAS AT THE BANK? THE LITTLE GIRL THAT SAVED HIM--THAT HAD TO BE AGATHA, THEN.
HAD TO BE.
LOOKS LIKE WE'RE NOT ALONE. THE OTHER REBORNS...
"...ARE *THE JONESES.*"

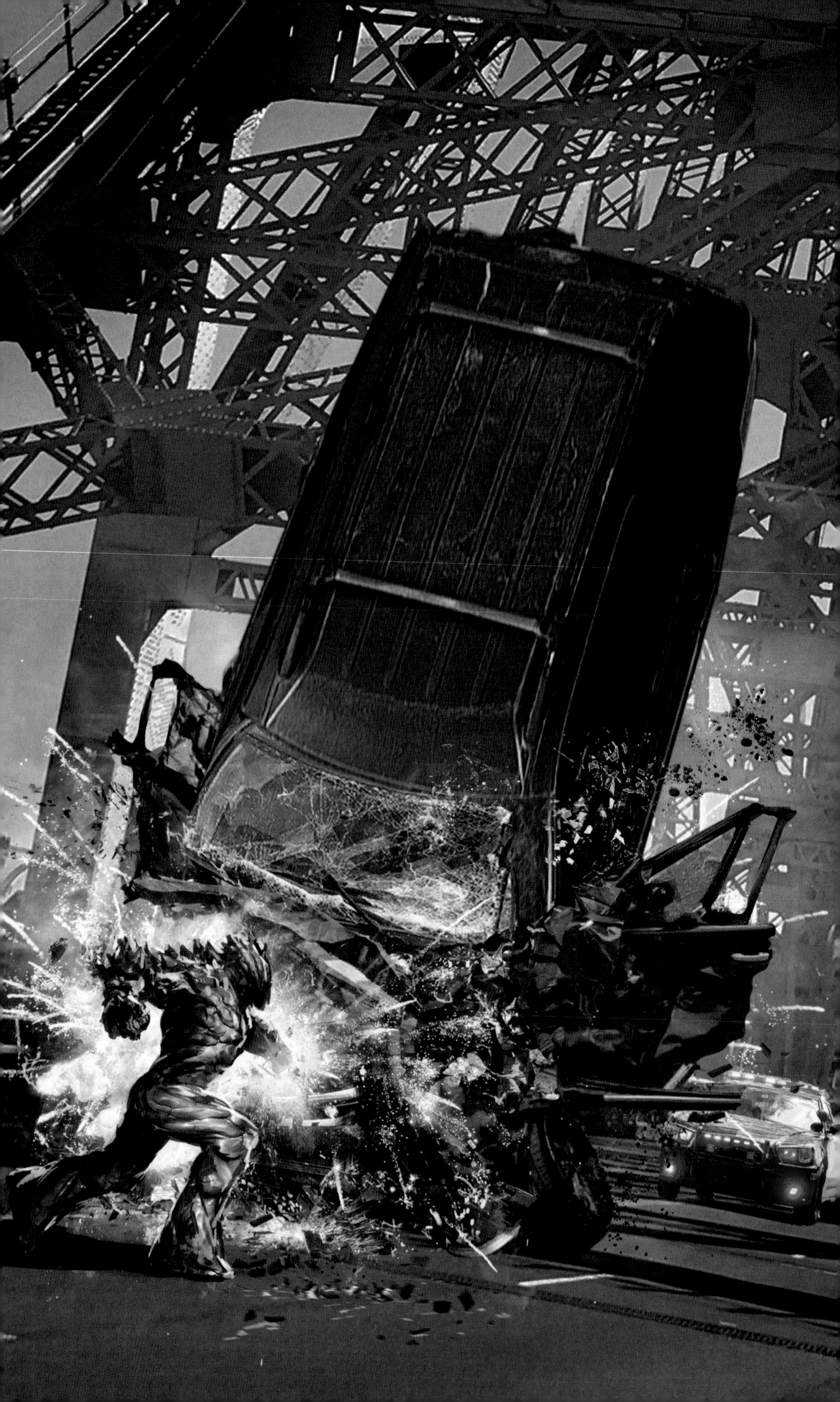

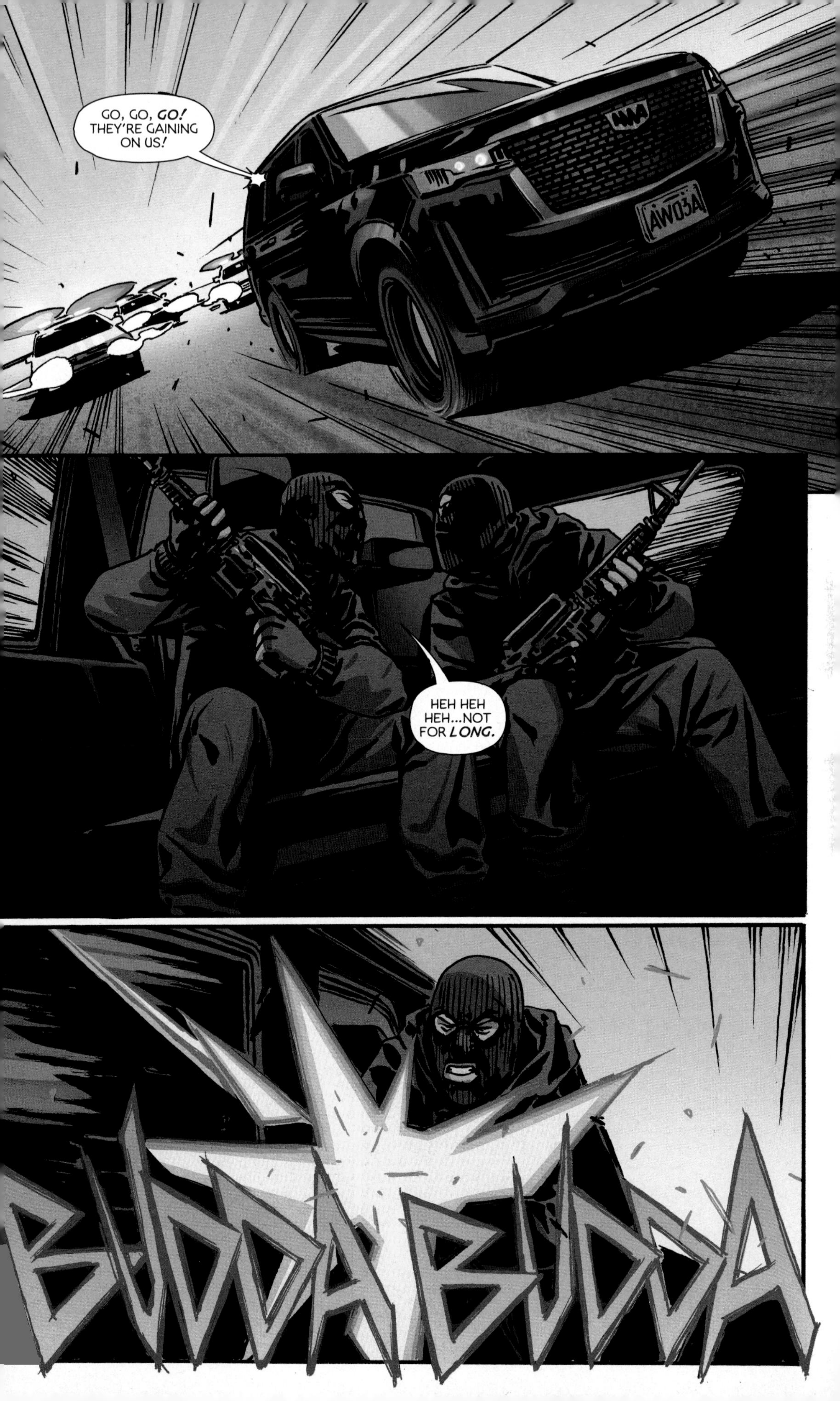
GO, GO, GO! THEY'RE GAINING ON US!
AW03A
HEH HEH HEH...NOT FOR LONG.
BUDDA BUDDA

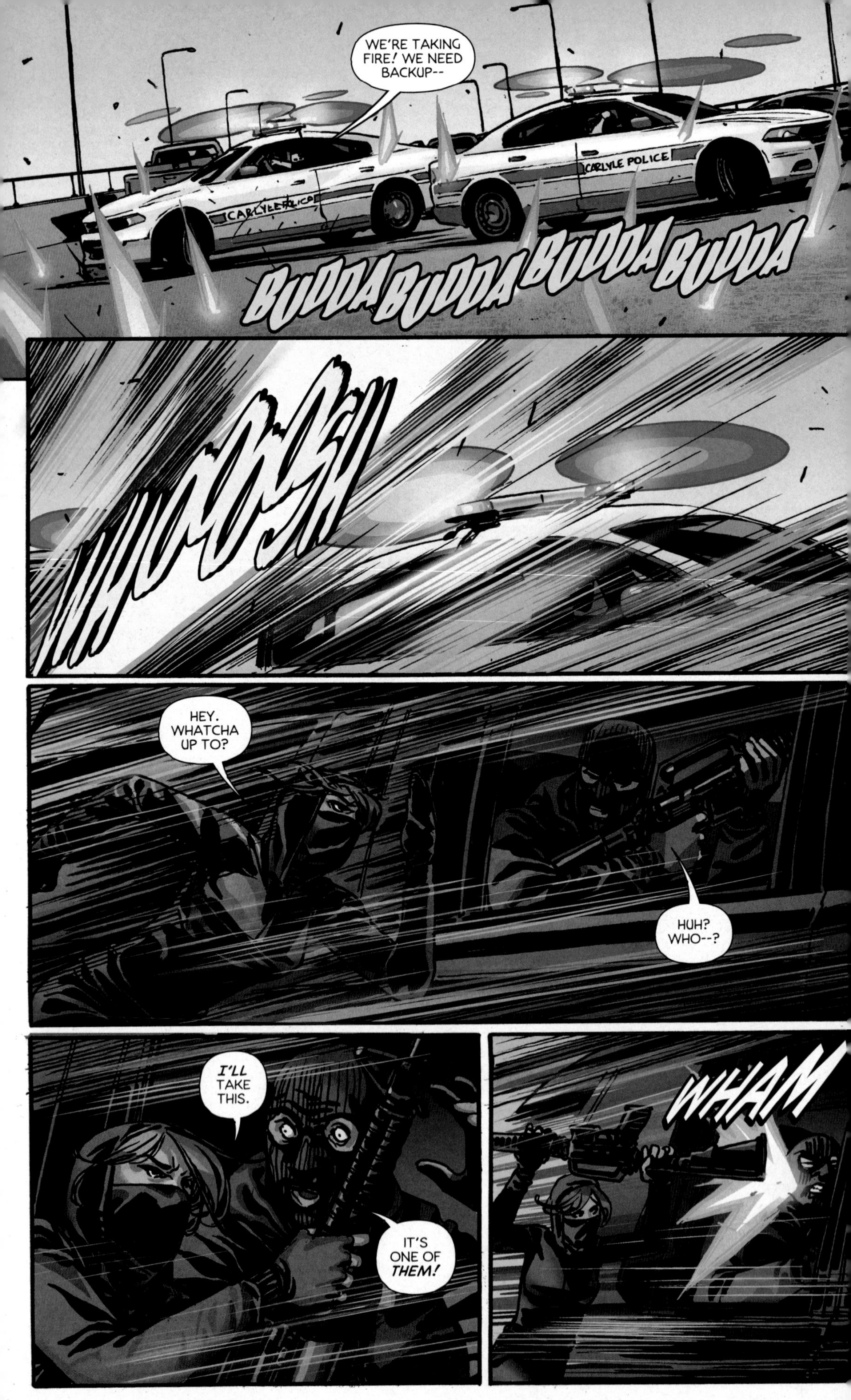
WE'RE TAKING FIRE! WE NEED BACKUP--
CARLYLE POLICE
CARLYLE POLICE
BUDDA BUDDA BUDDA BUDDA
WHOOSH
HEY. WHATCHA UP TO?
HUH? WHO--?
I'LL TAKE THIS.
IT'S ONE OF THEM!
WHAM

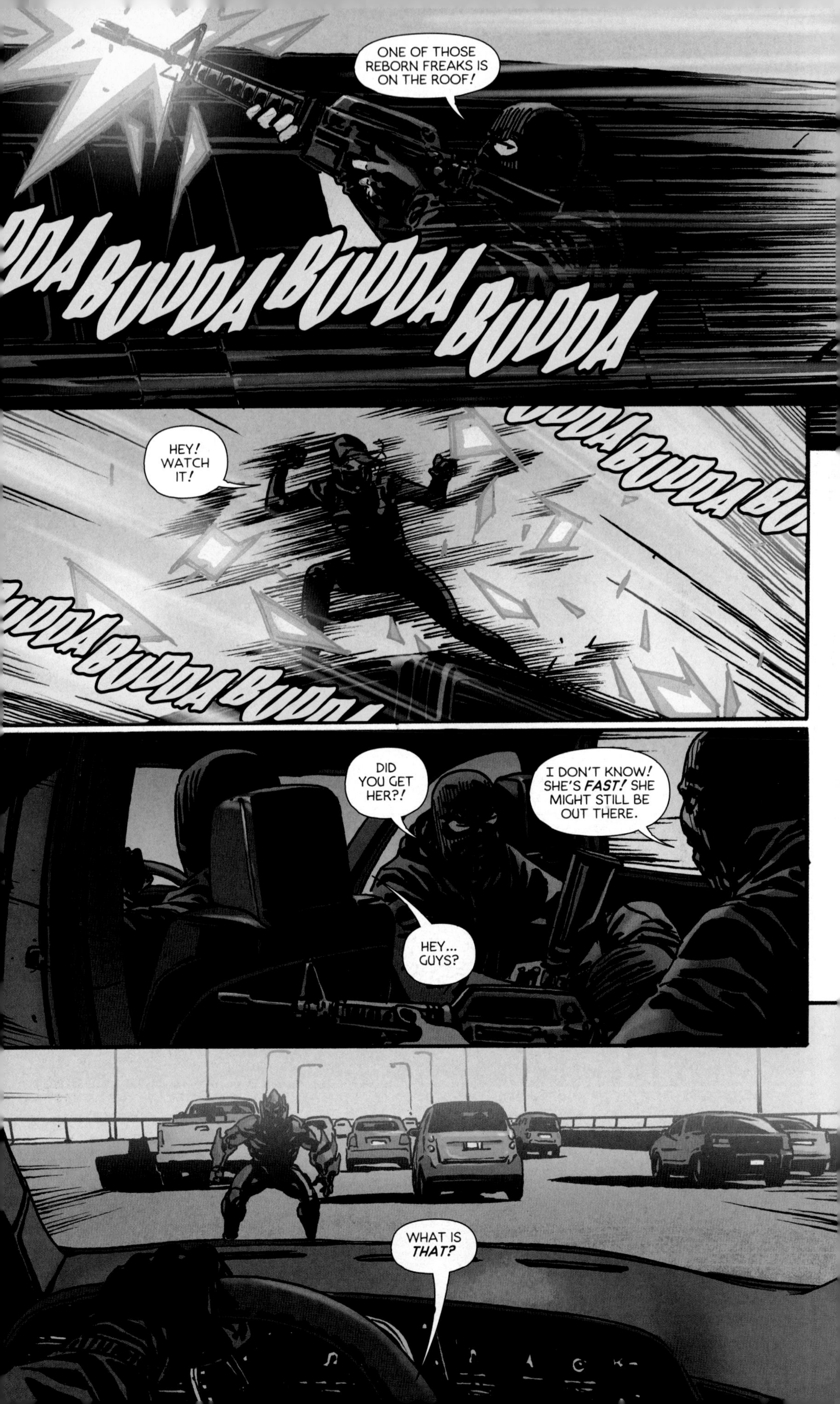
ONE OF THOSE REBORN FREAKS IS ON THE ROOF!
BUDDA BUDDA BUDDA
HEY! WATCH IT!
BUDDA BUDDA BU
BUDDA BUDDA BUDDA
DID YOU GET HER?!
I DON'T KNOW! SHE'S FAST! SHE MIGHT STILL BE OUT THERE.
HEY... GUYS?
WHAT IS THAT?

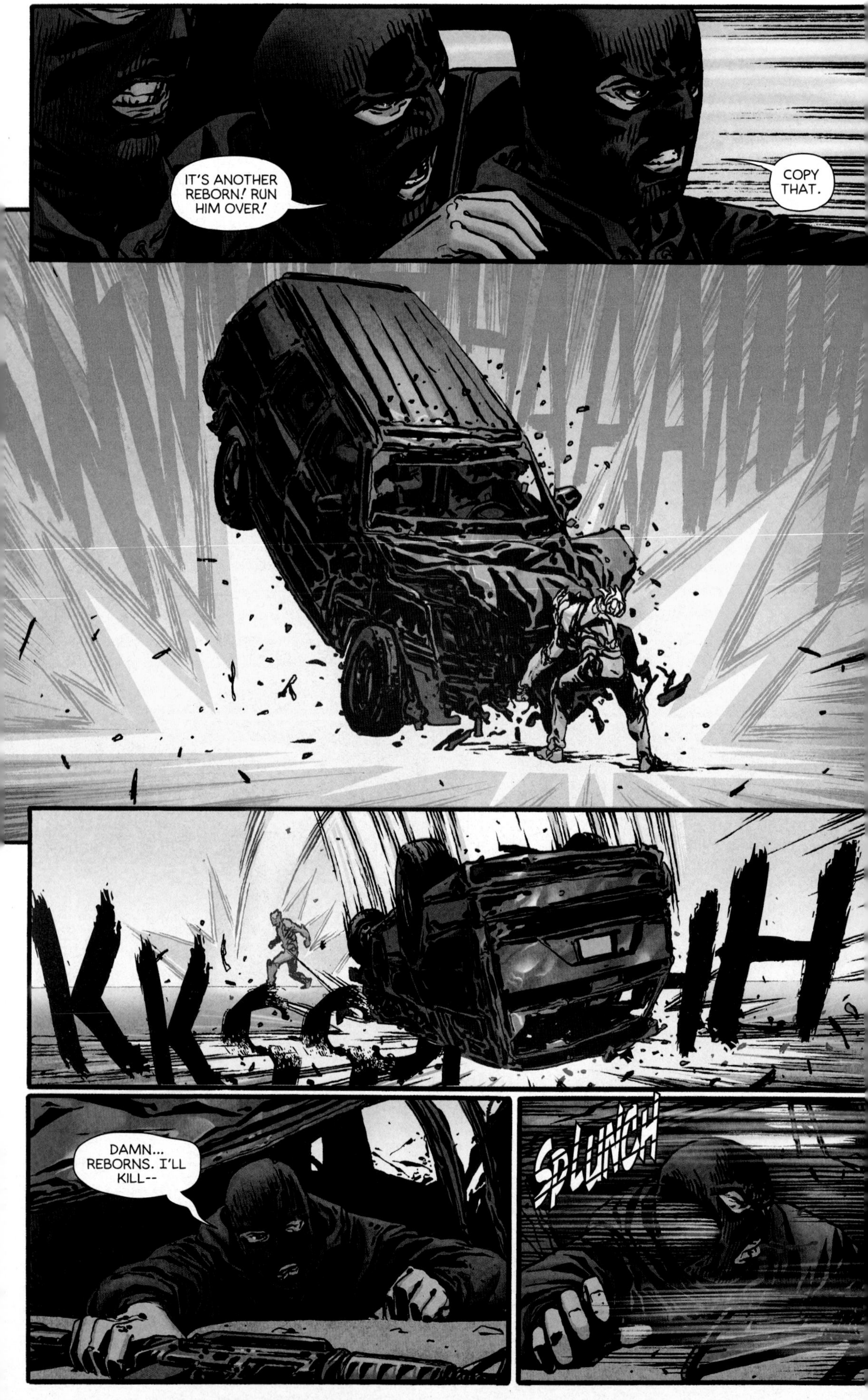

IT'S ANOTHER REBORN! RUN HIM OVER!
COPY THAT.
DAMN... REBORNS. I'LL KILL--
SPLUNCH

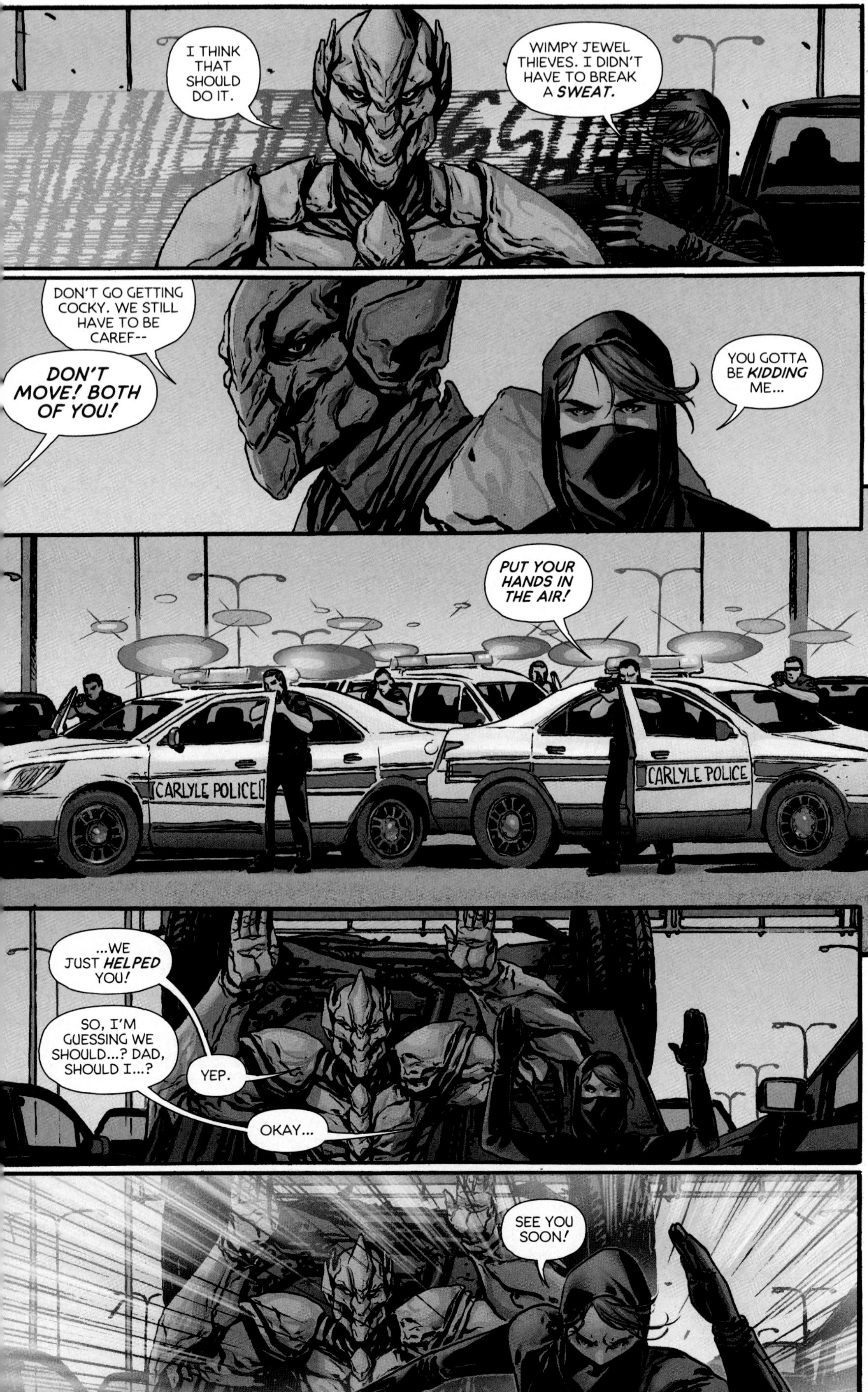
I THINK THAT SHOULD DO IT.
WIMPY JEWEL THIEVES. I DIDN'T HAVE TO BREAK A *SWEAT.*
DON'T GO GETTING COCKY. WE STILL HAVE TO BE CAREF--
DON'T MOVE! BOTH OF YOU!
YOU GOTTA BE *KIDDING* ME...
PUT YOUR HANDS IN THE AIR!
CARLYLE POLICE
CARLYLE POLICE
...WE JUST *HELPED* YOU!
SO, I'M GUESSING WE SHOULD...? DAD, SHOULD I...?
YEP.
OKAY...
SEE YOU SOON!

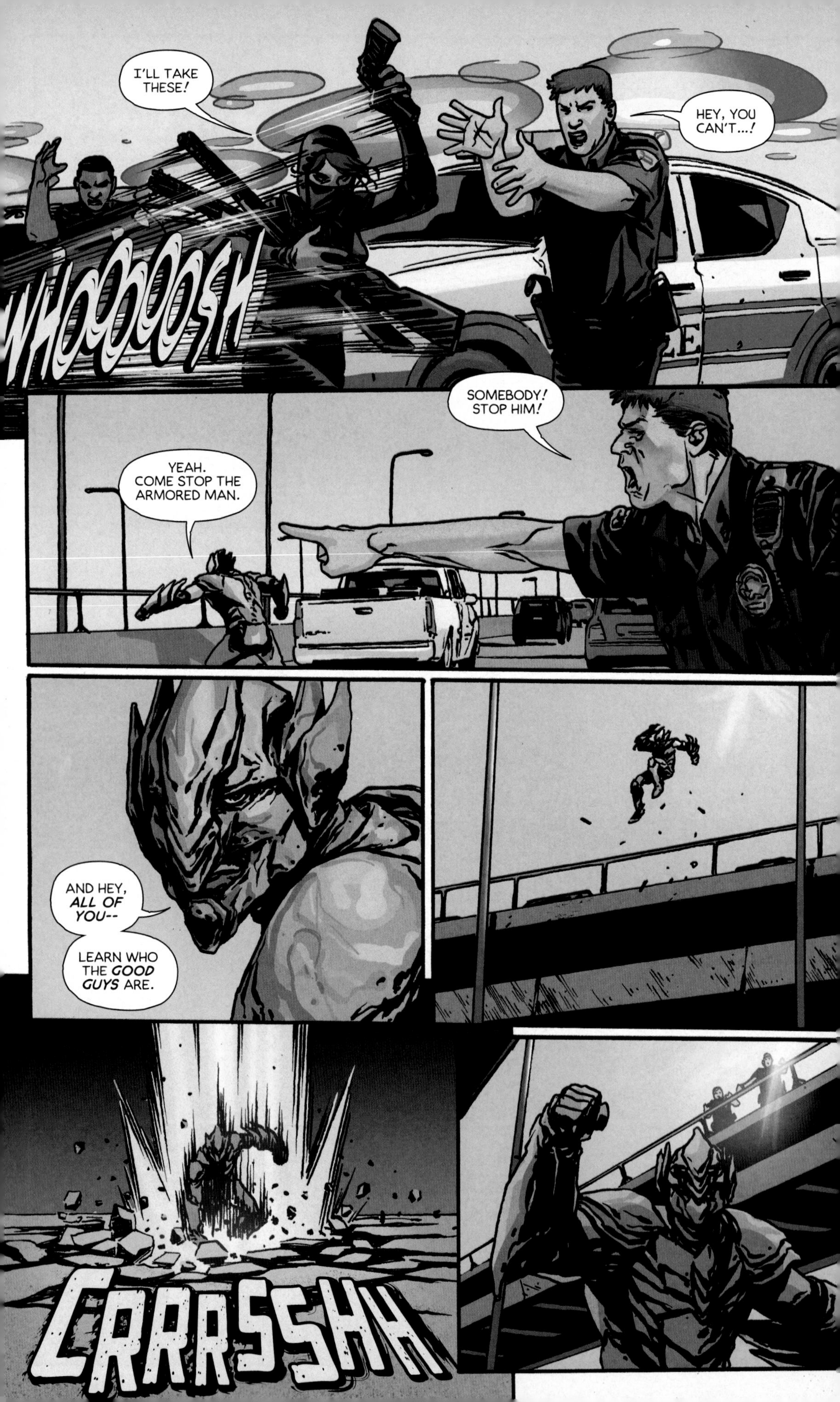
I'LL TAKE THESE!
HEY, YOU CAN'T...!
WHOOOOOSH
SOMEBODY! STOP HIM!
YEAH. COME STOP THE ARMORED MAN.
AND HEY, ALL OF YOU--
LEARN WHO THE GOOD GUYS ARE.
CRRRSSHH

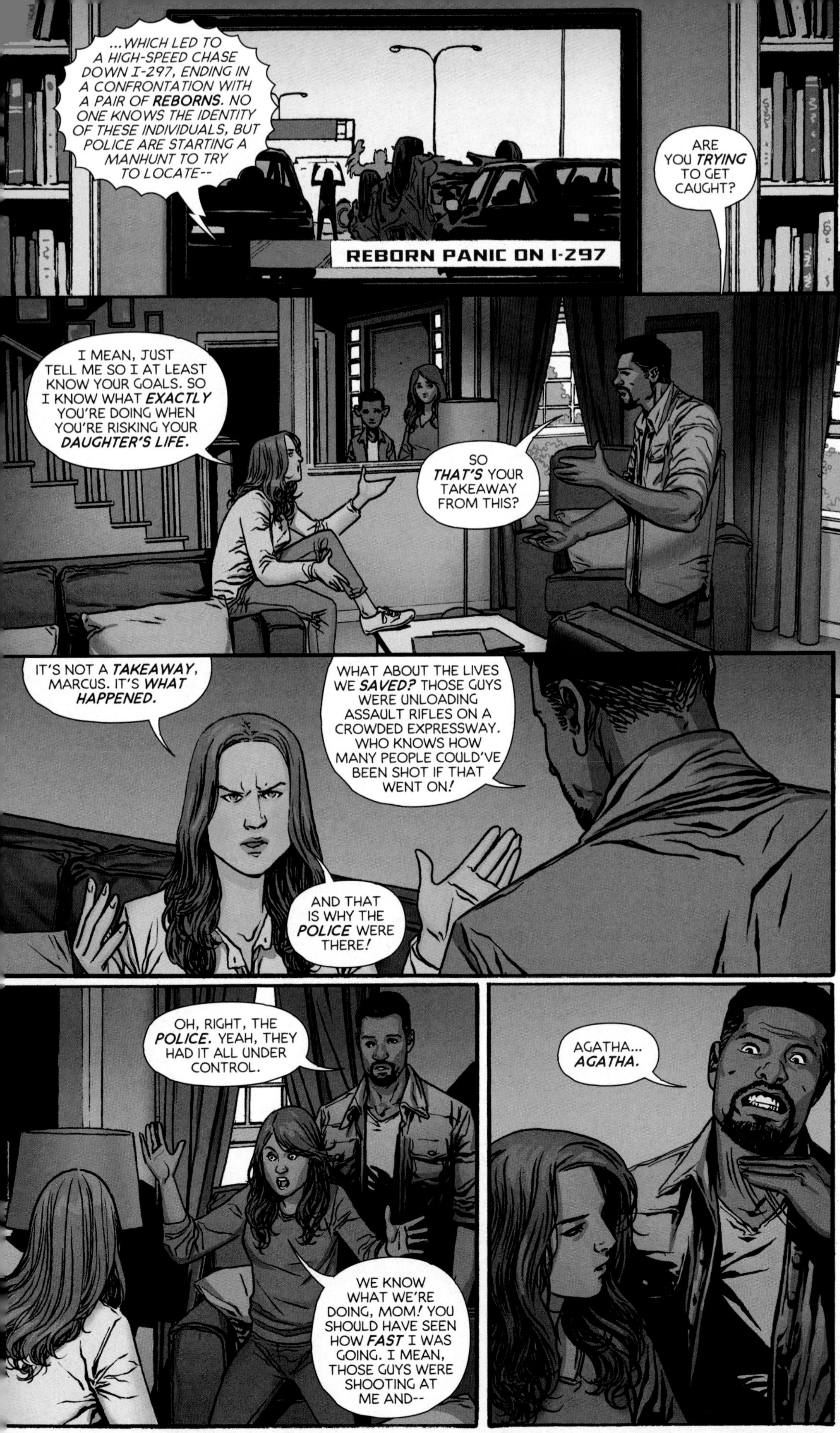
...WHICH LED TO A HIGH-SPEED CHASE DOWN I-297, ENDING IN A CONFRONTATION WITH A PAIR OF REBORNS. NO ONE KNOWS THE IDENTITY OF THESE INDIVIDUALS, BUT POLICE ARE STARTING A MANHUNT TO TRY TO LOCATE--
REBORN PANIC ON I-297
ARE YOU TRYING TO GET CAUGHT?
I MEAN, JUST TELL ME SO I AT LEAST KNOW YOUR GOALS. SO I KNOW WHAT EXACTLY YOU'RE DOING WHEN YOU'RE RISKING YOUR DAUGHTER'S LIFE.
SO THAT'S YOUR TAKEAWAY FROM THIS?
IT'S NOT A TAKEAWAY, MARCUS. IT'S WHAT HAPPENED.
WHAT ABOUT THE LIVES WE SAVED? THOSE GUYS WERE UNLOADING ASSAULT RIFLES ON A CROWDED EXPRESSWAY. WHO KNOWS HOW MANY PEOPLE COULD'VE BEEN SHOT IF THAT WENT ON!
AND THAT IS WHY THE POLICE WERE THERE!
OH, RIGHT, THE POLICE. YEAH, THEY HAD IT ALL UNDER CONTROL.
WE KNOW WHAT WE'RE DOING, MOM! YOU SHOULD HAVE SEEN HOW FAST I WAS GOING. I MEAN, THOSE GUYS WERE SHOOTING AT ME AND--
AGATHA... AGATHA.

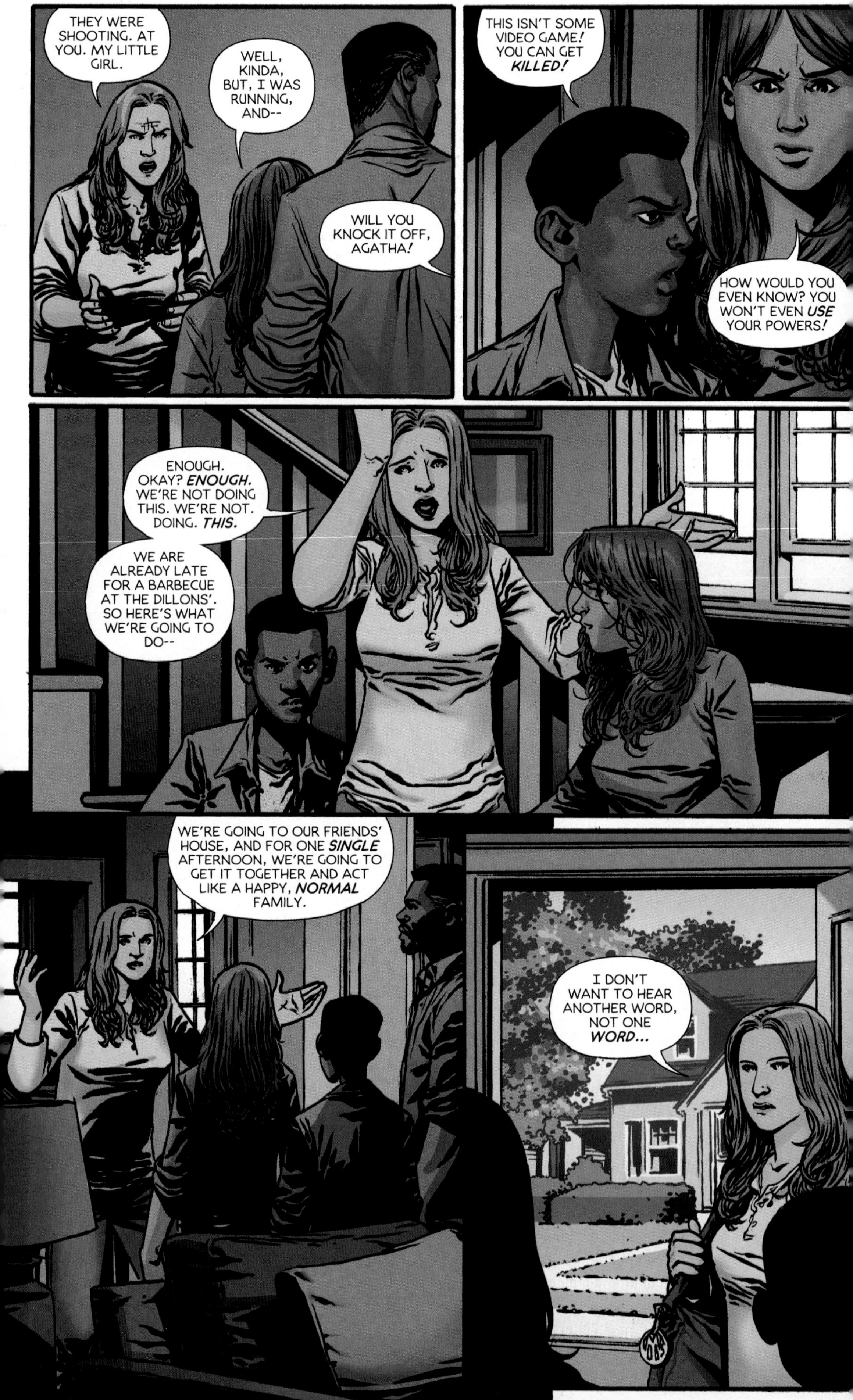
THEY WERE SHOOTING. AT YOU. MY LITTLE GIRL.
WELL, KINDA, BUT, I WAS RUNNING, AND--
WILL YOU KNOCK IT OFF, AGATHA!
THIS ISN'T SOME VIDEO GAME! YOU CAN GET KILLED!
HOW WOULD YOU EVEN KNOW? YOU WON'T EVEN USE YOUR POWERS!
ENOUGH. OKAY? ENOUGH. WE'RE NOT DOING THIS. WE'RE NOT. DOING. THIS.
WE ARE ALREADY LATE FOR A BARBECUE AT THE DILLONS'. SO HERE'S WHAT WE'RE GOING TO DO--
WE'RE GOING TO OUR FRIENDS' HOUSE, AND FOR ONE SINGLE AFTERNOON, WE'RE GOING TO GET IT TOGETHER AND ACT LIKE A HAPPY, NORMAL FAMILY.
I DON'T WANT TO HEAR ANOTHER WORD, NOT ONE WORD...

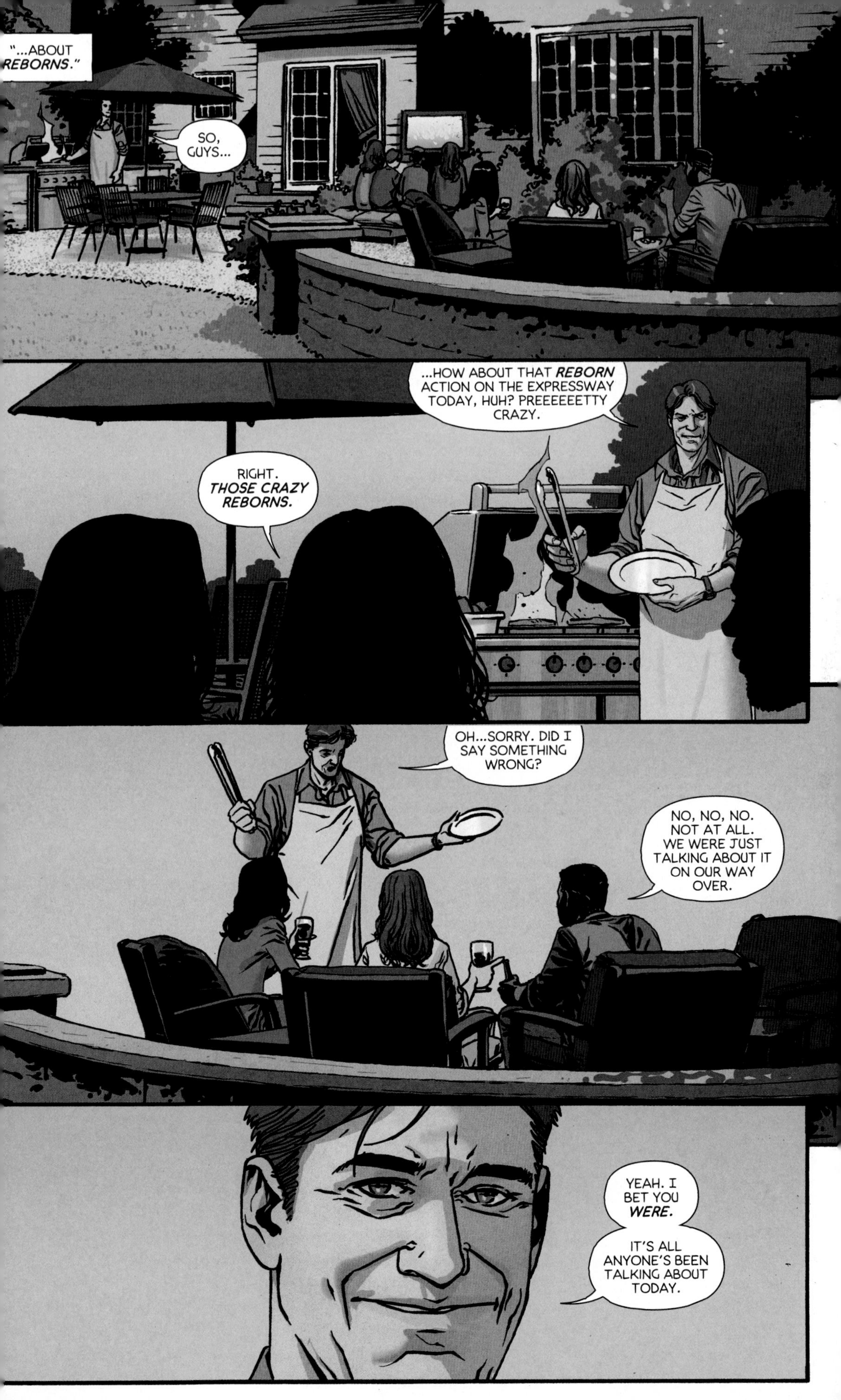
"...ABOUT *REBORNS*."
SO, GUYS...
...HOW ABOUT THAT *REBORN* ACTION ON THE EXPRESSWAY TODAY, HUH? PREEEEEETTY CRAZY.
RIGHT. *THOSE CRAZY REBORNS.*
OH...SORRY. DID I SAY SOMETHING WRONG?
NO, NO, NO. NOT AT ALL. WE WERE JUST TALKING ABOUT IT ON OUR WAY OVER.
YEAH. I BET YOU *WERE.*
IT'S ALL ANYONE'S BEEN TALKING ABOUT TODAY.

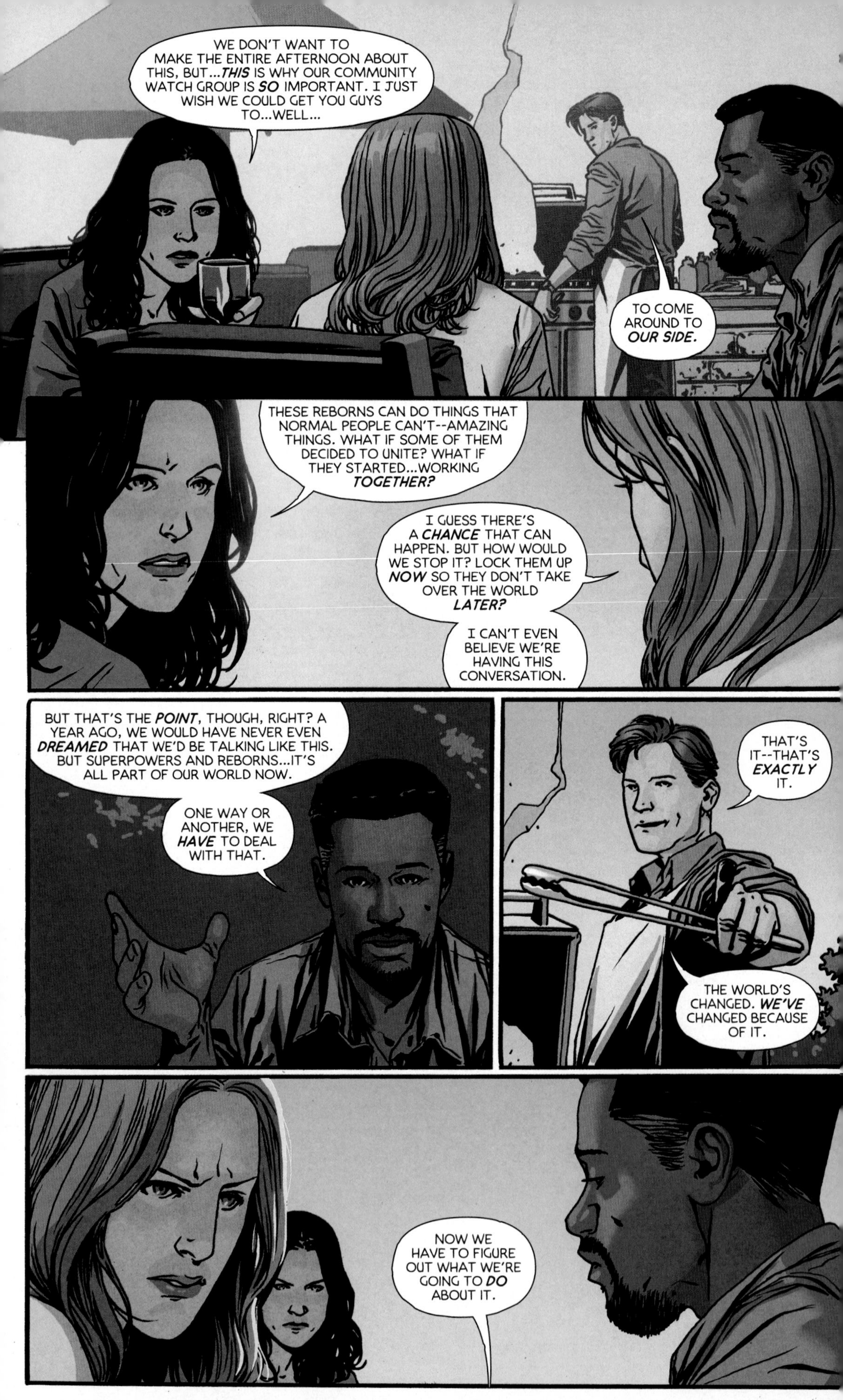
WE DON'T WANT TO MAKE THE ENTIRE AFTERNOON ABOUT THIS, BUT...*THIS* IS WHY OUR COMMUNITY WATCH GROUP IS *SO* IMPORTANT. I JUST WISH WE COULD GET YOU GUYS TO...WELL...
TO COME AROUND TO *OUR SIDE.*
THESE REBORNS CAN DO THINGS THAT NORMAL PEOPLE CAN'T--AMAZING THINGS. WHAT IF SOME OF THEM DECIDED TO UNITE? WHAT IF THEY STARTED...WORKING *TOGETHER?*
I GUESS THERE'S A *CHANCE* THAT CAN HAPPEN. BUT HOW WOULD WE STOP IT? LOCK THEM UP *NOW* SO THEY DON'T TAKE OVER THE WORLD *LATER?*
I CAN'T EVEN BELIEVE WE'RE HAVING THIS CONVERSATION.
BUT THAT'S THE *POINT*, THOUGH, RIGHT? A YEAR AGO, WE WOULD HAVE NEVER EVEN *DREAMED* THAT WE'D BE TALKING LIKE THIS. BUT SUPERPOWERS AND REBORNS...IT'S ALL PART OF OUR WORLD NOW.
ONE WAY OR ANOTHER, WE *HAVE* TO DEAL WITH THAT.
THAT'S IT--THAT'S *EXACTLY* IT.
THE WORLD'S CHANGED. *WE'VE* CHANGED BECAUSE OF IT.
NOW WE HAVE TO FIGURE OUT WHAT WE'RE GOING TO *DO* ABOUT IT.

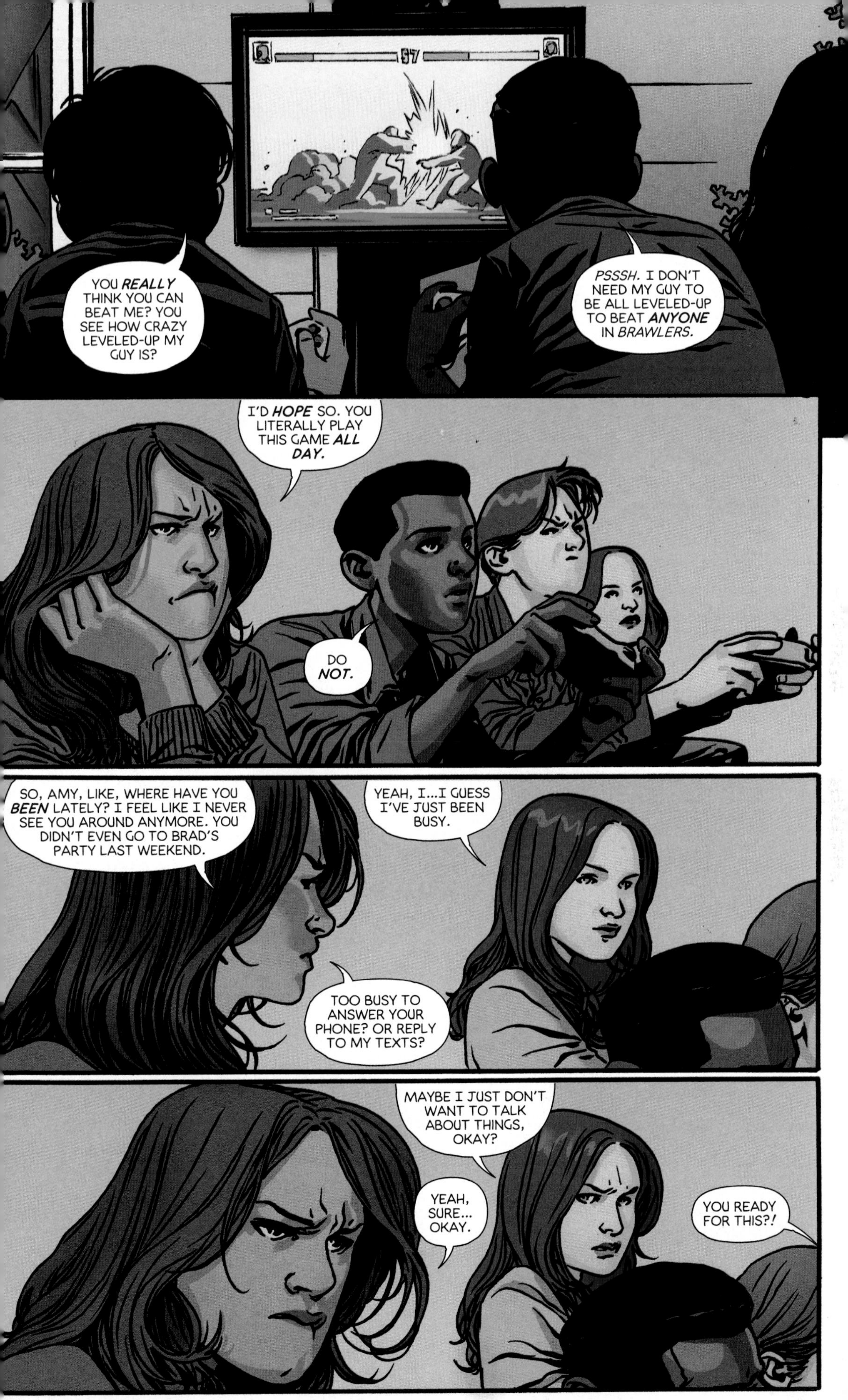
YOU REALLY THINK YOU CAN BEAT ME? YOU SEE HOW CRAZY LEVELED-UP MY GUY IS?
PSSSH. I DON'T NEED MY GUY TO BE ALL LEVELED-UP TO BEAT ANYONE IN BRAWLERS.
I'D HOPE SO. YOU LITERALLY PLAY THIS GAME ALL DAY.
DO NOT.
SO, AMY, LIKE, WHERE HAVE YOU BEEN LATELY? I FEEL LIKE I NEVER SEE YOU AROUND ANYMORE. YOU DIDN'T EVEN GO TO BRAD'S PARTY LAST WEEKEND.
YEAH, I...I GUESS I'VE JUST BEEN BUSY.
TOO BUSY TO ANSWER YOUR PHONE? OR REPLY TO MY TEXTS?
MAYBE I JUST DON'T WANT TO TALK ABOUT THINGS, OKAY?
YEAH, SURE... OKAY.
YOU READY FOR THIS?!

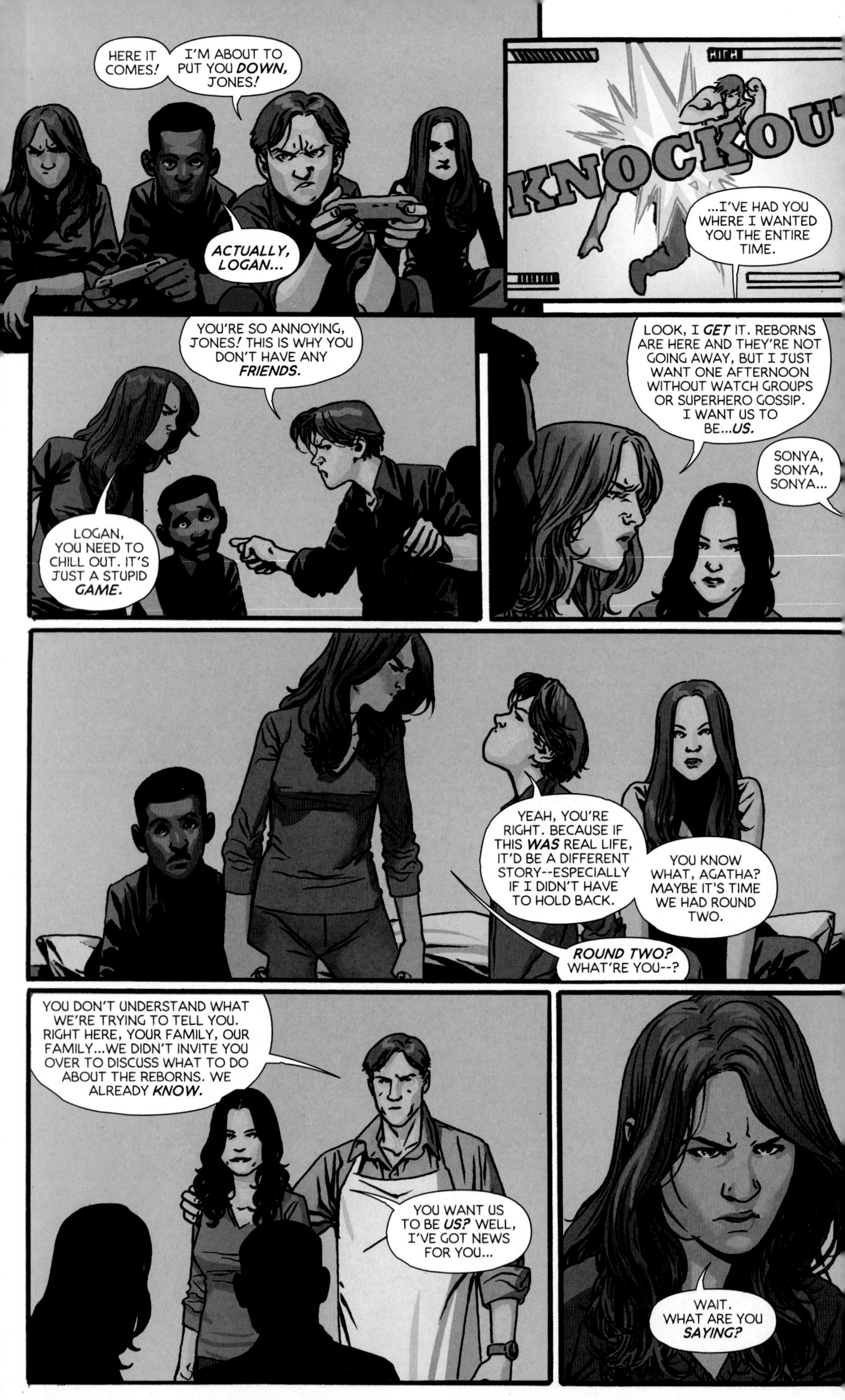
HERE IT COMES!
I'M ABOUT TO PUT YOU DOWN, JONES!
ACTUALLY, LOGAN...
KNOCKOUT
...I'VE HAD YOU WHERE I WANTED YOU THE ENTIRE TIME.
YOU'RE SO ANNOYING, JONES! THIS IS WHY YOU DON'T HAVE ANY FRIENDS.
LOGAN, YOU NEED TO CHILL OUT. IT'S JUST A STUPID GAME.
LOOK, I GET IT. REBORNS ARE HERE AND THEY'RE NOT GOING AWAY, BUT I JUST WANT ONE AFTERNOON WITHOUT WATCH GROUPS OR SUPERHERO GOSSIP. I WANT US TO BE...US.
SONYA, SONYA, SONYA...
YEAH, YOU'RE RIGHT. BECAUSE IF THIS WAS REAL LIFE, IT'D BE A DIFFERENT STORY--ESPECIALLY IF I DIDN'T HAVE TO HOLD BACK.
YOU KNOW WHAT, AGATHA? MAYBE IT'S TIME WE HAD ROUND TWO.
ROUND TWO? WHAT'RE YOU--?
YOU DON'T UNDERSTAND WHAT WE'RE TRYING TO TELL YOU. RIGHT HERE, YOUR FAMILY, OUR FAMILY...WE DIDN'T INVITE YOU OVER TO DISCUSS WHAT TO DO ABOUT THE REBORNS. WE ALREADY KNOW.
YOU WANT US TO BE US? WELL, I'VE GOT NEWS FOR YOU...
WAIT. WHAT ARE YOU SAYING?

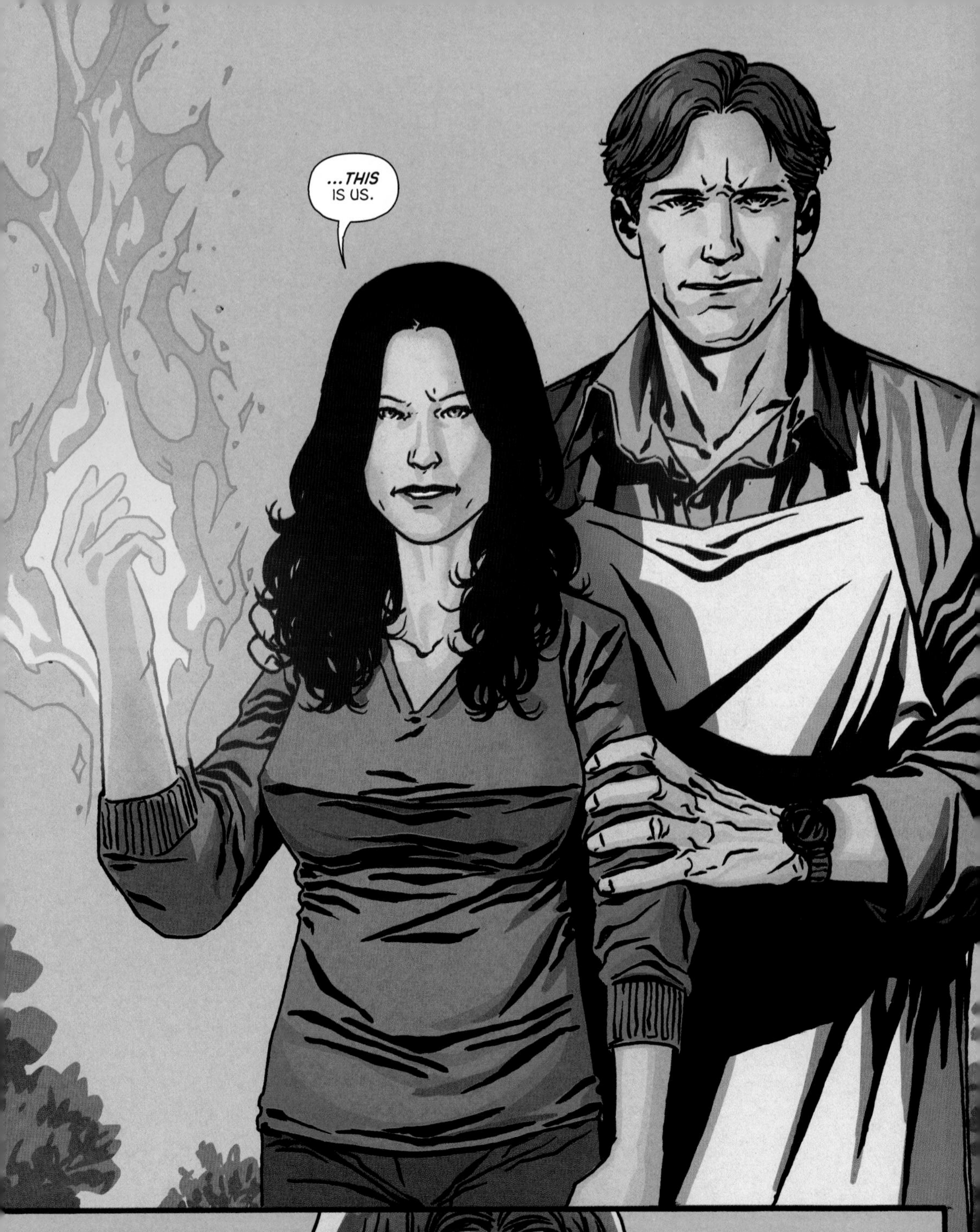
...THIS IS US.
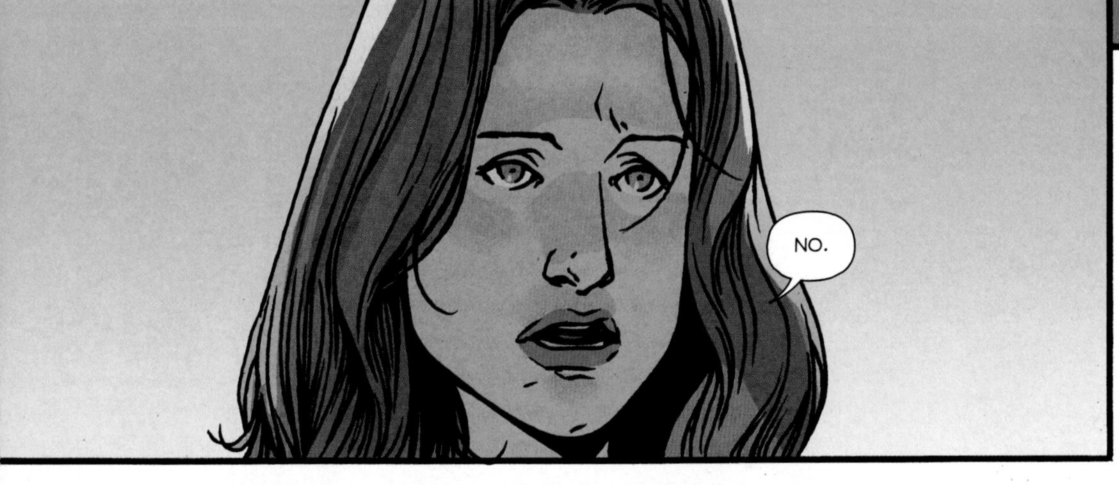
NO.

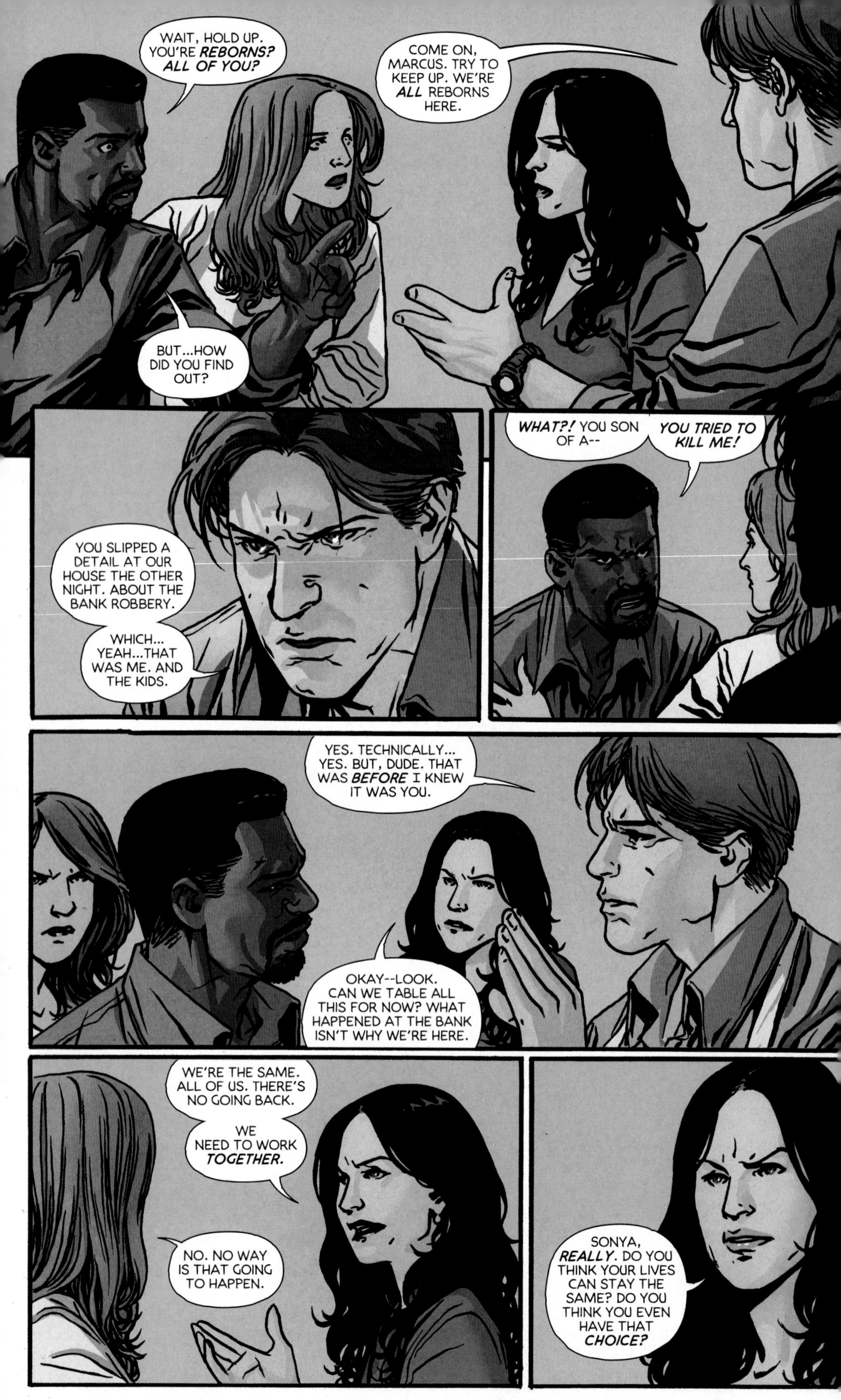
WAIT, HOLD UP. YOU'RE REBORNS? ALL OF YOU?
COME ON, MARCUS. TRY TO KEEP UP. WE'RE ALL REBORNS HERE.
BUT...HOW DID YOU FIND OUT?
YOU SLIPPED A DETAIL AT OUR HOUSE THE OTHER NIGHT. ABOUT THE BANK ROBBERY.
WHICH... YEAH...THAT WAS ME. AND THE KIDS.
WHAT?! YOU SON OF A--
YOU TRIED TO KILL ME!
YES. TECHNICALLY... YES. BUT, DUDE. THAT WAS BEFORE I KNEW IT WAS YOU.
OKAY--LOOK. CAN WE TABLE ALL THIS FOR NOW? WHAT HAPPENED AT THE BANK ISN'T WHY WE'RE HERE.
WE'RE THE SAME. ALL OF US. THERE'S NO GOING BACK.
WE NEED TO WORK TOGETHER.
NO. NO WAY IS THAT GOING TO HAPPEN.
SONYA, REALLY. DO YOU THINK YOUR LIVES CAN STAY THE SAME? DO YOU THINK YOU EVEN HAVE THAT CHOICE?

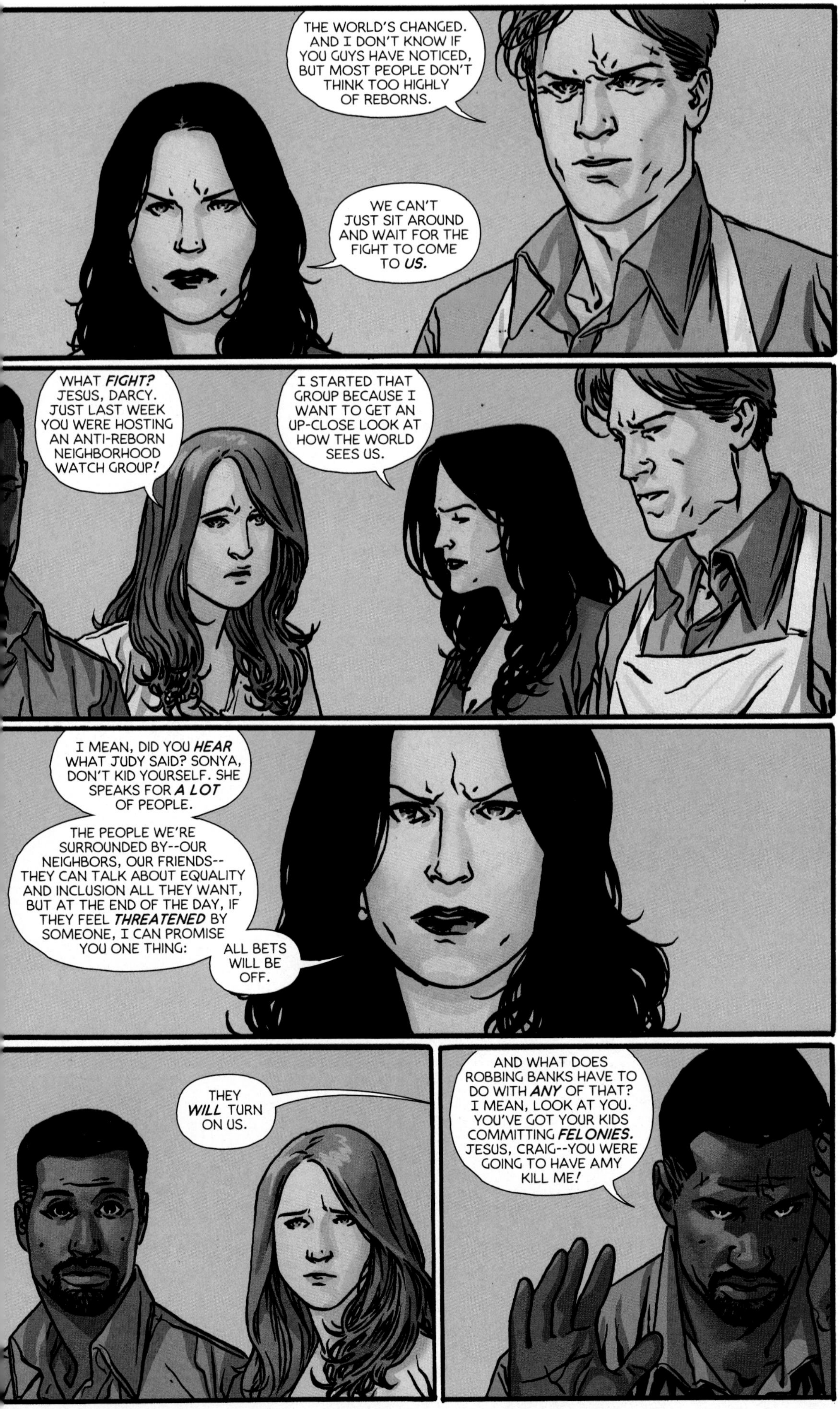
THE WORLD'S CHANGED. AND I DON'T KNOW IF YOU GUYS HAVE NOTICED, BUT MOST PEOPLE DON'T THINK TOO HIGHLY OF REBORNS.
WE CAN'T JUST SIT AROUND AND WAIT FOR THE FIGHT TO COME TO *US.*
WHAT *FIGHT?* JESUS, DARCY. JUST LAST WEEK YOU WERE HOSTING AN ANTI-REBORN NEIGHBORHOOD WATCH GROUP*!*
I STARTED THAT GROUP BECAUSE I WANT TO GET AN UP-CLOSE LOOK AT HOW THE WORLD SEES US.
I MEAN, DID YOU *HEAR* WHAT JUDY SAID? SONYA, DON'T KID YOURSELF. SHE SPEAKS FOR *A LOT* OF PEOPLE.
THE PEOPLE WE'RE SURROUNDED BY--OUR NEIGHBORS, OUR FRIENDS--THEY CAN TALK ABOUT EQUALITY AND INCLUSION ALL THEY WANT, BUT AT THE END OF THE DAY, IF THEY FEEL *THREATENED* BY SOMEONE, I CAN PROMISE YOU ONE THING:
ALL BETS WILL BE OFF.
THEY *WILL* TURN ON US.
AND WHAT DOES ROBBING BANKS HAVE TO DO WITH *ANY* OF THAT? I MEAN, LOOK AT YOU. YOU'VE GOT YOUR KIDS COMMITTING *FELONIES.* JESUS, CRAIG--YOU WERE GOING TO HAVE AMY KILL ME*!*

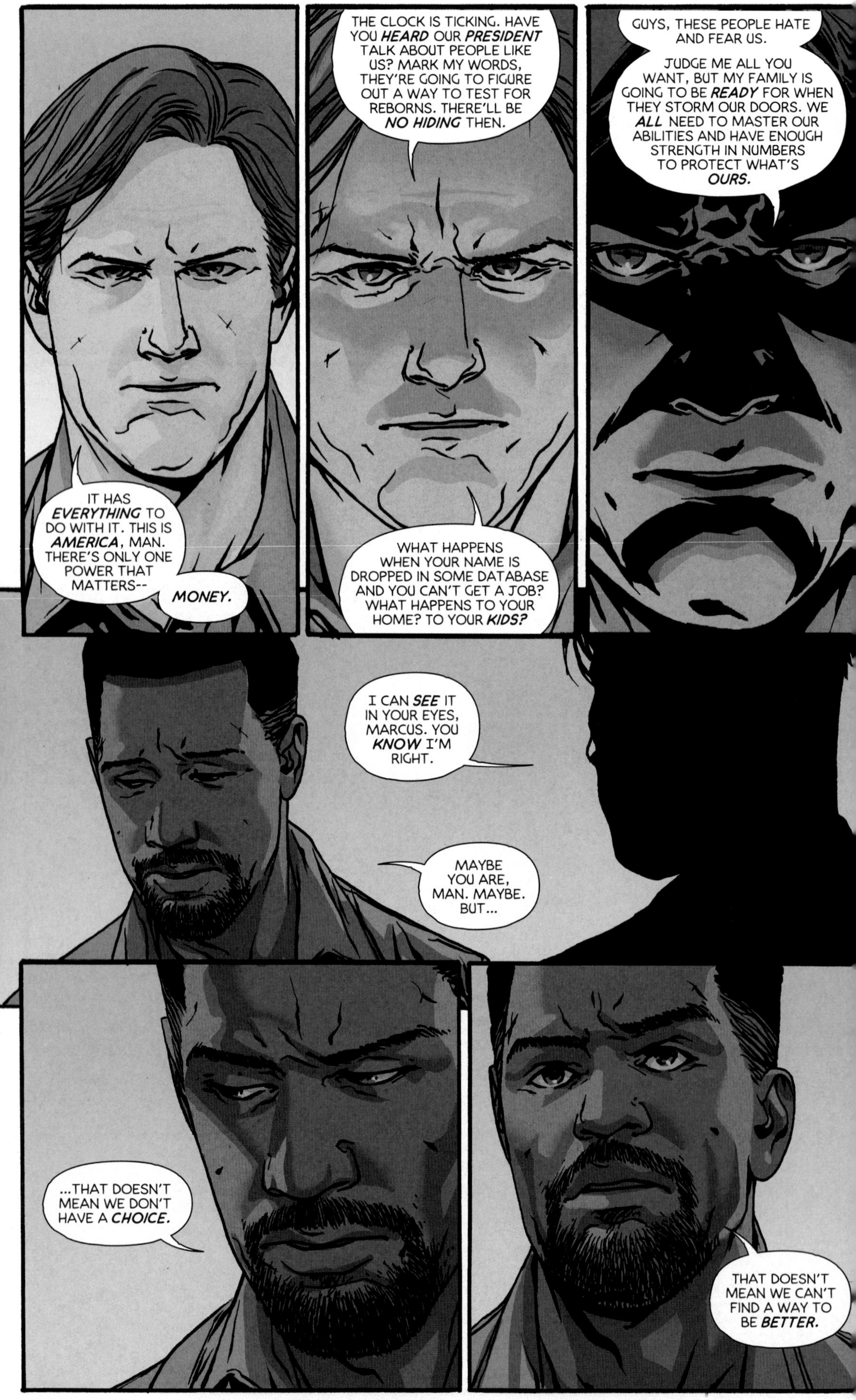
IT HAS EVERYTHING TO DO WITH IT. THIS IS AMERICA, MAN. THERE'S ONLY ONE POWER THAT MATTERS--
MONEY.
THE CLOCK IS TICKING. HAVE YOU HEARD OUR PRESIDENT TALK ABOUT PEOPLE LIKE US? MARK MY WORDS, THEY'RE GOING TO FIGURE OUT A WAY TO TEST FOR REBORNS. THERE'LL BE NO HIDING THEN.
WHAT HAPPENS WHEN YOUR NAME IS DROPPED IN SOME DATABASE AND YOU CAN'T GET A JOB? WHAT HAPPENS TO YOUR HOME? TO YOUR KIDS?
GUYS, THESE PEOPLE HATE AND FEAR US.
JUDGE ME ALL YOU WANT, BUT MY FAMILY IS GOING TO BE READY FOR WHEN THEY STORM OUR DOORS. WE ALL NEED TO MASTER OUR ABILITIES AND HAVE ENOUGH STRENGTH IN NUMBERS TO PROTECT WHAT'S OURS.
I CAN SEE IT IN YOUR EYES, MARCUS. YOU KNOW I'M RIGHT.
MAYBE YOU ARE, MAN. MAYBE. BUT...
...THAT DOESN'T MEAN WE DON'T HAVE A CHOICE.
THAT DOESN'T MEAN WE CAN'T FIND A WAY TO BE BETTER.

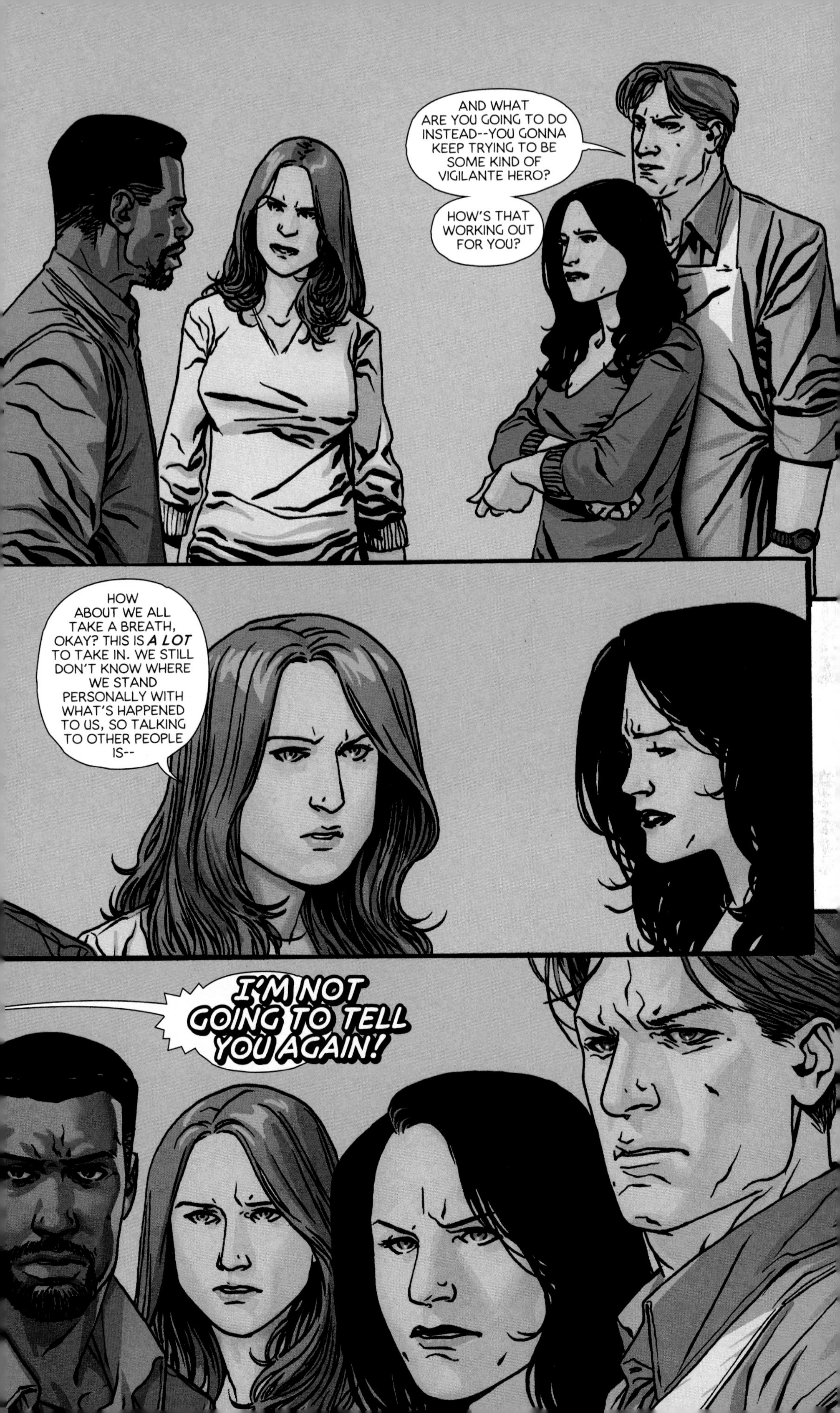
AND WHAT ARE YOU GOING TO DO INSTEAD--YOU GONNA KEEP TRYING TO BE SOME KIND OF VIGILANTE HERO?
HOW'S THAT WORKING OUT FOR YOU?
HOW ABOUT WE ALL TAKE A BREATH, OKAY? THIS IS *A LOT* TO TAKE IN. WE STILL DON'T KNOW WHERE WE STAND PERSONALLY WITH WHAT'S HAPPENED TO US, SO TALKING TO OTHER PEOPLE IS--
I'M NOT GOING TO TELL YOU AGAIN!

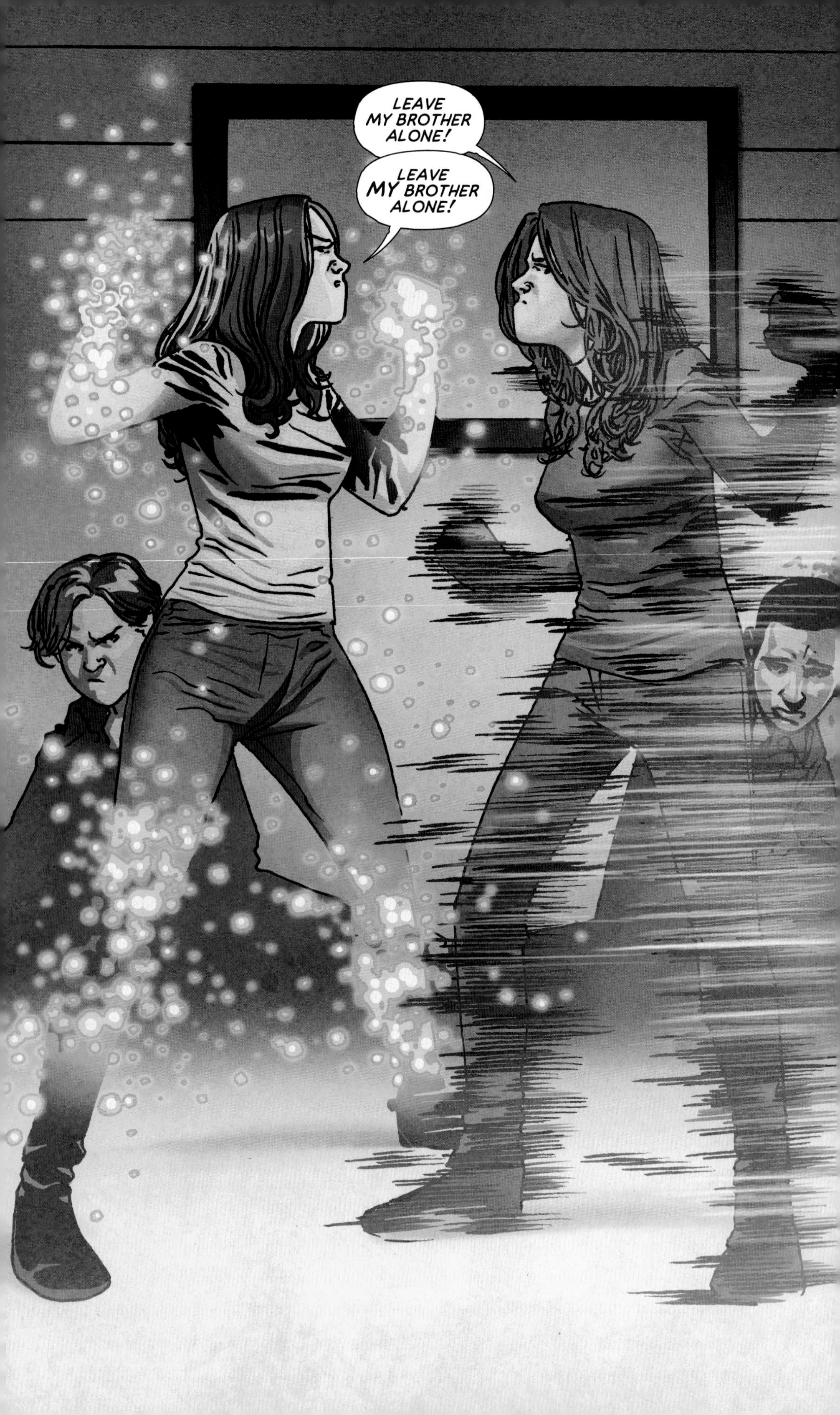
LEAVE MY BROTHER ALONE!
LEAVE MY BROTHER ALONE!

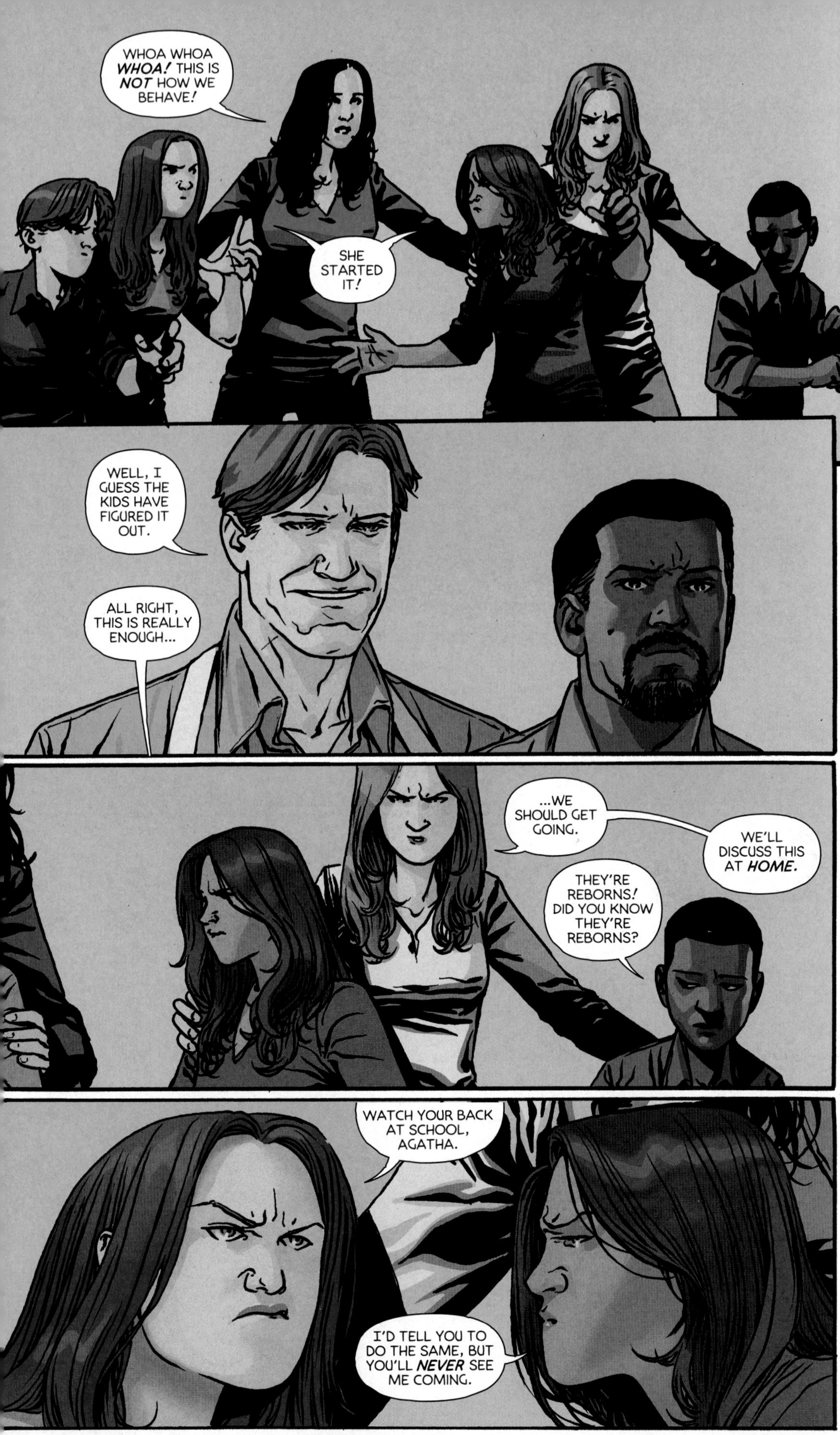

WHOA WHOA **WHOA!** THIS IS **NOT** HOW WE BEHAVE!
SHE STARTED IT!
WELL, I GUESS THE KIDS HAVE FIGURED IT OUT.
ALL RIGHT, THIS IS REALLY ENOUGH...
...WE SHOULD GET GOING.
WE'LL DISCUSS THIS AT **HOME.**
THEY'RE REBORNS! DID YOU KNOW THEY'RE REBORNS?
WATCH YOUR BACK AT SCHOOL, AGATHA.
I'D TELL YOU TO DO THE SAME, BUT YOU'LL **NEVER** SEE ME COMING.

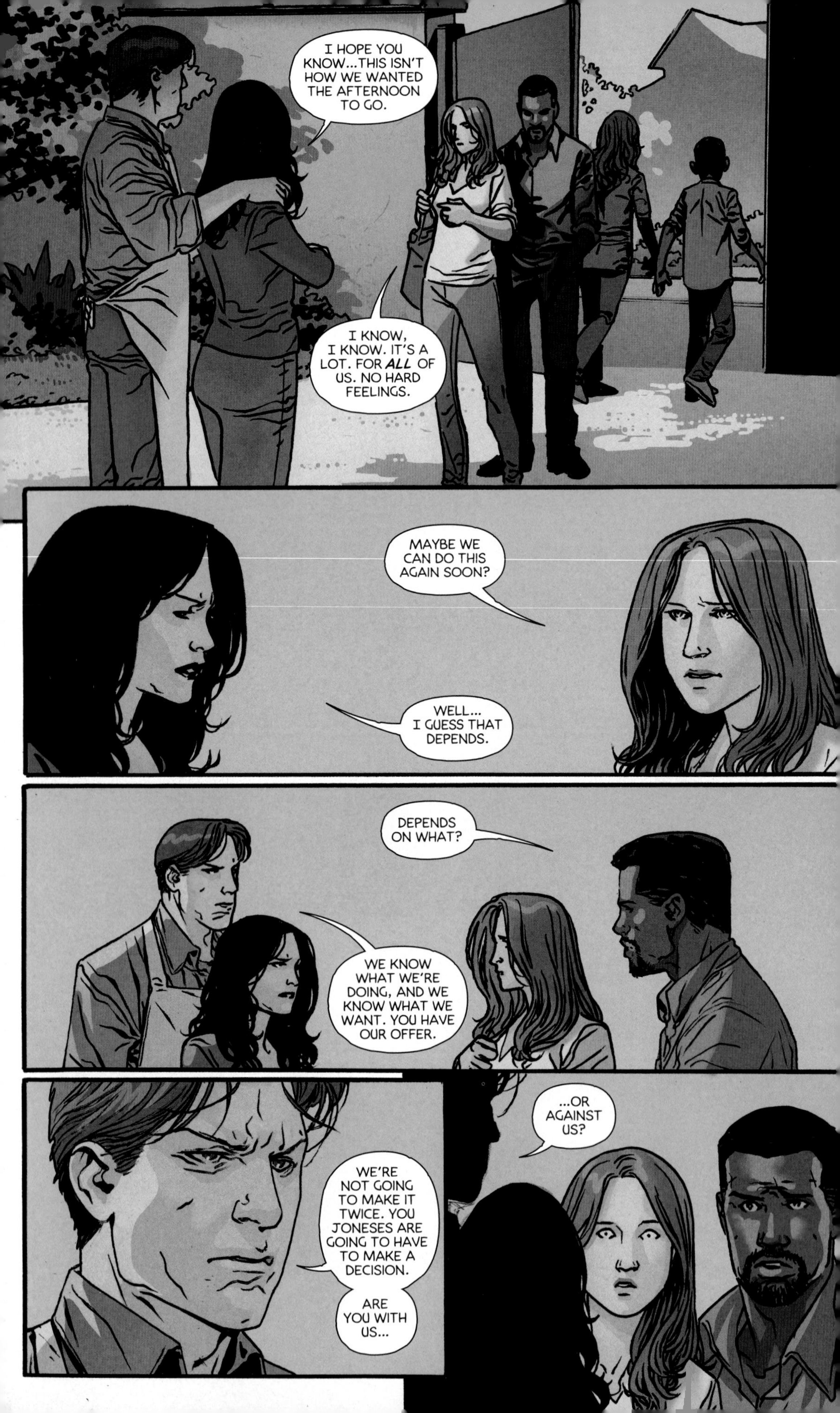
I HOPE YOU KNOW...THIS ISN'T HOW WE WANTED THE AFTERNOON TO GO.
I KNOW, I KNOW. IT'S A LOT. FOR *ALL* OF US. NO HARD FEELINGS.
MAYBE WE CAN DO THIS AGAIN SOON?
WELL... I GUESS THAT DEPENDS.
DEPENDS ON WHAT?
WE KNOW WHAT WE'RE DOING, AND WE KNOW WHAT WE WANT. YOU HAVE OUR OFFER.
WE'RE NOT GOING TO MAKE IT TWICE. YOU JONESES ARE GOING TO HAVE TO MAKE A DECISION.
ARE YOU WITH US...
...OR AGAINST US?

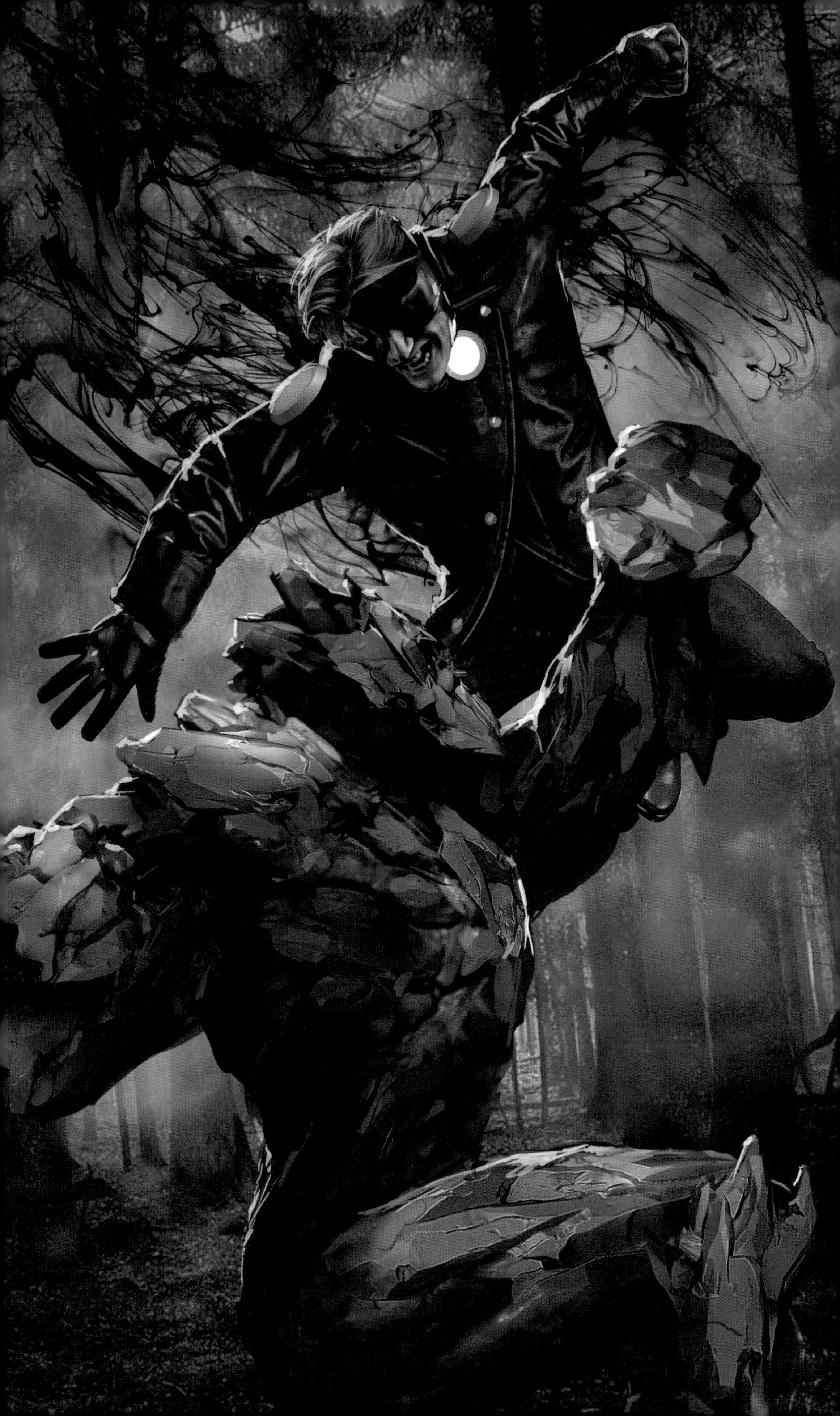

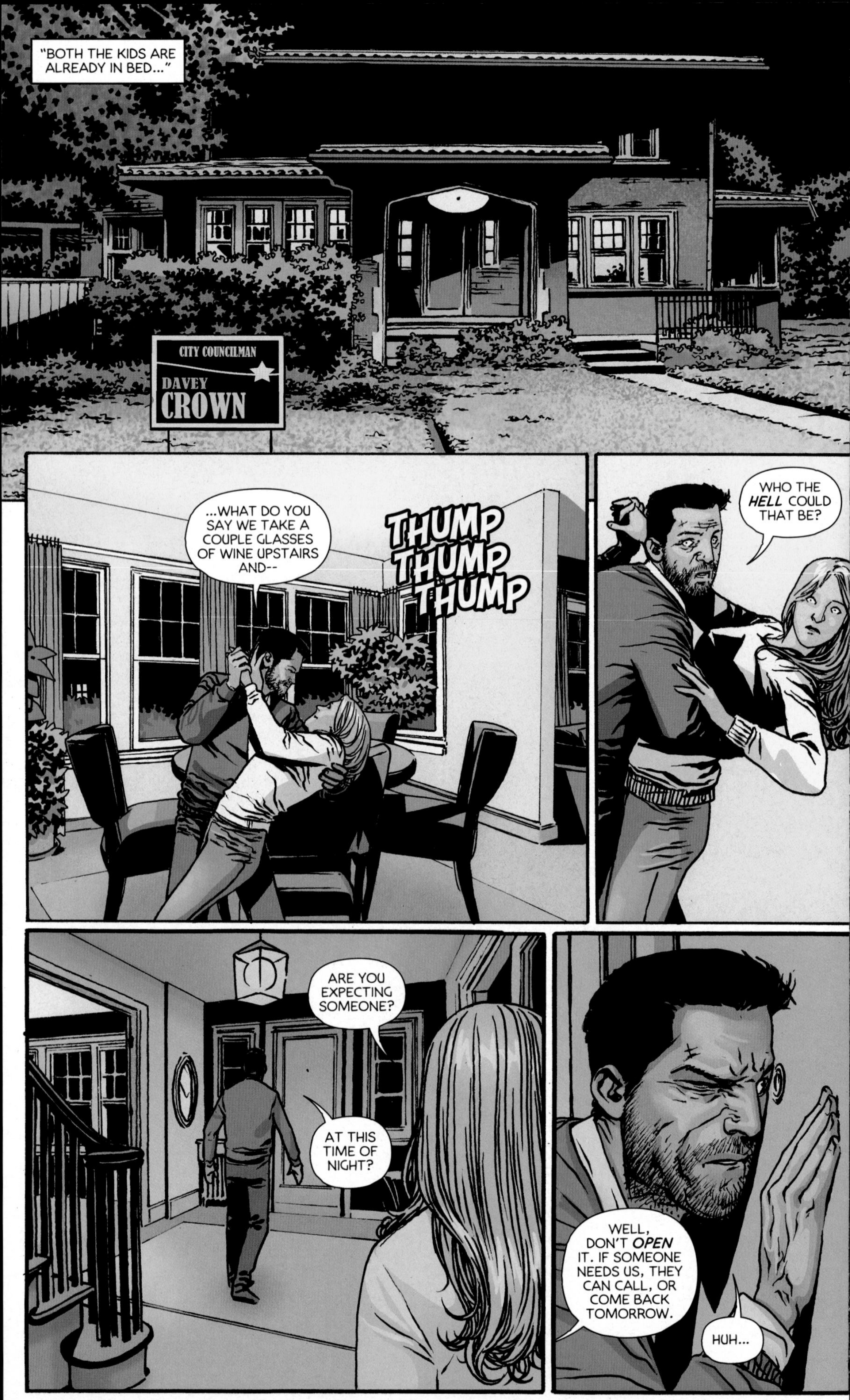
"BOTH THE KIDS ARE ALREADY IN BED..."
CITY COUNCILMAN DAVEY CROWN
...WHAT DO YOU SAY WE TAKE A COUPLE GLASSES OF WINE UPSTAIRS AND--
THUMP THUMP THUMP
WHO THE HELL COULD THAT BE?
ARE YOU EXPECTING SOMEONE?
AT THIS TIME OF NIGHT?
WELL, DON'T OPEN IT. IF SOMEONE NEEDS US, THEY CAN CALL, OR COME BACK TOMORROW.
HUH...

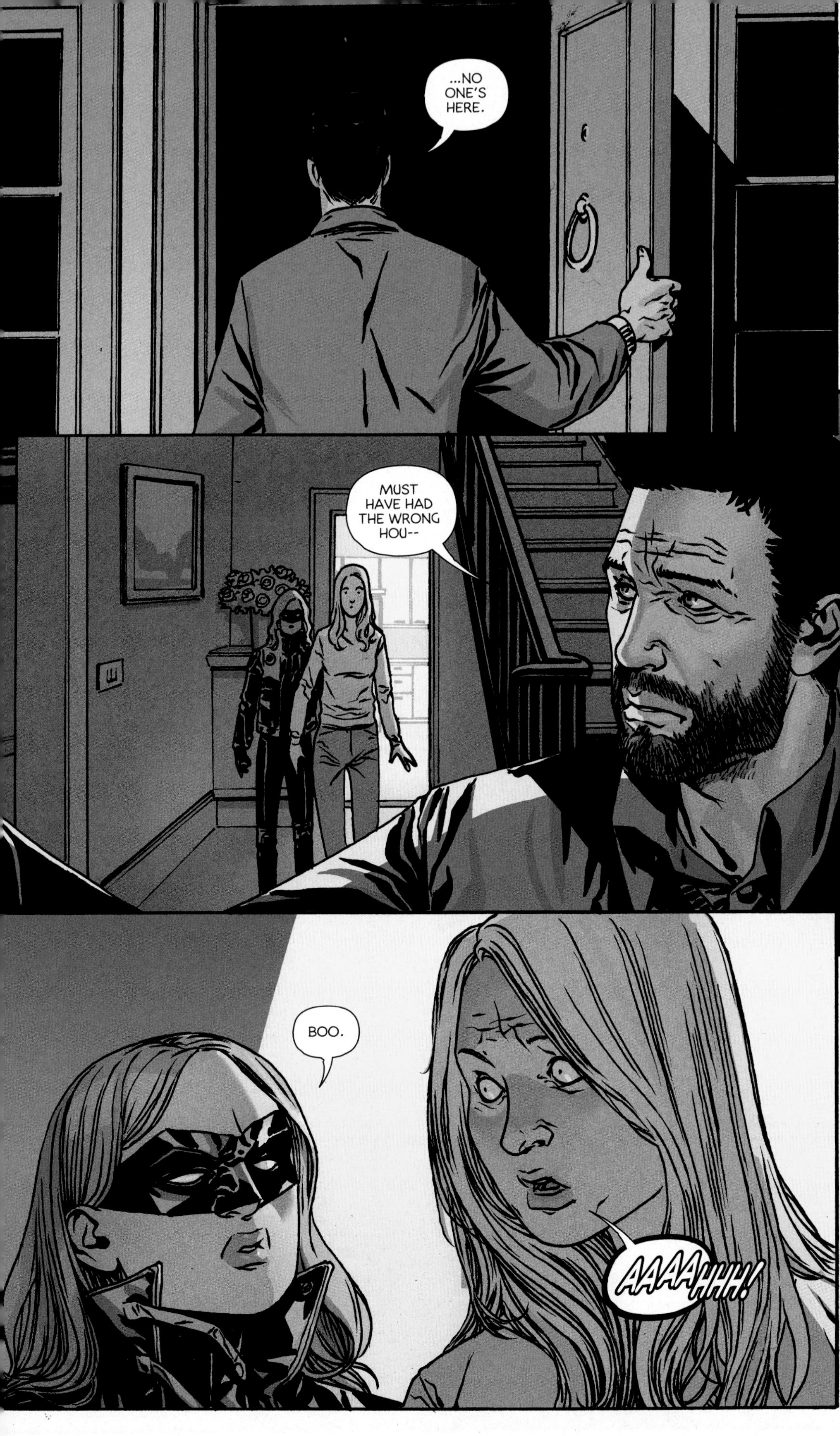
...NO ONE'S HERE.
MUST HAVE HAD THE WRONG HOU--
BOO.
AAAAHHH!

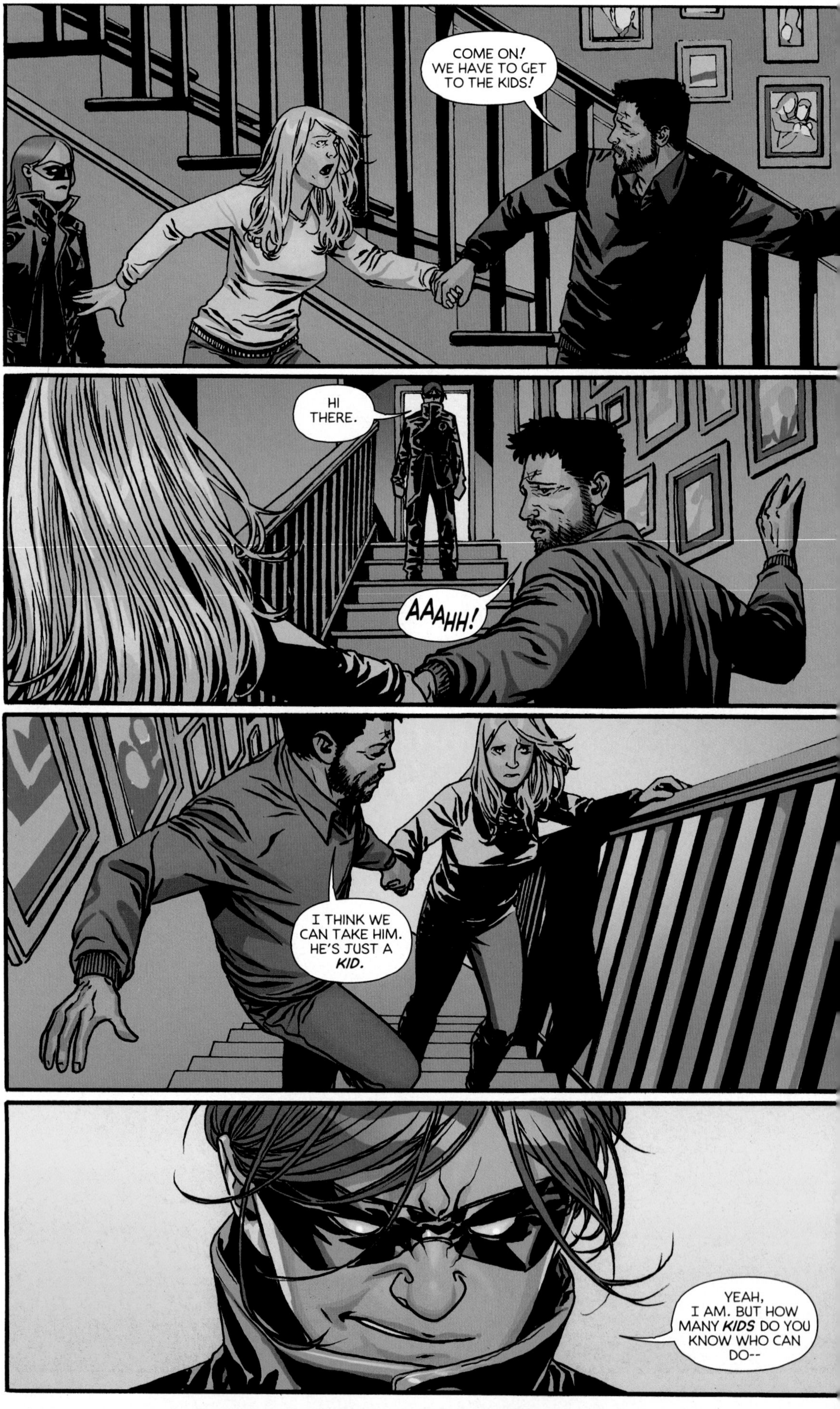
COME ON! WE HAVE TO GET TO THE KIDS!
HI THERE.
AAAHH!
I THINK WE CAN TAKE HIM. HE'S JUST A KID.
YEAH, I AM. BUT HOW MANY KIDS DO YOU KNOW WHO CAN DO--

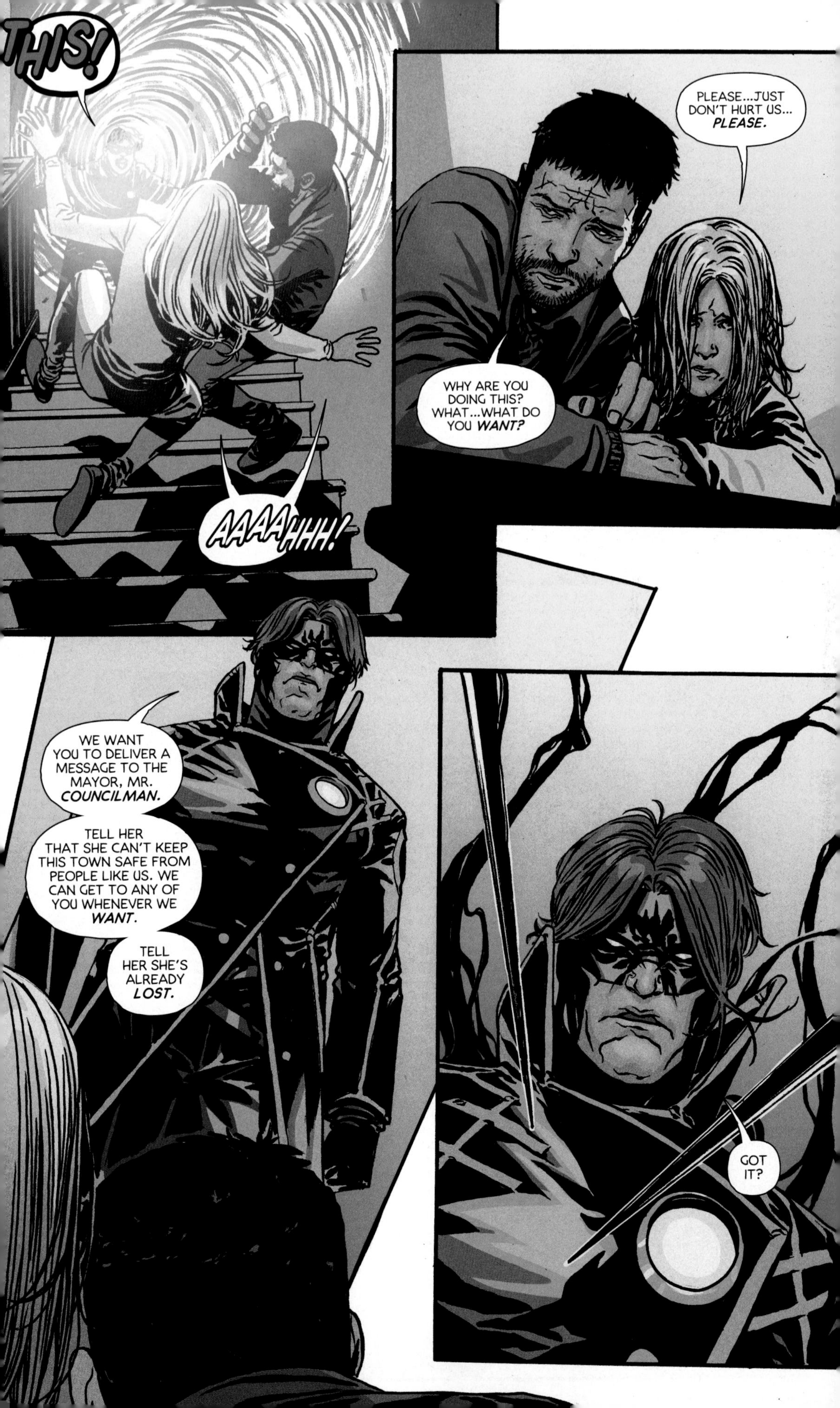
THIS!
PLEASE...JUST DON'T HURT US... PLEASE.
WHY ARE YOU DOING THIS? WHAT...WHAT DO YOU WANT?
AAAAHHH!
WE WANT YOU TO DELIVER A MESSAGE TO THE MAYOR, MR. COUNCILMAN.
TELL HER THAT SHE CAN'T KEEP THIS TOWN SAFE FROM PEOPLE LIKE US. WE CAN GET TO ANY OF YOU WHENEVER WE WANT.
TELL HER SHE'S ALREADY LOST.
GOT IT?

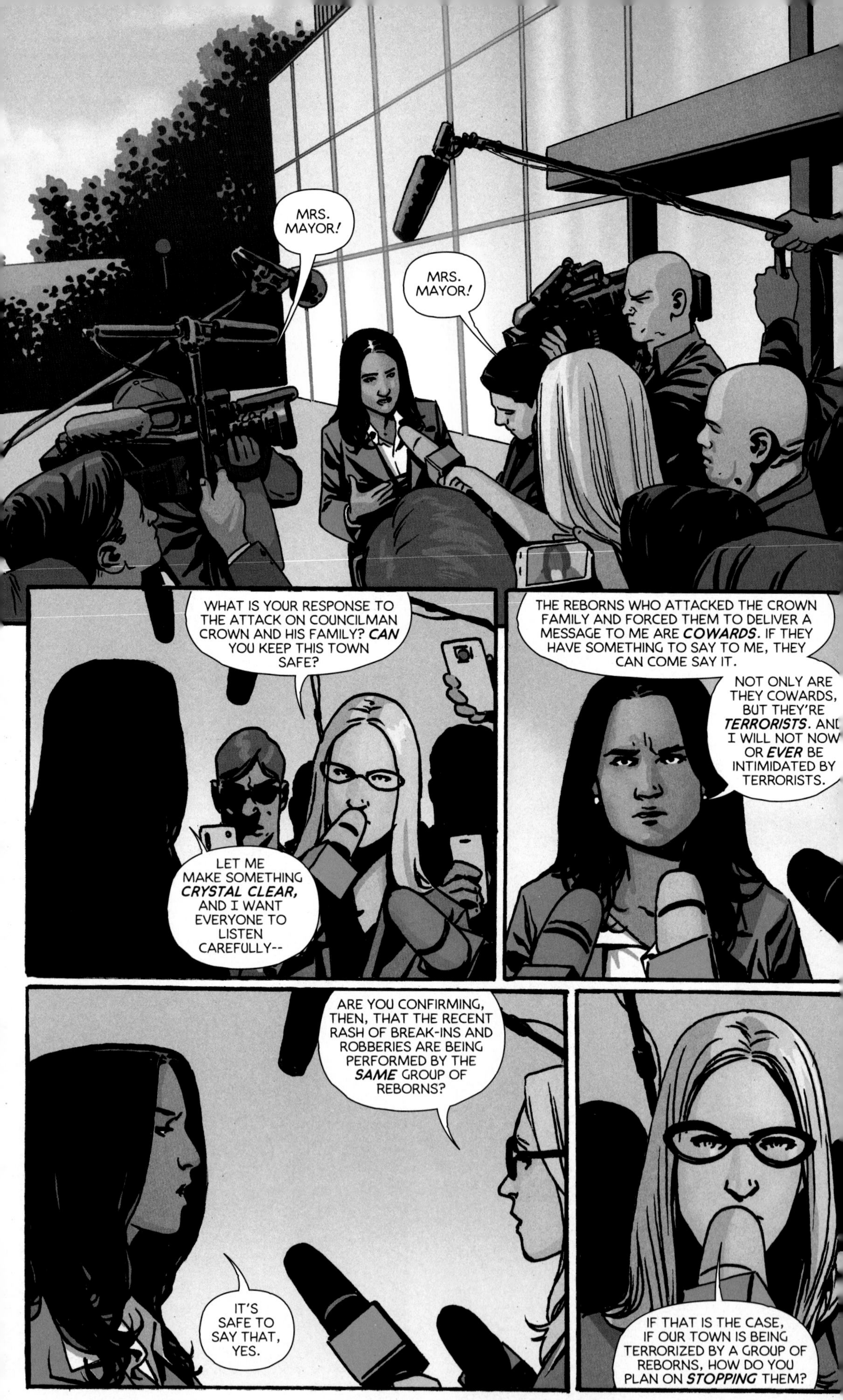
MRS. MAYOR!
MRS. MAYOR!
WHAT IS YOUR RESPONSE TO THE ATTACK ON COUNCILMAN CROWN AND HIS FAMILY? CAN YOU KEEP THIS TOWN SAFE?
LET ME MAKE SOMETHING CRYSTAL CLEAR, AND I WANT EVERYONE TO LISTEN CAREFULLY--
THE REBORNS WHO ATTACKED THE CROWN FAMILY AND FORCED THEM TO DELIVER A MESSAGE TO ME ARE COWARDS. IF THEY HAVE SOMETHING TO SAY TO ME, THEY CAN COME SAY IT.
NOT ONLY ARE THEY COWARDS, BUT THEY'RE TERRORISTS. AND I WILL NOT NOW OR EVER BE INTIMIDATED BY TERRORISTS.
ARE YOU CONFIRMING, THEN, THAT THE RECENT RASH OF BREAK-INS AND ROBBERIES ARE BEING PERFORMED BY THE SAME GROUP OF REBORNS?
IT'S SAFE TO SAY THAT, YES.
IF THAT IS THE CASE, IF OUR TOWN IS BEING TERRORIZED BY A GROUP OF REBORNS, HOW DO YOU PLAN ON STOPPING THEM?

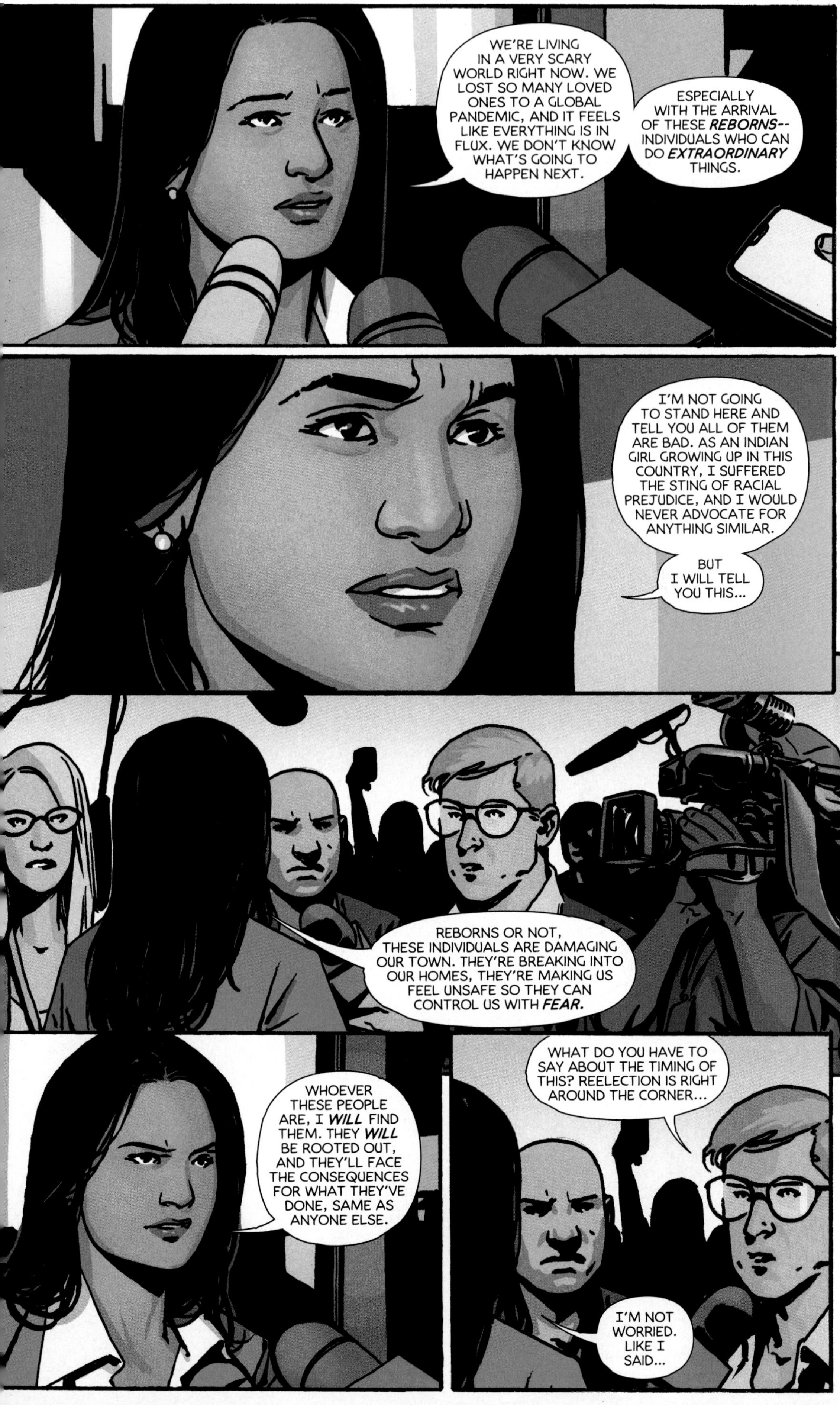
WE'RE LIVING IN A VERY SCARY WORLD RIGHT NOW. WE LOST SO MANY LOVED ONES TO A GLOBAL PANDEMIC, AND IT FEELS LIKE EVERYTHING IS IN FLUX. WE DON'T KNOW WHAT'S GOING TO HAPPEN NEXT.
ESPECIALLY WITH THE ARRIVAL OF THESE *REBORNS*--INDIVIDUALS WHO CAN DO *EXTRAORDINARY* THINGS.
I'M NOT GOING TO STAND HERE AND TELL YOU ALL OF THEM ARE BAD. AS AN INDIAN GIRL GROWING UP IN THIS COUNTRY, I SUFFERED THE STING OF RACIAL PREJUDICE, AND I WOULD NEVER ADVOCATE FOR ANYTHING SIMILAR.
BUT I WILL TELL YOU THIS...
REBORNS OR NOT, THESE INDIVIDUALS ARE DAMAGING OUR TOWN. THEY'RE BREAKING INTO OUR HOMES, THEY'RE MAKING US FEEL UNSAFE SO THEY CAN CONTROL US WITH *FEAR.*
WHOEVER THESE PEOPLE ARE, I *WILL* FIND THEM. THEY *WILL* BE ROOTED OUT, AND THEY'LL FACE THE CONSEQUENCES FOR WHAT THEY'VE DONE, SAME AS ANYONE ELSE.
WHAT DO YOU HAVE TO SAY ABOUT THE TIMING OF THIS? REELECTION IS RIGHT AROUND THE CORNER...
I'M NOT WORRIED. LIKE I SAID...

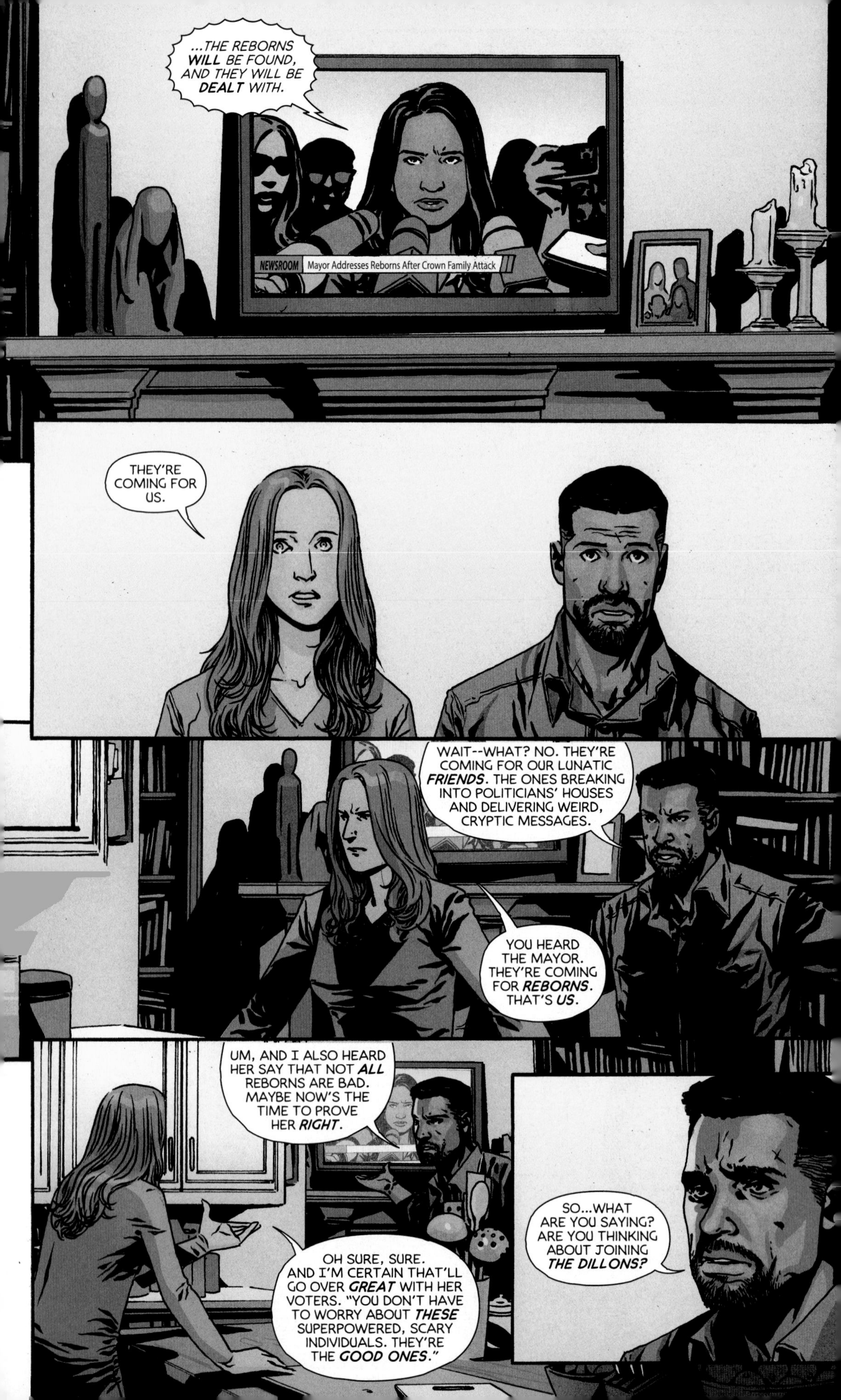
...THE REBORNS *WILL* BE FOUND, AND THEY WILL BE *DEALT* WITH.
NEWSROOM Mayor Addresses Reborns After Crown Family Attack
THEY'RE COMING FOR US.
WAIT--WHAT? NO. THEY'RE COMING FOR OUR LUNATIC *FRIENDS*. THE ONES BREAKING INTO POLITICIANS' HOUSES AND DELIVERING WEIRD, CRYPTIC MESSAGES.
YOU HEARD THE MAYOR. THEY'RE COMING FOR *REBORNS*. THAT'S *US*.
UM, AND I ALSO HEARD HER SAY THAT NOT *ALL* REBORNS ARE BAD. MAYBE NOW'S THE TIME TO PROVE HER *RIGHT*.
OH SURE, SURE. AND I'M CERTAIN THAT'LL GO OVER *GREAT* WITH HER VOTERS. "YOU DON'T HAVE TO WORRY ABOUT *THESE* SUPERPOWERED, SCARY INDIVIDUALS. THEY'RE THE *GOOD ONES*."
SO...WHAT ARE YOU SAYING? ARE YOU THINKING ABOUT JOINING *THE DILLONS?*

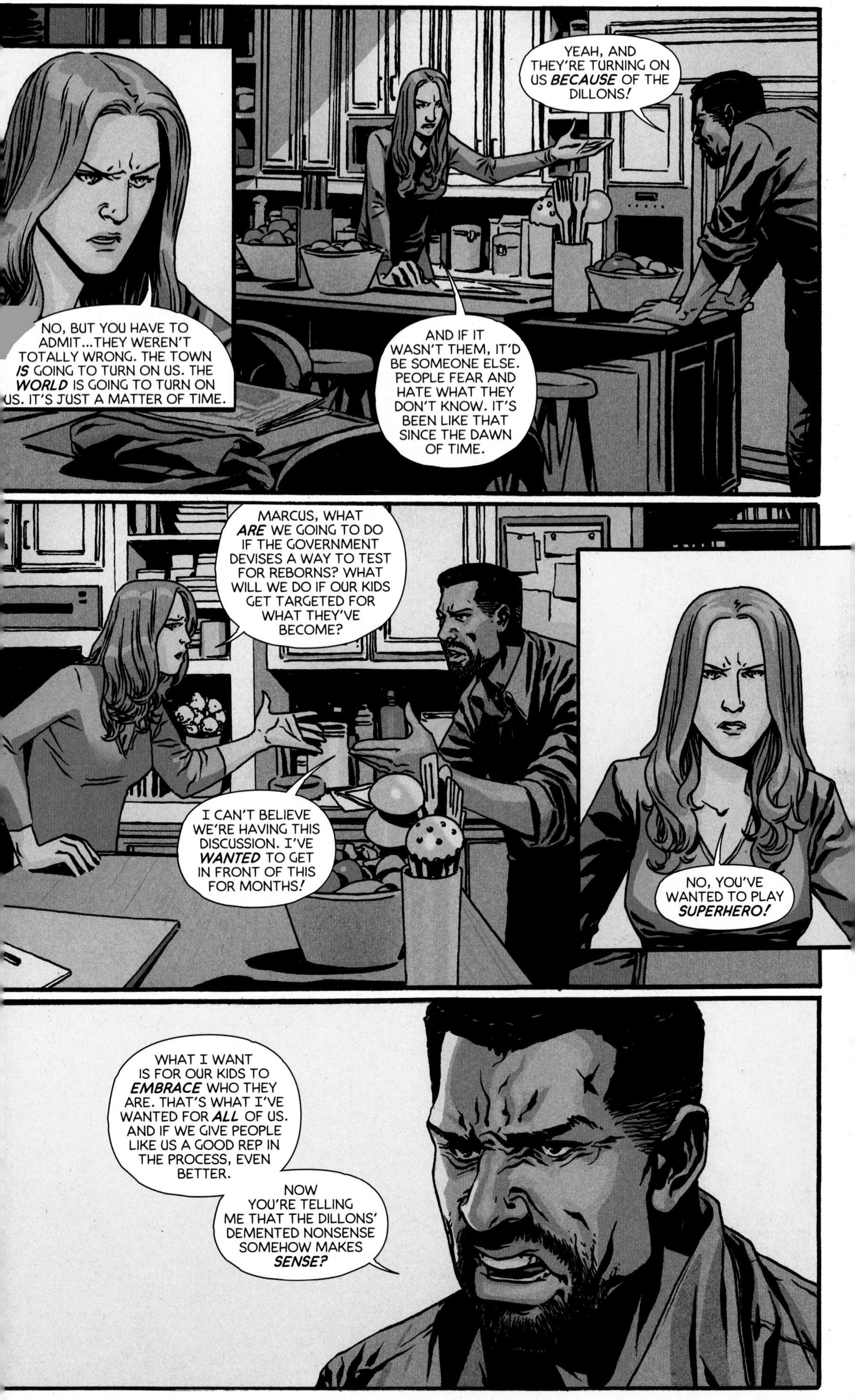
NO, BUT YOU HAVE TO ADMIT...THEY WEREN'T TOTALLY WRONG. THE TOWN *IS* GOING TO TURN ON US. THE *WORLD* IS GOING TO TURN ON US. IT'S JUST A MATTER OF TIME.
YEAH, AND THEY'RE TURNING ON US *BECAUSE* OF THE DILLONS!
AND IF IT WASN'T THEM, IT'D BE SOMEONE ELSE. PEOPLE FEAR AND HATE WHAT THEY DON'T KNOW. IT'S BEEN LIKE THAT SINCE THE DAWN OF TIME.
MARCUS, WHAT *ARE* WE GOING TO DO IF THE GOVERNMENT DEVISES A WAY TO TEST FOR REBORNS? WHAT WILL WE DO IF OUR KIDS GET TARGETED FOR WHAT THEY'VE BECOME?
I CAN'T BELIEVE WE'RE HAVING THIS DISCUSSION. I'VE *WANTED* TO GET IN FRONT OF THIS FOR MONTHS!
NO, YOU'VE WANTED TO PLAY *SUPERHERO!*
WHAT I WANT IS FOR OUR KIDS TO *EMBRACE* WHO THEY ARE. THAT'S WHAT I'VE WANTED FOR *ALL* OF US. AND IF WE GIVE PEOPLE LIKE US A GOOD REP IN THE PROCESS, EVEN BETTER.
NOW YOU'RE TELLING ME THAT THE DILLONS' DEMENTED NONSENSE SOMEHOW MAKES *SENSE?*

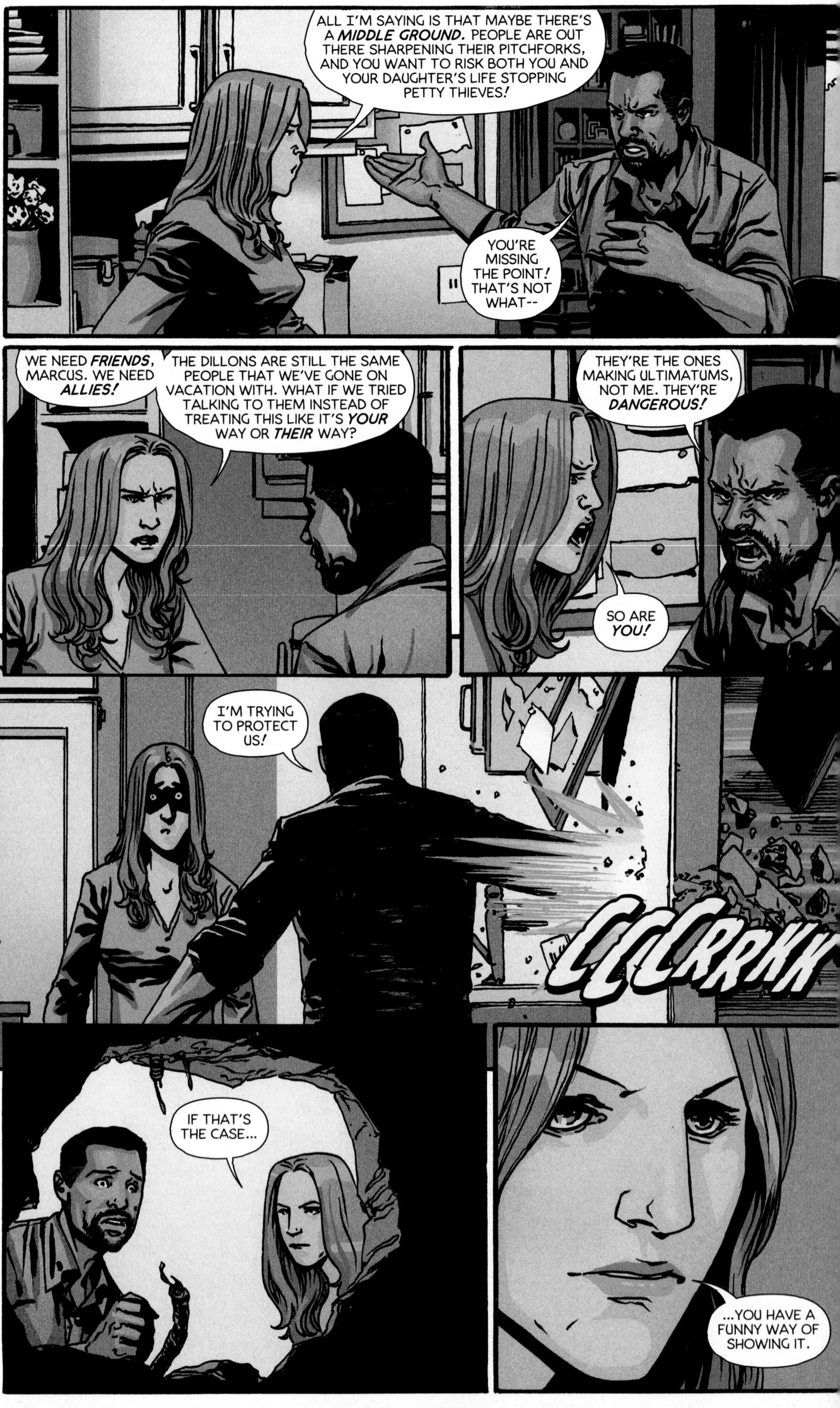
ALL I'M SAYING IS THAT MAYBE THERE'S A MIDDLE GROUND. PEOPLE ARE OUT THERE SHARPENING THEIR PITCHFORKS, AND YOU WANT TO RISK BOTH YOU AND YOUR DAUGHTER'S LIFE STOPPING PETTY THIEVES!
YOU'RE MISSING THE POINT! THAT'S NOT WHAT--
WE NEED FRIENDS, MARCUS. WE NEED ALLIES!
THE DILLONS ARE STILL THE SAME PEOPLE THAT WE'VE GONE ON VACATION WITH. WHAT IF WE TRIED TALKING TO THEM INSTEAD OF TREATING THIS LIKE IT'S YOUR WAY OR THEIR WAY?
THEY'RE THE ONES MAKING ULTIMATUMS, NOT ME. THEY'RE DANGEROUS!
SO ARE YOU!
I'M TRYING TO PROTECT US!
CCCRRRKK
IF THAT'S THE CASE...
...YOU HAVE A FUNNY WAY OF SHOWING IT.

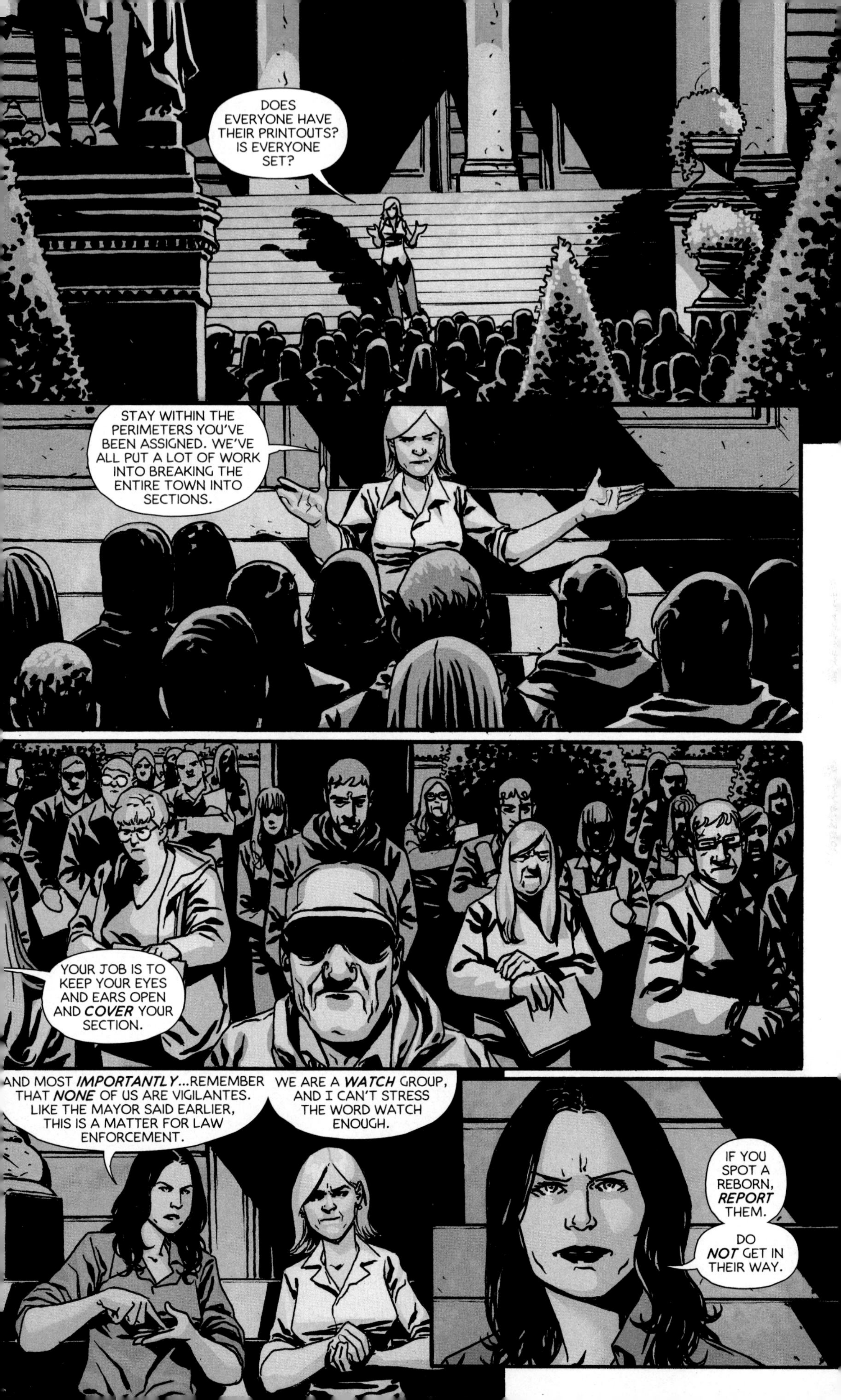
DOES EVERYONE HAVE THEIR PRINTOUTS? IS EVERYONE SET?
STAY WITHIN THE PERIMETERS YOU'VE BEEN ASSIGNED. WE'VE ALL PUT A LOT OF WORK INTO BREAKING THE ENTIRE TOWN INTO SECTIONS.
YOUR JOB IS TO KEEP YOUR EYES AND EARS OPEN AND *COVER* YOUR SECTION.
AND MOST *IMPORTANTLY*...REMEMBER THAT *NONE* OF US ARE VIGILANTES. LIKE THE MAYOR SAID EARLIER, THIS IS A MATTER FOR LAW ENFORCEMENT.
WE ARE A *WATCH* GROUP, AND I CAN'T STRESS THE WORD WATCH ENOUGH.
IF YOU SPOT A REBORN, *REPORT* THEM.
DO *NOT* GET IN THEIR WAY.

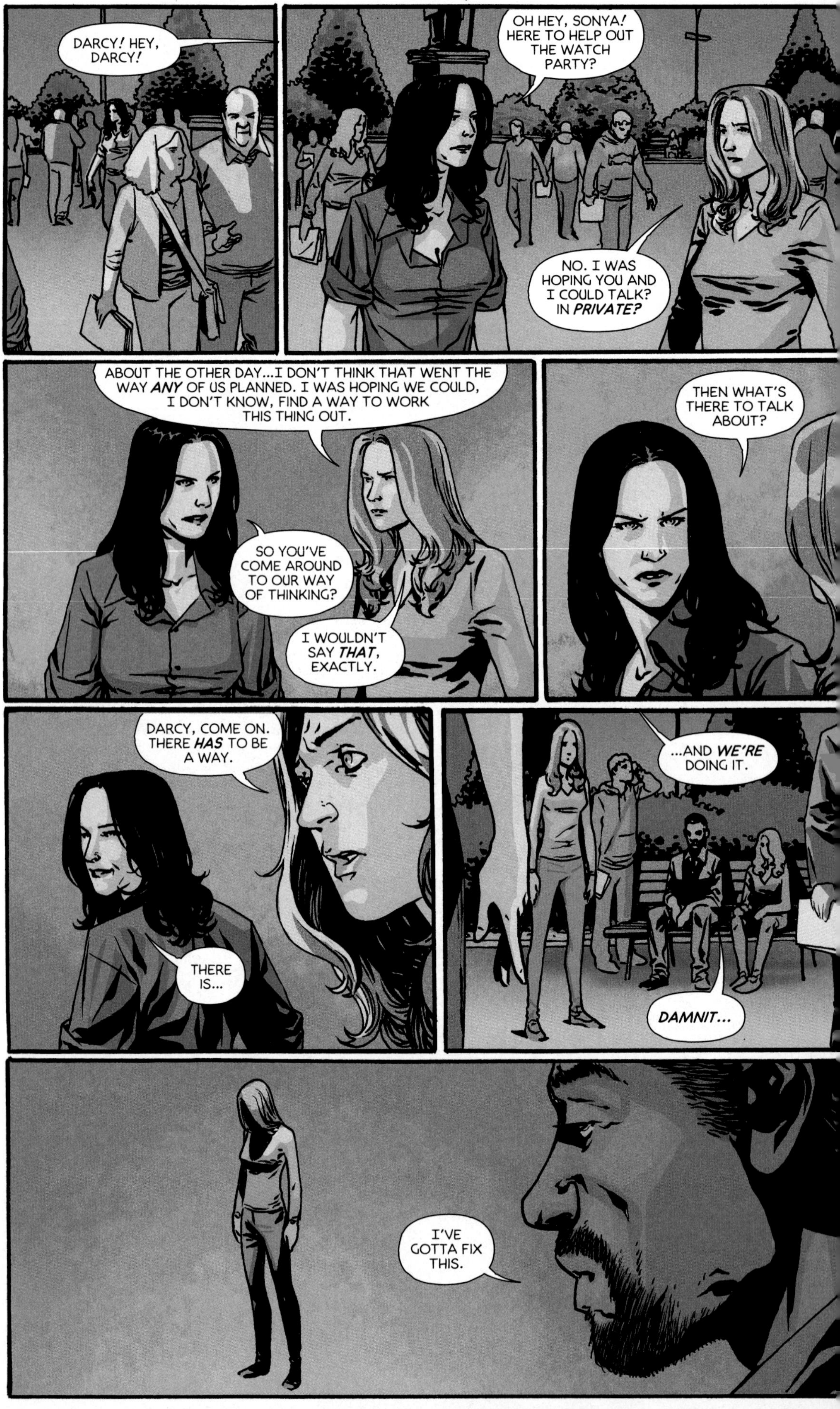
DARCY! HEY, DARCY!
OH HEY, SONYA! HERE TO HELP OUT THE WATCH PARTY?
NO. I WAS HOPING YOU AND I COULD TALK? IN PRIVATE?
ABOUT THE OTHER DAY...I DON'T THINK THAT WENT THE WAY ANY OF US PLANNED. I WAS HOPING WE COULD, I DON'T KNOW, FIND A WAY TO WORK THIS THING OUT.
SO YOU'VE COME AROUND TO OUR WAY OF THINKING?
I WOULDN'T SAY THAT, EXACTLY.
THEN WHAT'S THERE TO TALK ABOUT?
DARCY, COME ON. THERE HAS TO BE A WAY.
THERE IS...
...AND WE'RE DOING IT.
DAMNIT...
I'VE GOTTA FIX THIS.

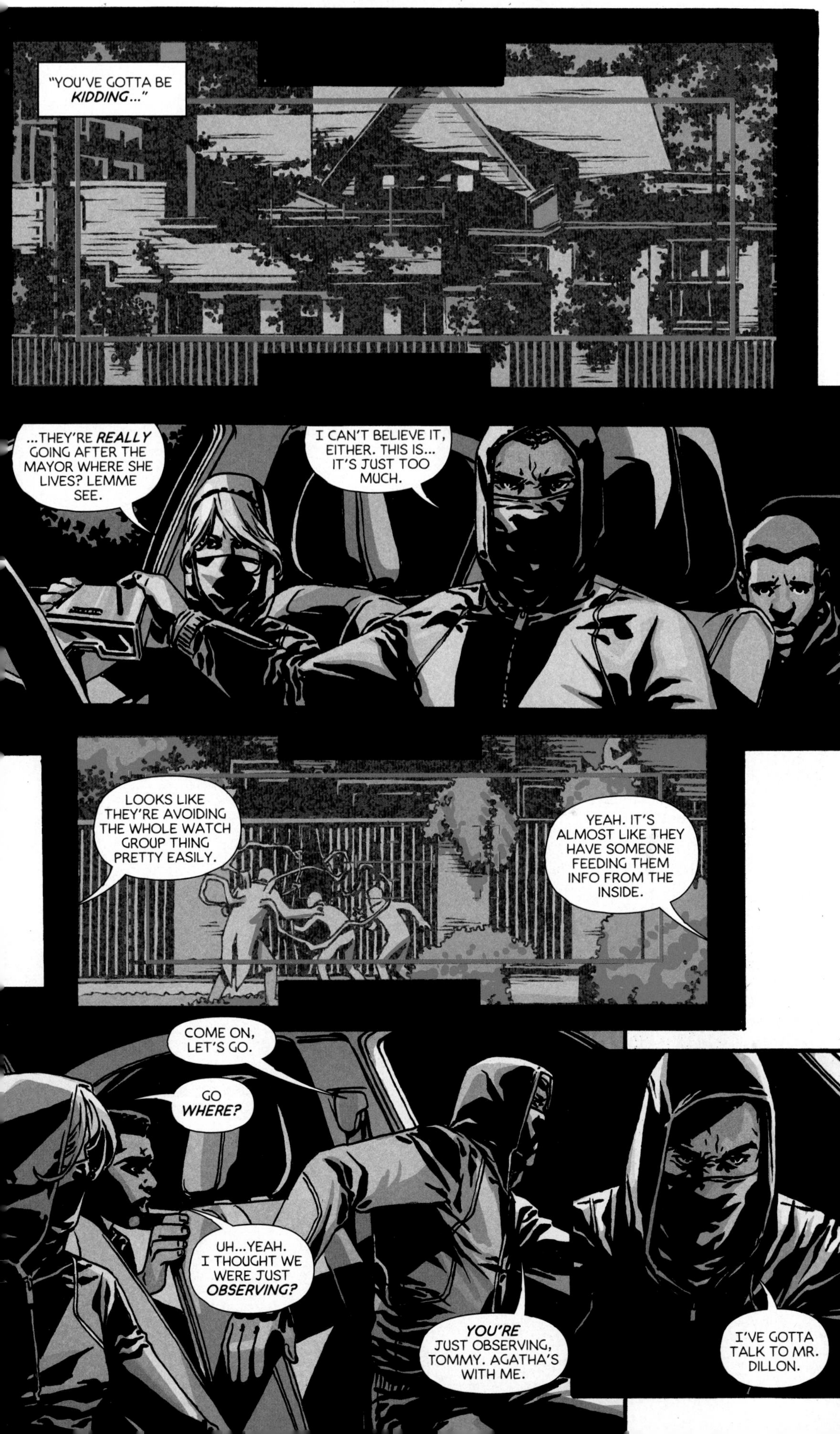
"YOU'VE GOTTA BE *KIDDING...*"
...THEY'RE *REALLY* GOING AFTER THE MAYOR WHERE SHE LIVES? LEMME SEE.
I CAN'T BELIEVE IT, EITHER. THIS IS... IT'S JUST TOO MUCH.
LOOKS LIKE THEY'RE AVOIDING THE WHOLE WATCH GROUP THING PRETTY EASILY.
YEAH. IT'S ALMOST LIKE THEY HAVE SOMEONE FEEDING THEM INFO FROM THE INSIDE.
COME ON, LET'S GO.
GO *WHERE?*
UH...YEAH. I THOUGHT WE WERE JUST *OBSERVING?*
YOU'RE JUST OBSERVING, TOMMY. AGATHA'S WITH ME.
I'VE GOTTA TALK TO MR. DILLON.

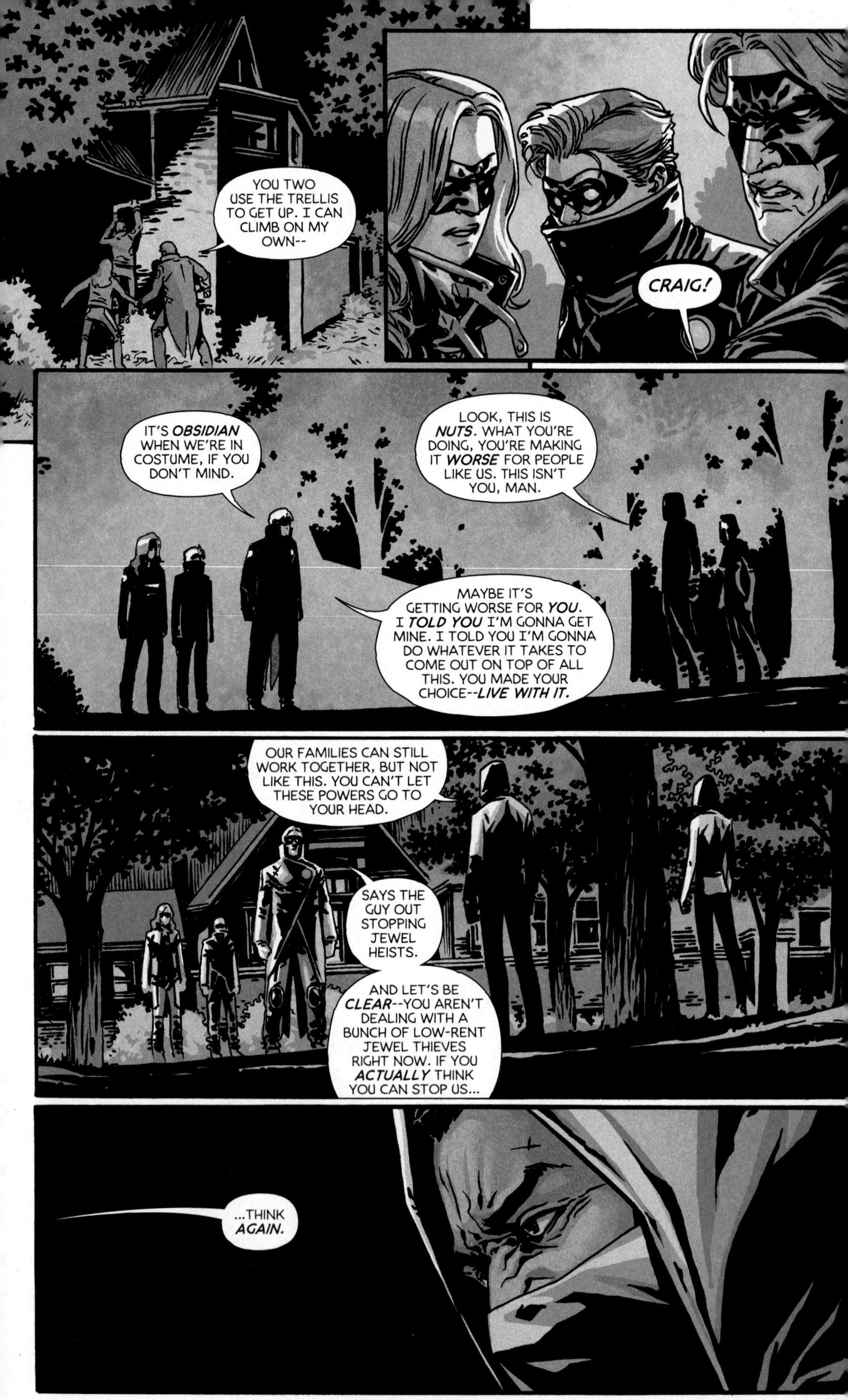
YOU TWO USE THE TRELLIS TO GET UP. I CAN CLIMB ON MY OWN--
CRAIG!
IT'S OBSIDIAN WHEN WE'RE IN COSTUME, IF YOU DON'T MIND.
LOOK, THIS IS NUTS. WHAT YOU'RE DOING, YOU'RE MAKING IT WORSE FOR PEOPLE LIKE US. THIS ISN'T YOU, MAN.
MAYBE IT'S GETTING WORSE FOR YOU. I TOLD YOU I'M GONNA GET MINE. I TOLD YOU I'M GONNA DO WHATEVER IT TAKES TO COME OUT ON TOP OF ALL THIS. YOU MADE YOUR CHOICE--LIVE WITH IT.
OUR FAMILIES CAN STILL WORK TOGETHER, BUT NOT LIKE THIS. YOU CAN'T LET THESE POWERS GO TO YOUR HEAD.
SAYS THE GUY OUT STOPPING JEWEL HEISTS.
AND LET'S BE CLEAR--YOU AREN'T DEALING WITH A BUNCH OF LOW-RENT JEWEL THIEVES RIGHT NOW. IF YOU ACTUALLY THINK YOU CAN STOP US...
...THINK AGAIN.

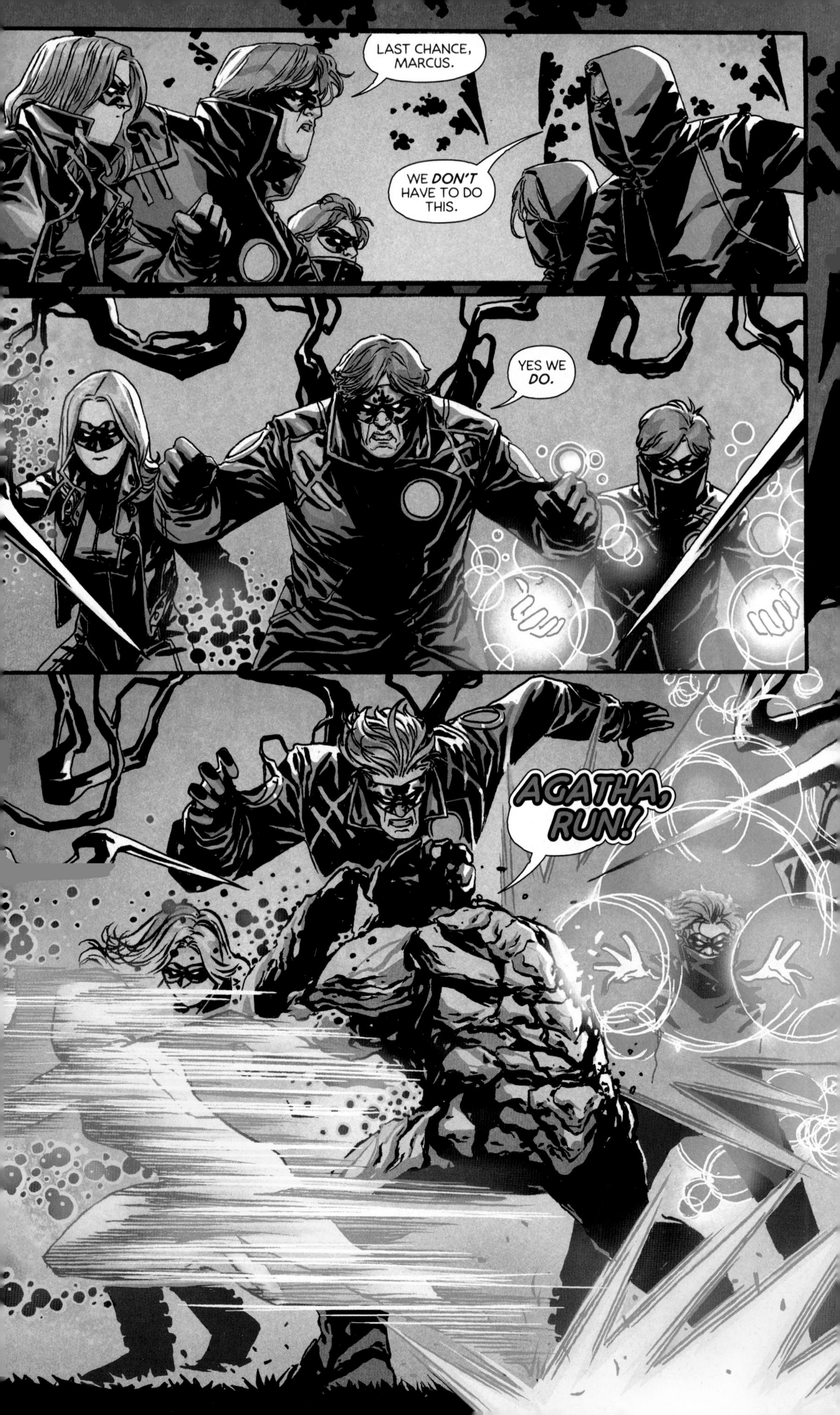
LAST CHANCE, MARCUS.
WE *DON'T* HAVE TO DO THIS.
YES WE *DO.*
AGATHA, RUN!

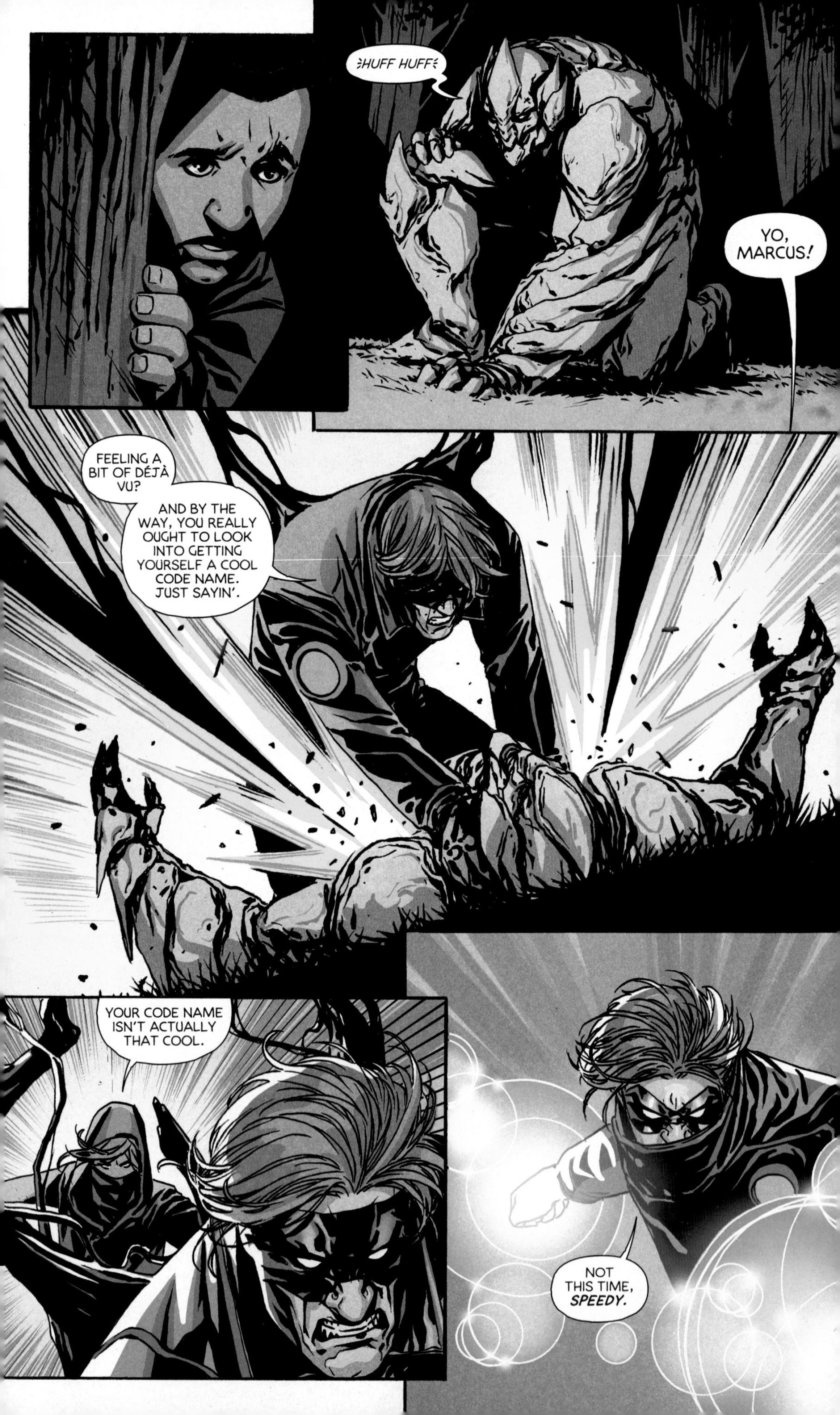
HUFF HUFF
YO, MARCUS!
FEELING A BIT OF DÉJÀ VU?
AND BY THE WAY, YOU REALLY OUGHT TO LOOK INTO GETTING YOURSELF A COOL CODE NAME. JUST SAYIN'.
YOUR CODE NAME ISN'T ACTUALLY THAT COOL.
NOT THIS TIME, *SPEEDY*.

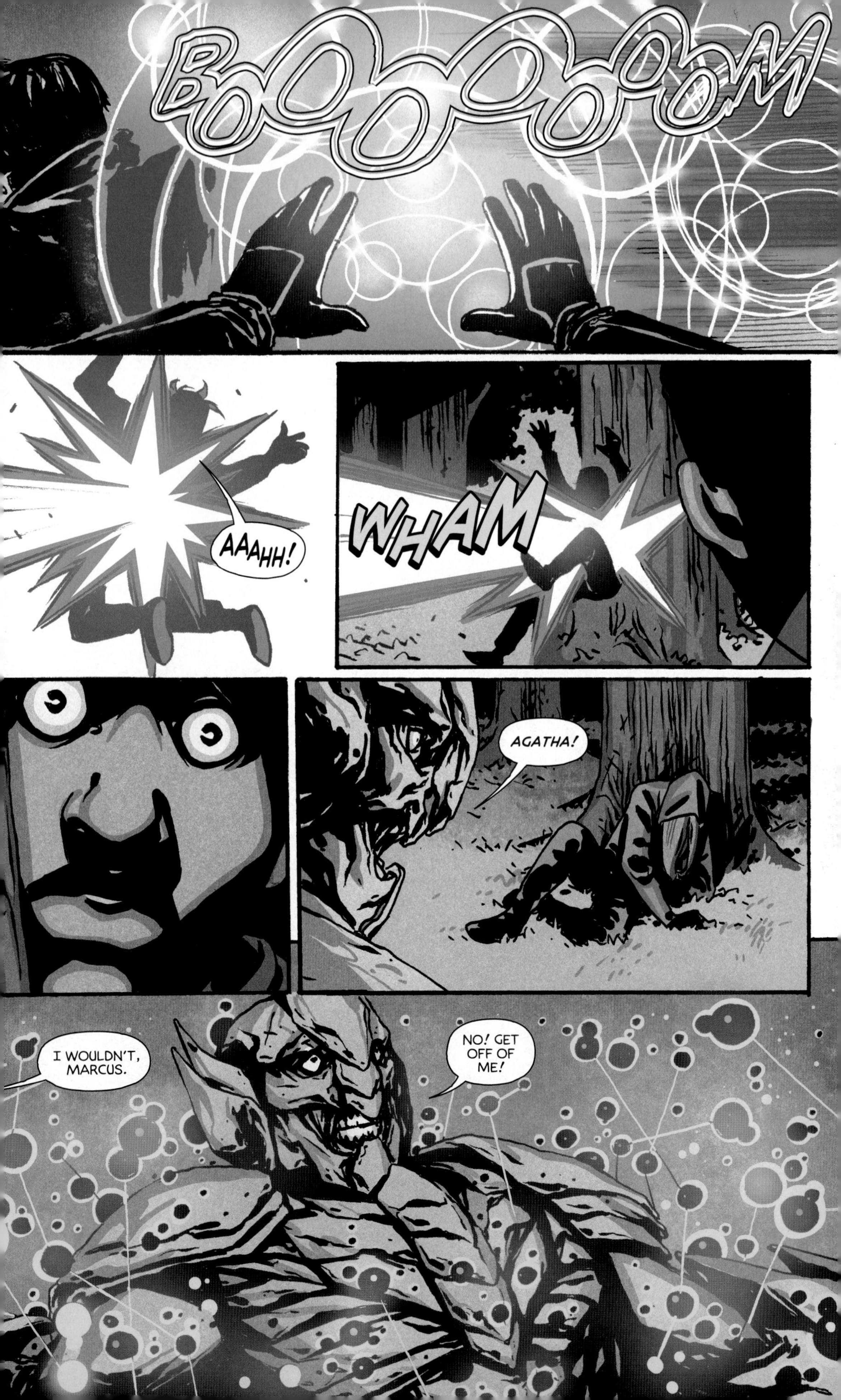
BOOOOOOOOM
AAAHH!
WHAM
AGATHA!
I WOULDN'T, MARCUS.
NO! GET OFF OF ME!

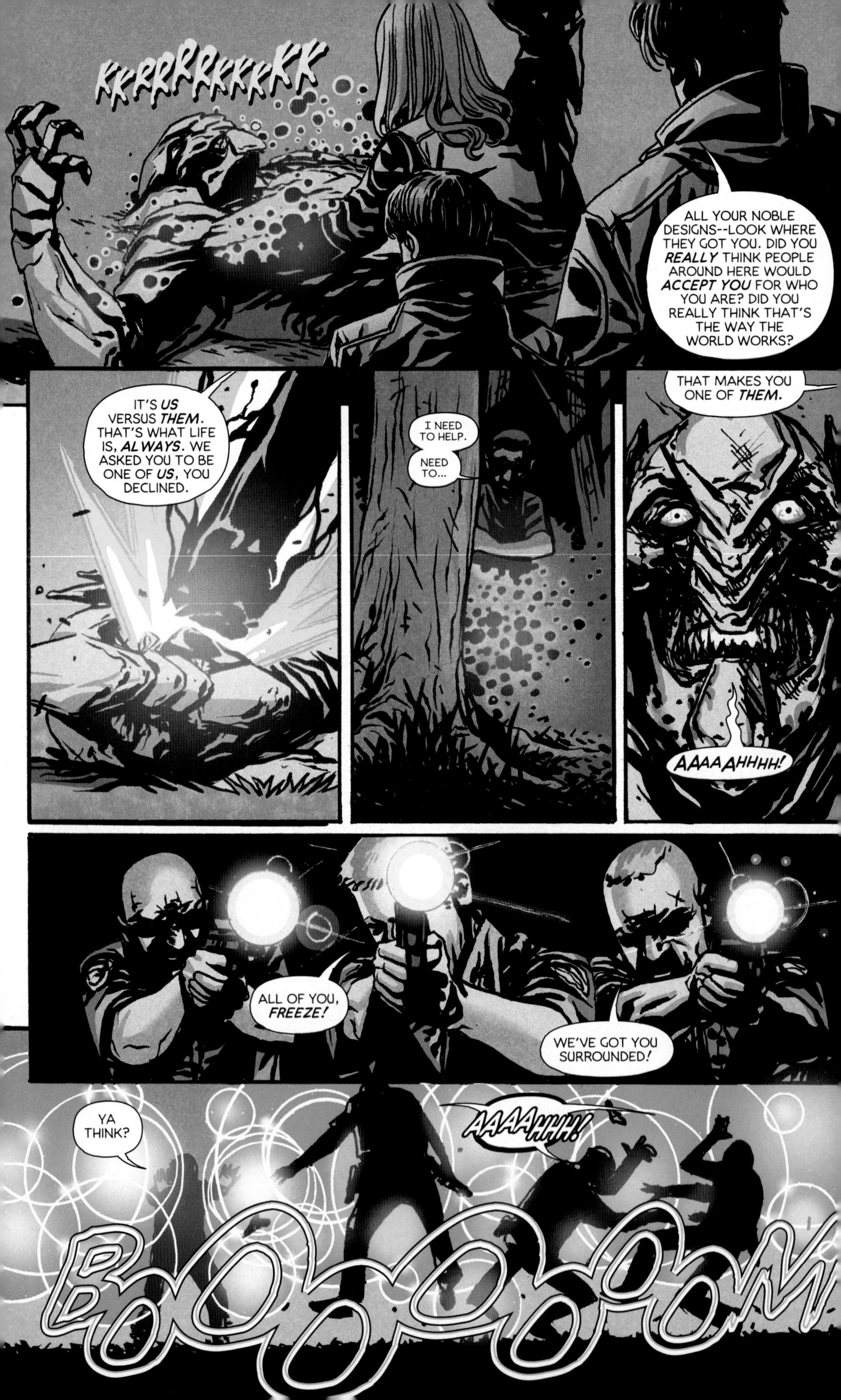
KKRRRRKKKKKK
ALL YOUR NOBLE DESIGNS--LOOK WHERE THEY GOT YOU. DID YOU REALLY THINK PEOPLE AROUND HERE WOULD ACCEPT YOU FOR WHO YOU ARE? DID YOU REALLY THINK THAT'S THE WAY THE WORLD WORKS?
IT'S US VERSUS THEM. THAT'S WHAT LIFE IS, ALWAYS. WE ASKED YOU TO BE ONE OF US, YOU DECLINED.
I NEED TO HELP.
NEED TO...
THAT MAKES YOU ONE OF THEM.
AAAAHHHH!
ALL OF YOU, FREEZE!
WE'VE GOT YOU SURROUNDED!
YA THINK?
AAAAHHH!
BOOOOOOOOM

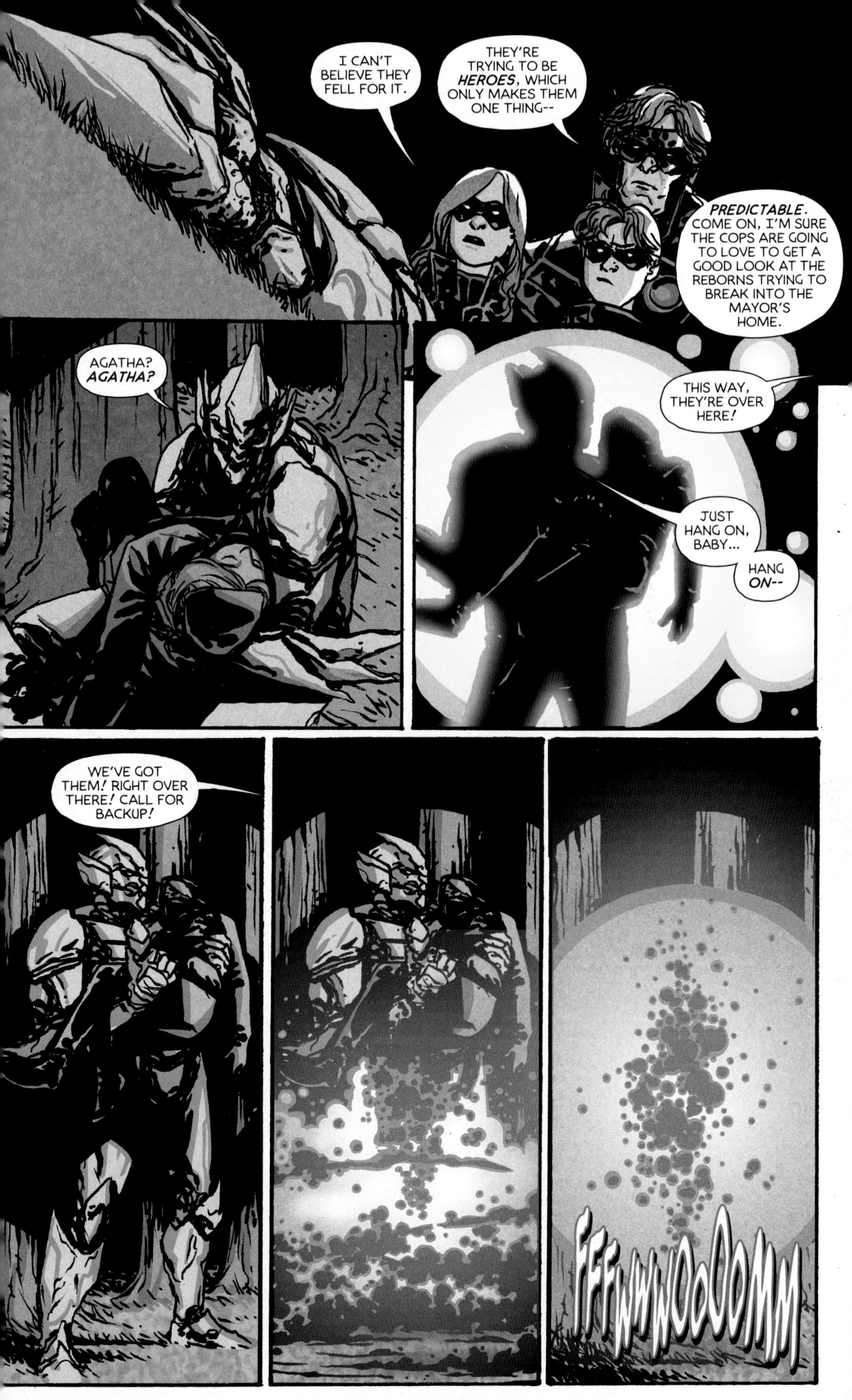

I CAN'T BELIEVE THEY FELL FOR IT.
THEY'RE TRYING TO BE *HEROES*, WHICH ONLY MAKES THEM ONE THING--
PREDICTABLE. COME ON, I'M SURE THE COPS ARE GOING TO LOVE TO GET A GOOD LOOK AT THE REBORNS TRYING TO BREAK INTO THE MAYOR'S HOME.
AGATHA? *AGATHA?*
THIS WAY, THEY'RE OVER HERE!
JUST HANG ON, BABY...
HANG *ON*--
WE'VE GOT THEM! RIGHT OVER THERE! CALL FOR BACKUP!
FFFWWWOOOOMM

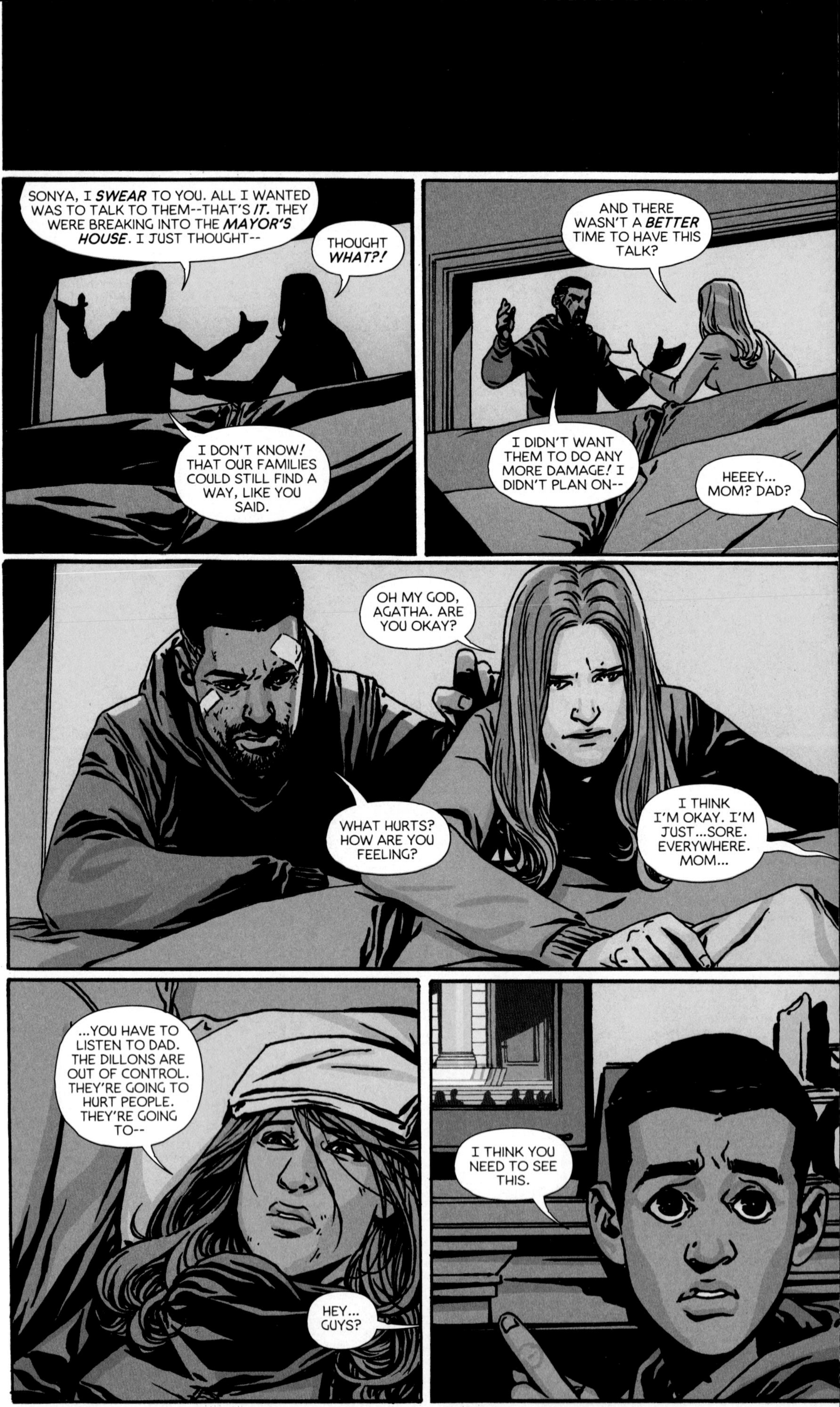
SONYA, I SWEAR TO YOU. ALL I WANTED WAS TO TALK TO THEM--THAT'S IT. THEY WERE BREAKING INTO THE MAYOR'S HOUSE. I JUST THOUGHT--
THOUGHT WHAT?!
I DON'T KNOW! THAT OUR FAMILIES COULD STILL FIND A WAY, LIKE YOU SAID.
AND THERE WASN'T A BETTER TIME TO HAVE THIS TALK?
I DIDN'T WANT THEM TO DO ANY MORE DAMAGE! I DIDN'T PLAN ON--
HEEEY... MOM? DAD?
OH MY GOD, AGATHA. ARE YOU OKAY?
WHAT HURTS? HOW ARE YOU FEELING?
I THINK I'M OKAY. I'M JUST...SORE. EVERYWHERE. MOM...
...YOU HAVE TO LISTEN TO DAD. THE DILLONS ARE OUT OF CONTROL. THEY'RE GOING TO HURT PEOPLE. THEY'RE GOING TO--
HEY... GUYS?
I THINK YOU NEED TO SEE THIS.

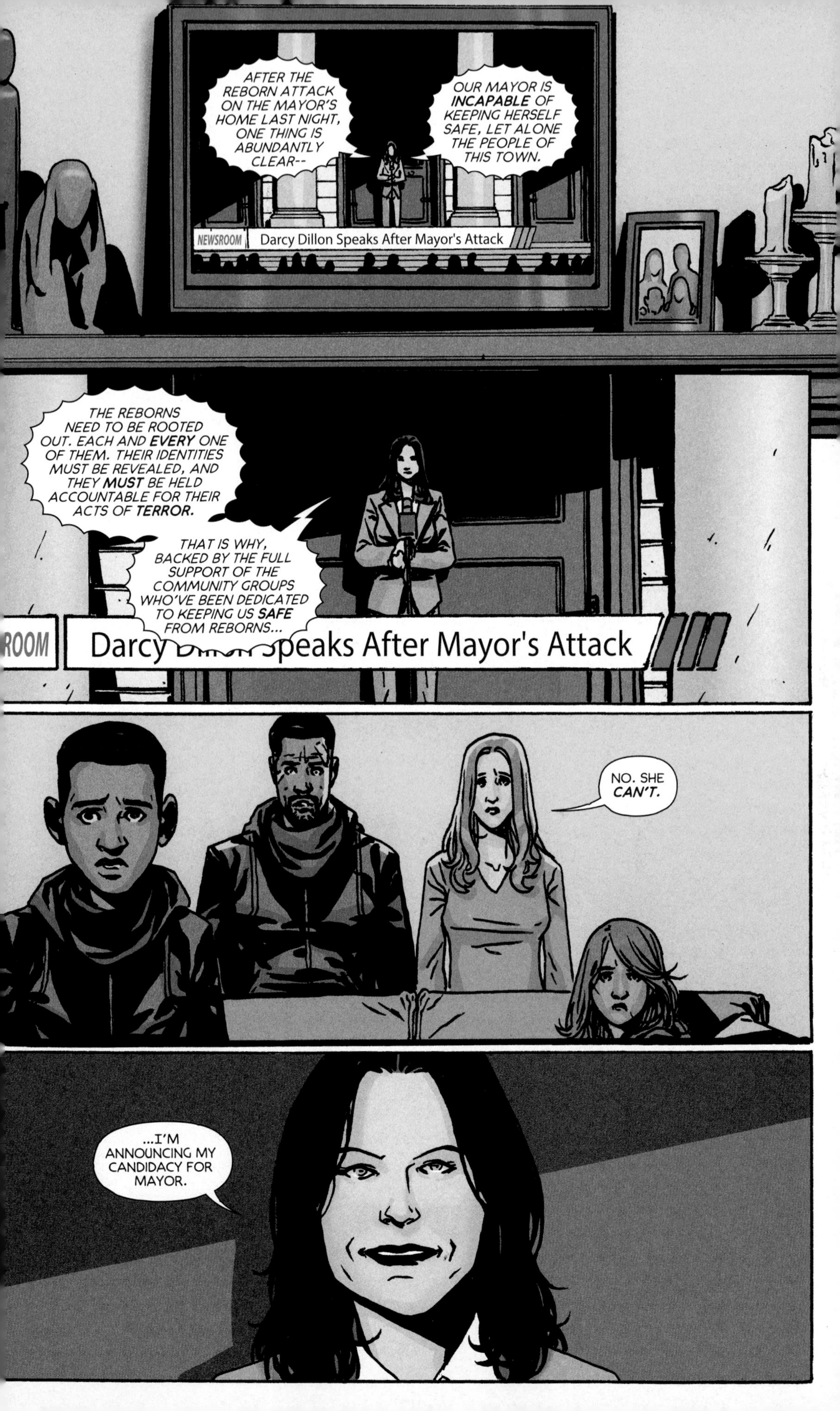
AFTER THE REBORN ATTACK ON THE MAYOR'S HOME LAST NIGHT, ONE THING IS ABUNDANTLY CLEAR--
OUR MAYOR IS **INCAPABLE** OF KEEPING HERSELF SAFE, LET ALONE THE PEOPLE OF THIS TOWN.
NEWSROOM
Darcy Dillon Speaks After Mayor's Attack
THE REBORNS NEED TO BE ROOTED OUT. EACH AND **EVERY** ONE OF THEM. THEIR IDENTITIES MUST BE REVEALED, AND THEY **MUST** BE HELD ACCOUNTABLE FOR THEIR ACTS OF **TERROR.**
THAT IS WHY, BACKED BY THE FULL SUPPORT OF THE COMMUNITY GROUPS WHO'VE BEEN DEDICATED TO KEEPING US **SAFE** FROM REBORNS...
ROOM
NO. SHE **CAN'T.**
...I'M ANNOUNCING MY CANDIDACY FOR MAYOR.

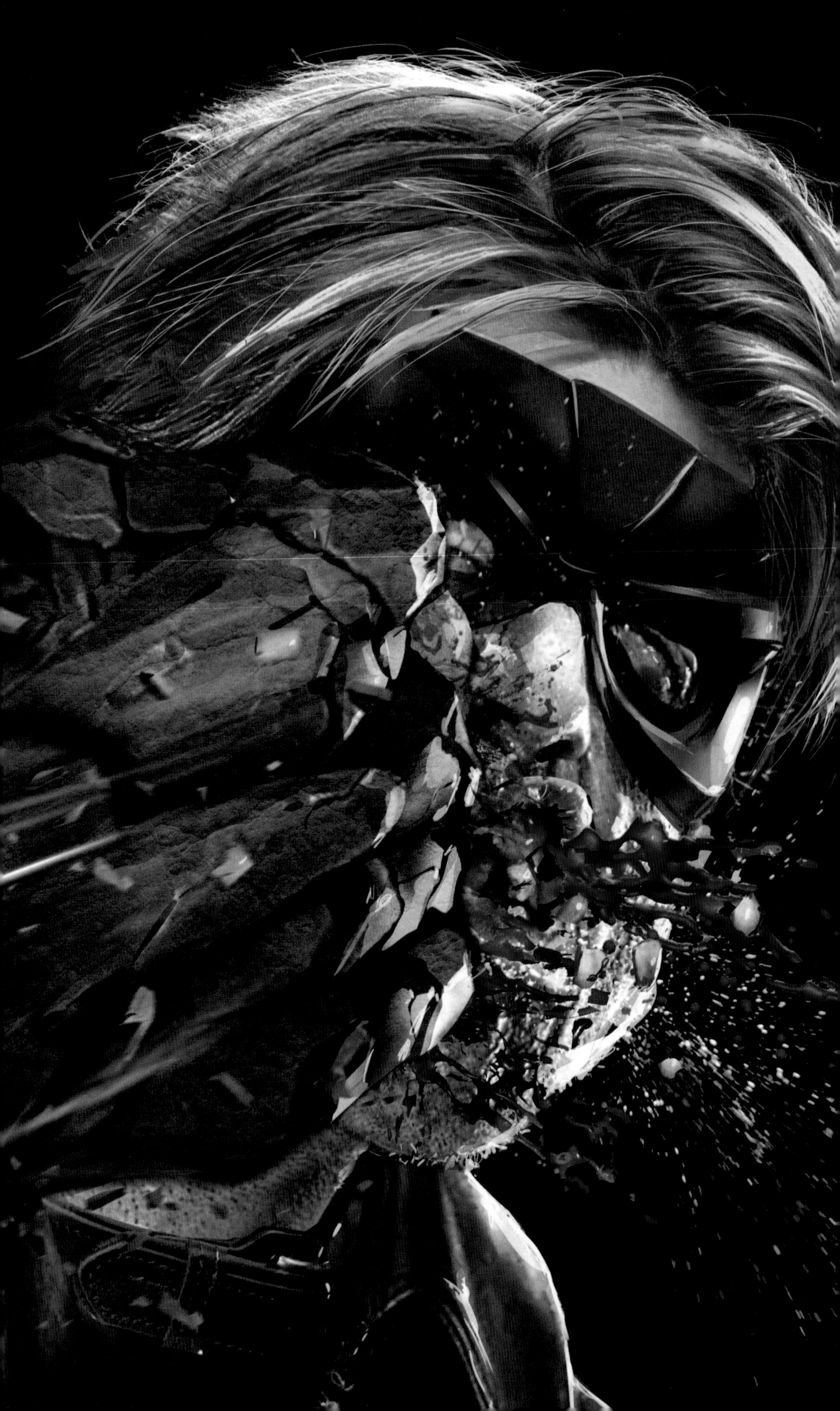

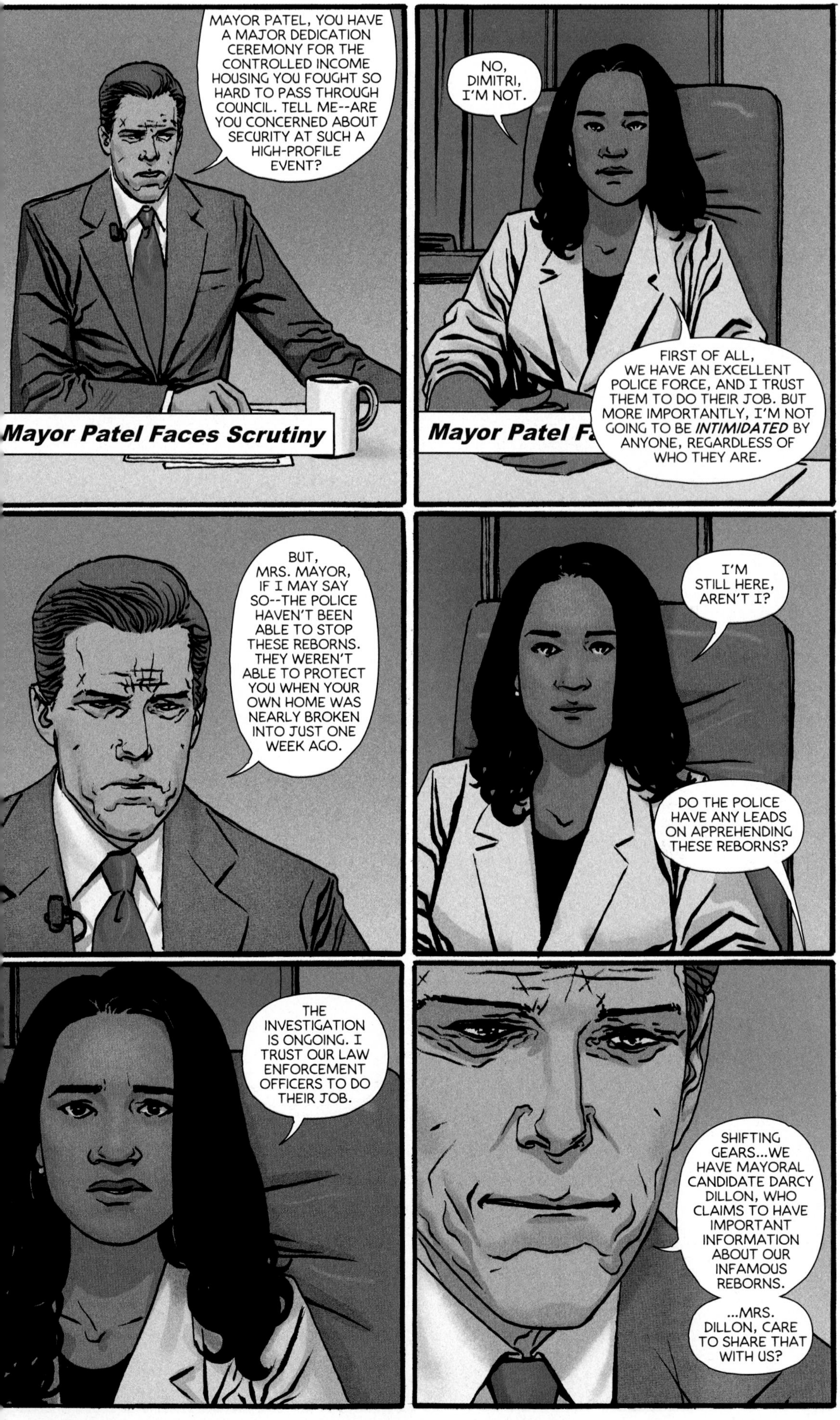
MAYOR PATEL, YOU HAVE A MAJOR DEDICATION CEREMONY FOR THE CONTROLLED INCOME HOUSING YOU FOUGHT SO HARD TO PASS THROUGH COUNCIL. TELL ME--ARE YOU CONCERNED ABOUT SECURITY AT SUCH A HIGH-PROFILE EVENT?
Mayor Patel Faces Scrutiny
NO, DIMITRI, I'M NOT.
Mayor Patel Fa
FIRST OF ALL, WE HAVE AN EXCELLENT POLICE FORCE, AND I TRUST THEM TO DO THEIR JOB. BUT MORE IMPORTANTLY, I'M NOT GOING TO BE *INTIMIDATED* BY ANYONE, REGARDLESS OF WHO THEY ARE.
BUT, MRS. MAYOR, IF I MAY SAY SO--THE POLICE HAVEN'T BEEN ABLE TO STOP THESE REBORNS. THEY WEREN'T ABLE TO PROTECT YOU WHEN YOUR OWN HOME WAS NEARLY BROKEN INTO JUST ONE WEEK AGO.
I'M STILL HERE, AREN'T I?
DO THE POLICE HAVE ANY LEADS ON APPREHENDING THESE REBORNS?
THE INVESTIGATION IS ONGOING. I TRUST OUR LAW ENFORCEMENT OFFICERS TO DO THEIR JOB.
SHIFTING GEARS...WE HAVE MAYORAL CANDIDATE DARCY DILLON, WHO CLAIMS TO HAVE IMPORTANT INFORMATION ABOUT OUR INFAMOUS REBORNS.
...MRS. DILLON, CARE TO SHARE THAT WITH US?

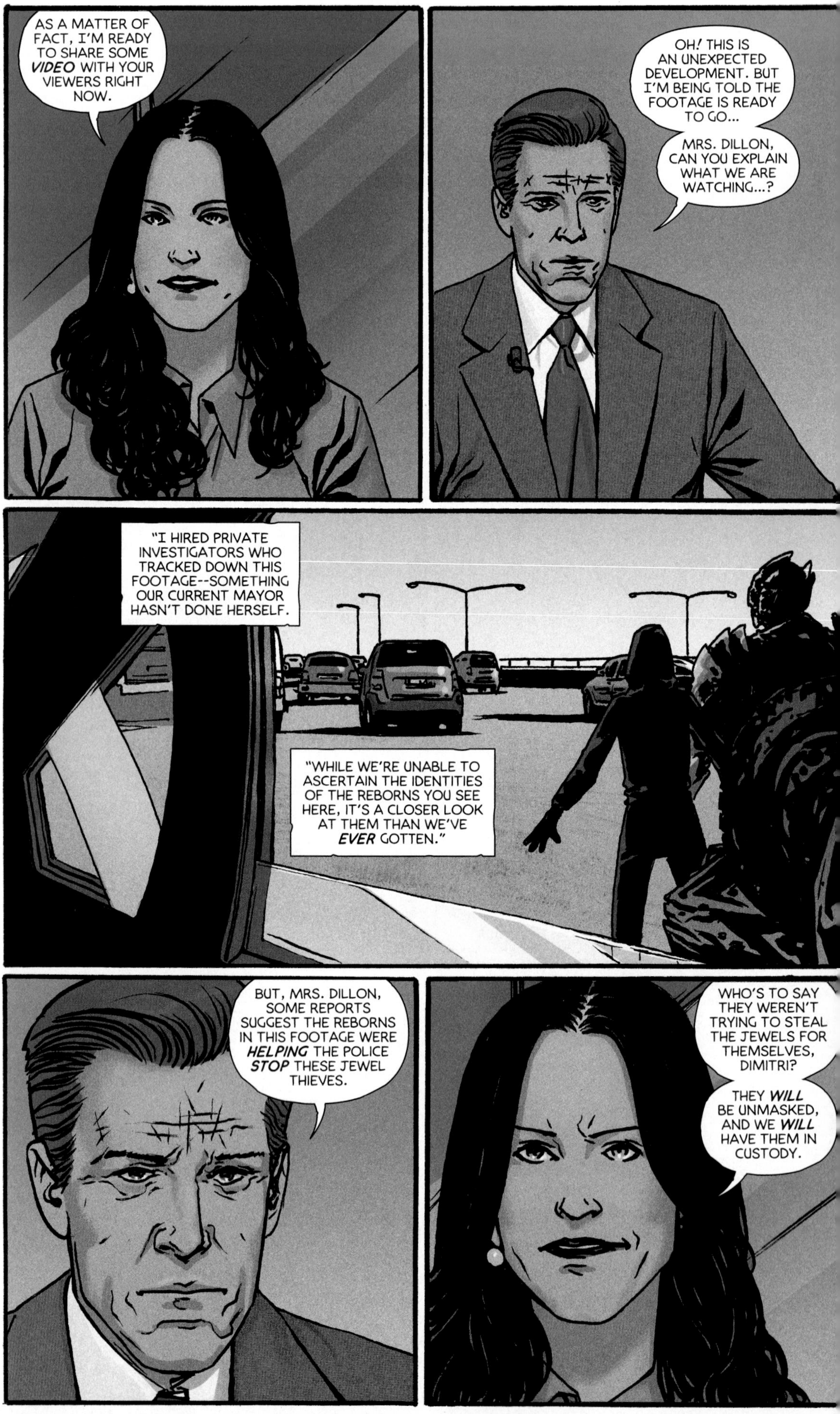
AS A MATTER OF FACT, I'M READY TO SHARE SOME VIDEO WITH YOUR VIEWERS RIGHT NOW.
OH! THIS IS AN UNEXPECTED DEVELOPMENT. BUT I'M BEING TOLD THE FOOTAGE IS READY TO GO...
MRS. DILLON, CAN YOU EXPLAIN WHAT WE ARE WATCHING...?
"I HIRED PRIVATE INVESTIGATORS WHO TRACKED DOWN THIS FOOTAGE--SOMETHING OUR CURRENT MAYOR HASN'T DONE HERSELF.
"WHILE WE'RE UNABLE TO ASCERTAIN THE IDENTITIES OF THE REBORNS YOU SEE HERE, IT'S A CLOSER LOOK AT THEM THAN WE'VE EVER GOTTEN."
BUT, MRS. DILLON, SOME REPORTS SUGGEST THE REBORNS IN THIS FOOTAGE WERE HELPING THE POLICE STOP THESE JEWEL THIEVES.
WHO'S TO SAY THEY WEREN'T TRYING TO STEAL THE JEWELS FOR THEMSELVES, DIMITRI?
THEY WILL BE UNMASKED, AND WE WILL HAVE THEM IN CUSTODY.

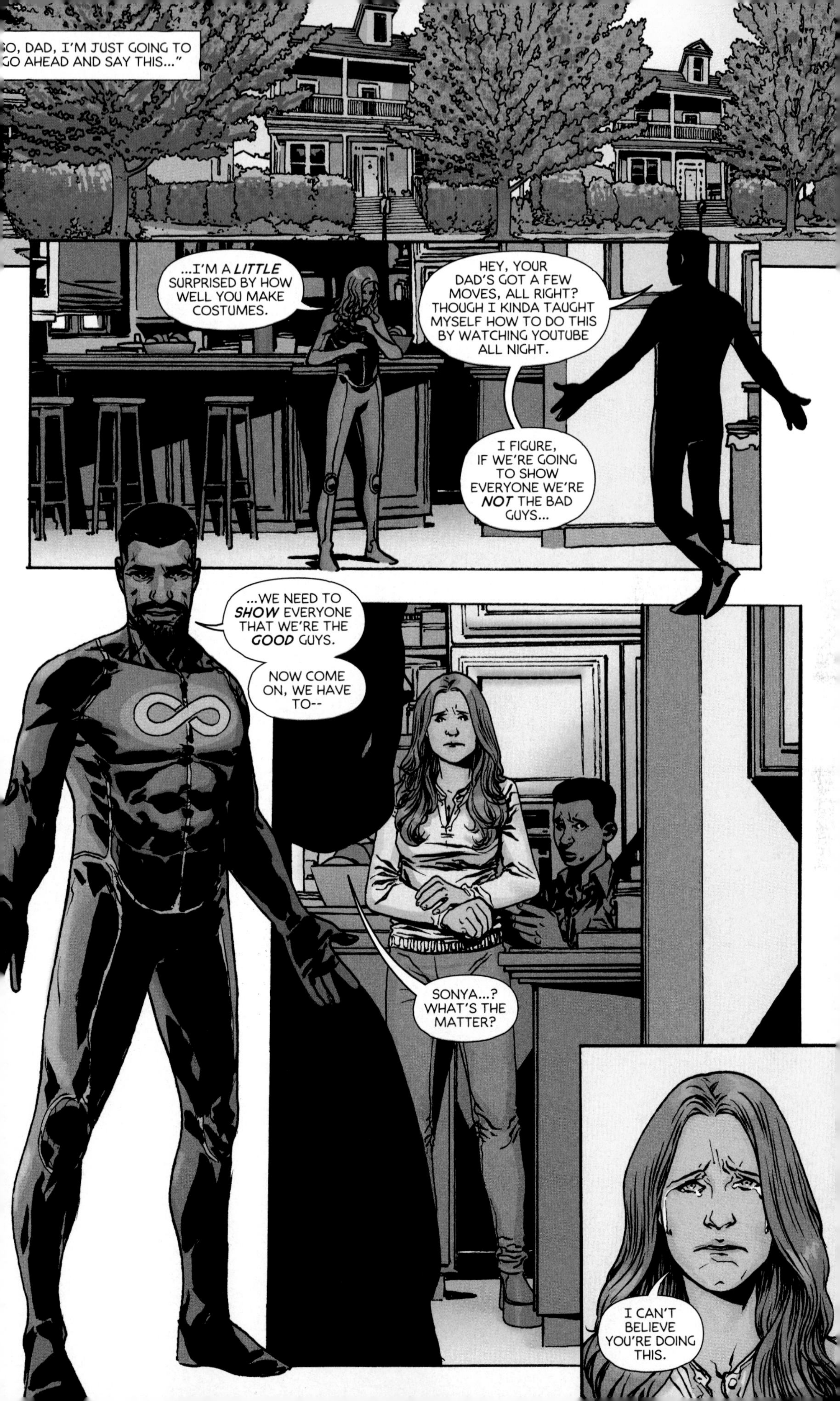
SO, DAD, I'M JUST GOING TO GO AHEAD AND SAY THIS..."
...I'M A *LITTLE* SURPRISED BY HOW WELL YOU MAKE COSTUMES.
HEY, YOUR DAD'S GOT A FEW MOVES, ALL RIGHT? THOUGH I KINDA TAUGHT MYSELF HOW TO DO THIS BY WATCHING YOUTUBE ALL NIGHT.
I FIGURE, IF WE'RE GOING TO SHOW EVERYONE WE'RE *NOT* THE BAD GUYS...
...WE NEED TO *SHOW* EVERYONE THAT WE'RE THE *GOOD* GUYS.
NOW COME ON, WE HAVE TO--
SONYA...? WHAT'S THE MATTER?
I CAN'T BELIEVE YOU'RE DOING THIS.

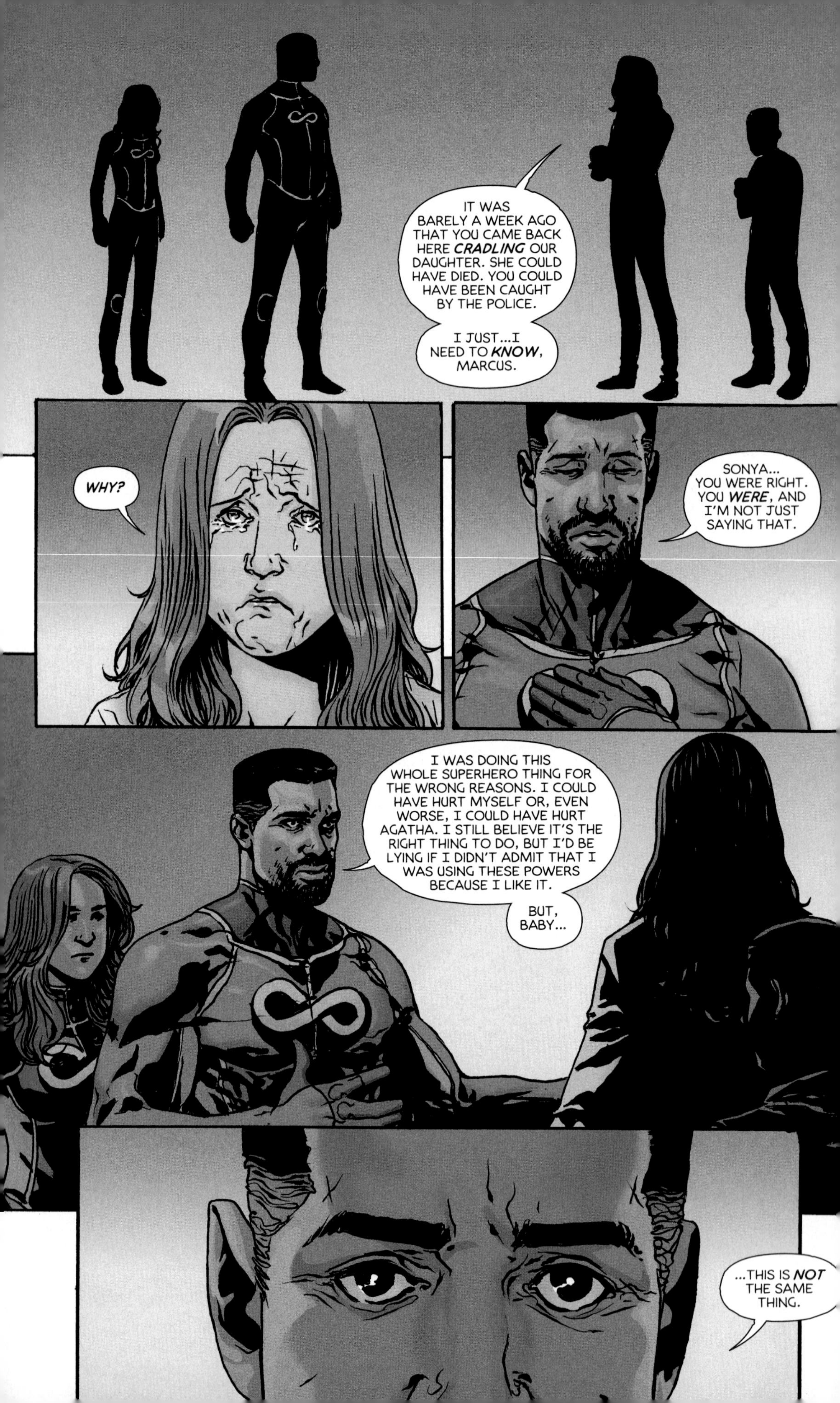

IT WAS BARELY A WEEK AGO THAT YOU CAME BACK HERE *CRADLING* OUR DAUGHTER. SHE COULD HAVE DIED. YOU COULD HAVE BEEN CAUGHT BY THE POLICE.
I JUST...I NEED TO *KNOW*, MARCUS.
WHY?
SONYA... YOU WERE RIGHT. YOU *WERE*, AND I'M NOT JUST SAYING THAT.
I WAS DOING THIS WHOLE SUPERHERO THING FOR THE WRONG REASONS. I COULD HAVE HURT MYSELF OR, EVEN WORSE, I COULD HAVE HURT AGATHA. I STILL BELIEVE IT'S THE RIGHT THING TO DO, BUT I'D BE LYING IF I DIDN'T ADMIT THAT I WAS USING THESE POWERS BECAUSE I LIKE IT.
BUT, BABY...
...THIS IS *NOT* THE SAME THING.

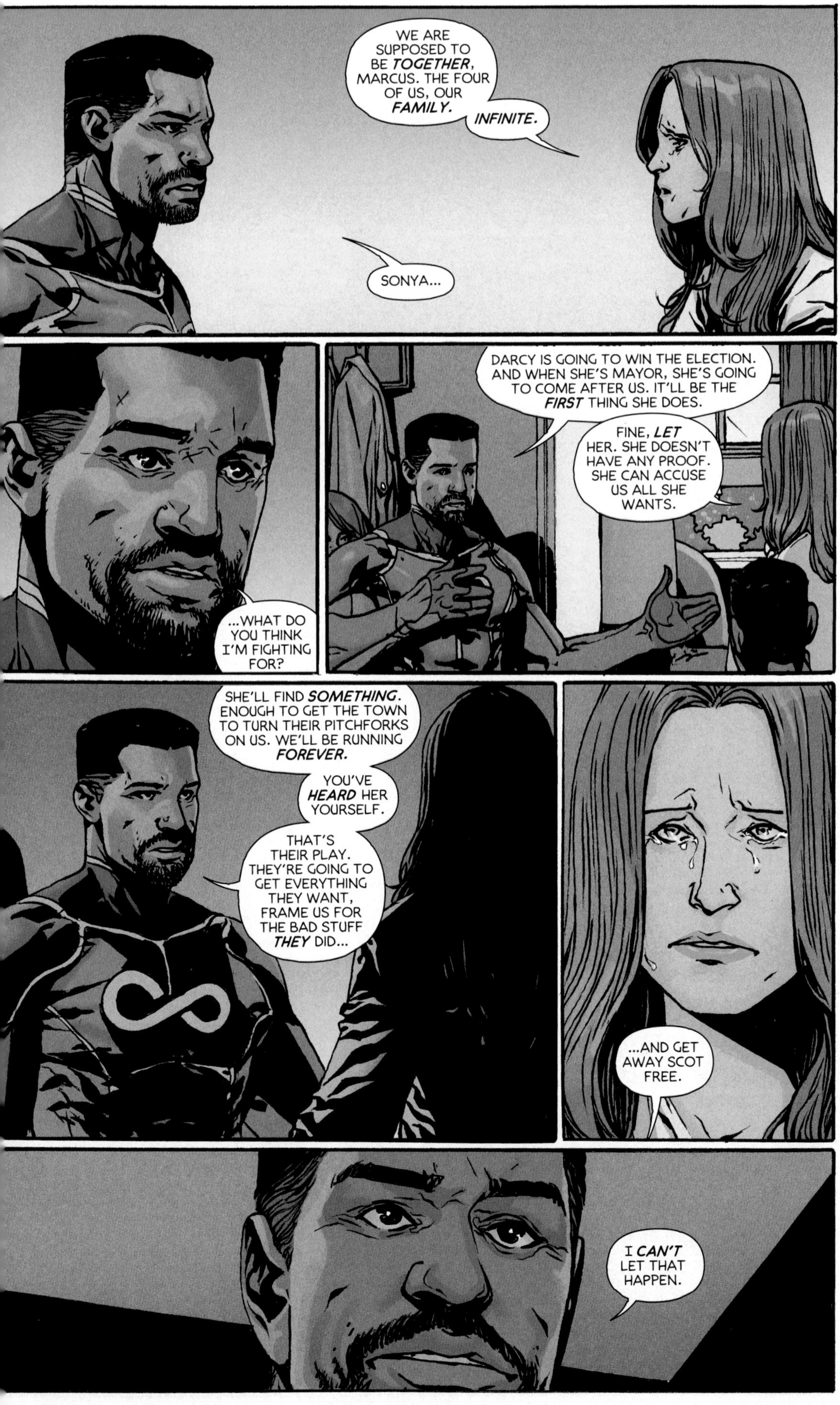

WE ARE SUPPOSED TO BE TOGETHER, MARCUS. THE FOUR OF US, OUR FAMILY.
INFINITE.
SONYA...
...WHAT DO YOU THINK I'M FIGHTING FOR?
DARCY IS GOING TO WIN THE ELECTION. AND WHEN SHE'S MAYOR, SHE'S GOING TO COME AFTER US. IT'LL BE THE FIRST THING SHE DOES.
FINE, LET HER. SHE DOESN'T HAVE ANY PROOF. SHE CAN ACCUSE US ALL SHE WANTS.
SHE'LL FIND SOMETHING. ENOUGH TO GET THE TOWN TO TURN THEIR PITCHFORKS ON US. WE'LL BE RUNNING FOREVER.
YOU'VE HEARD HER YOURSELF.
THAT'S THEIR PLAY. THEY'RE GOING TO GET EVERYTHING THEY WANT, FRAME US FOR THE BAD STUFF THEY DID...
...AND GET AWAY SCOT FREE.
I CAN'T LET THAT HAPPEN.

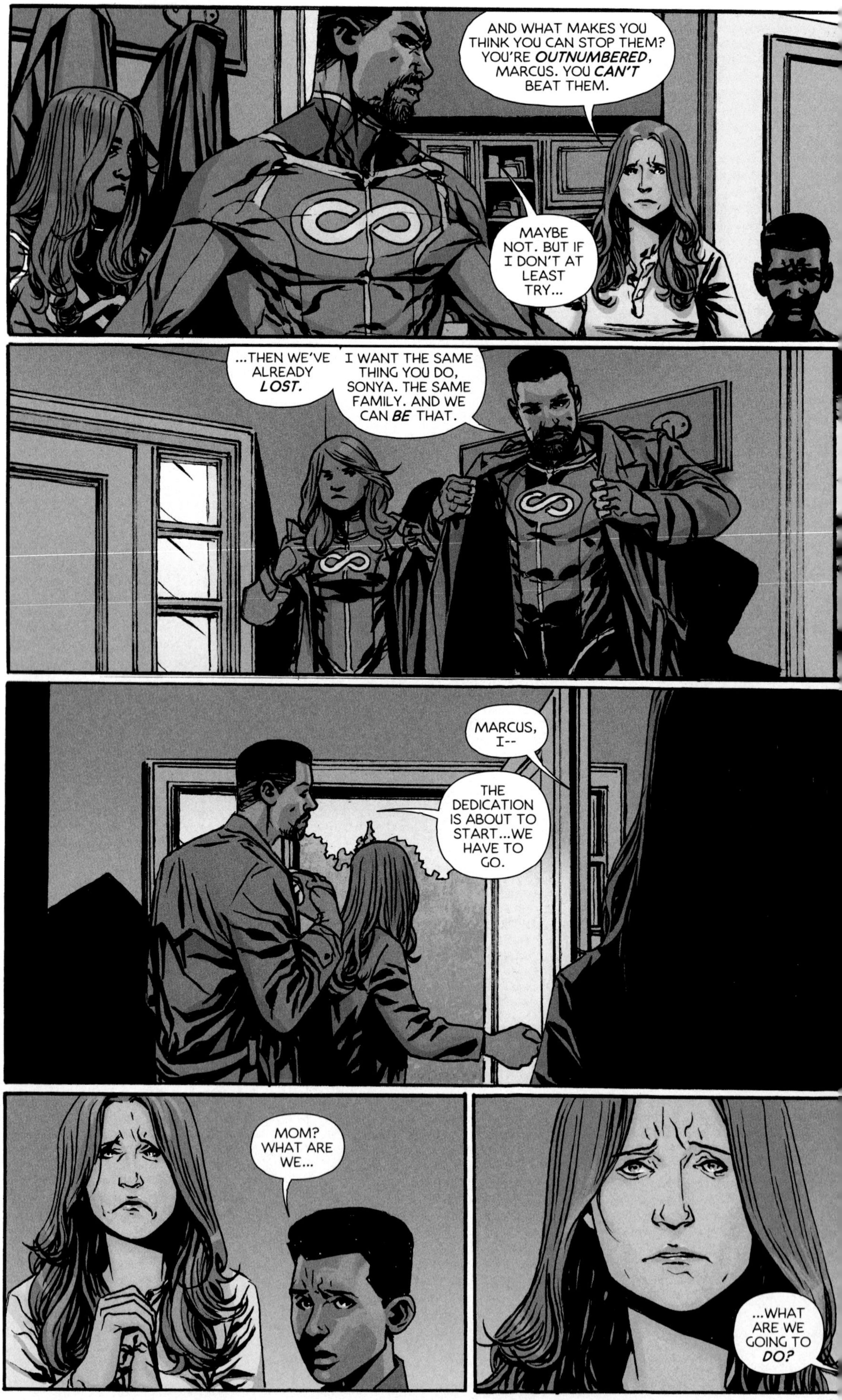
AND WHAT MAKES YOU THINK YOU CAN STOP THEM? YOU'RE ***OUTNUMBERED***, MARCUS. YOU ***CAN'T*** BEAT THEM.
MAYBE NOT. BUT IF I DON'T AT LEAST TRY...
...THEN WE'VE ALREADY ***LOST.***
I WANT THE SAME THING YOU DO, SONYA. THE SAME FAMILY. AND WE CAN ***BE*** THAT.
MARCUS, I--
THE DEDICATION IS ABOUT TO START...WE HAVE TO GO.
MOM? WHAT ARE WE...
...WHAT ARE WE GOING TO ***DO?***

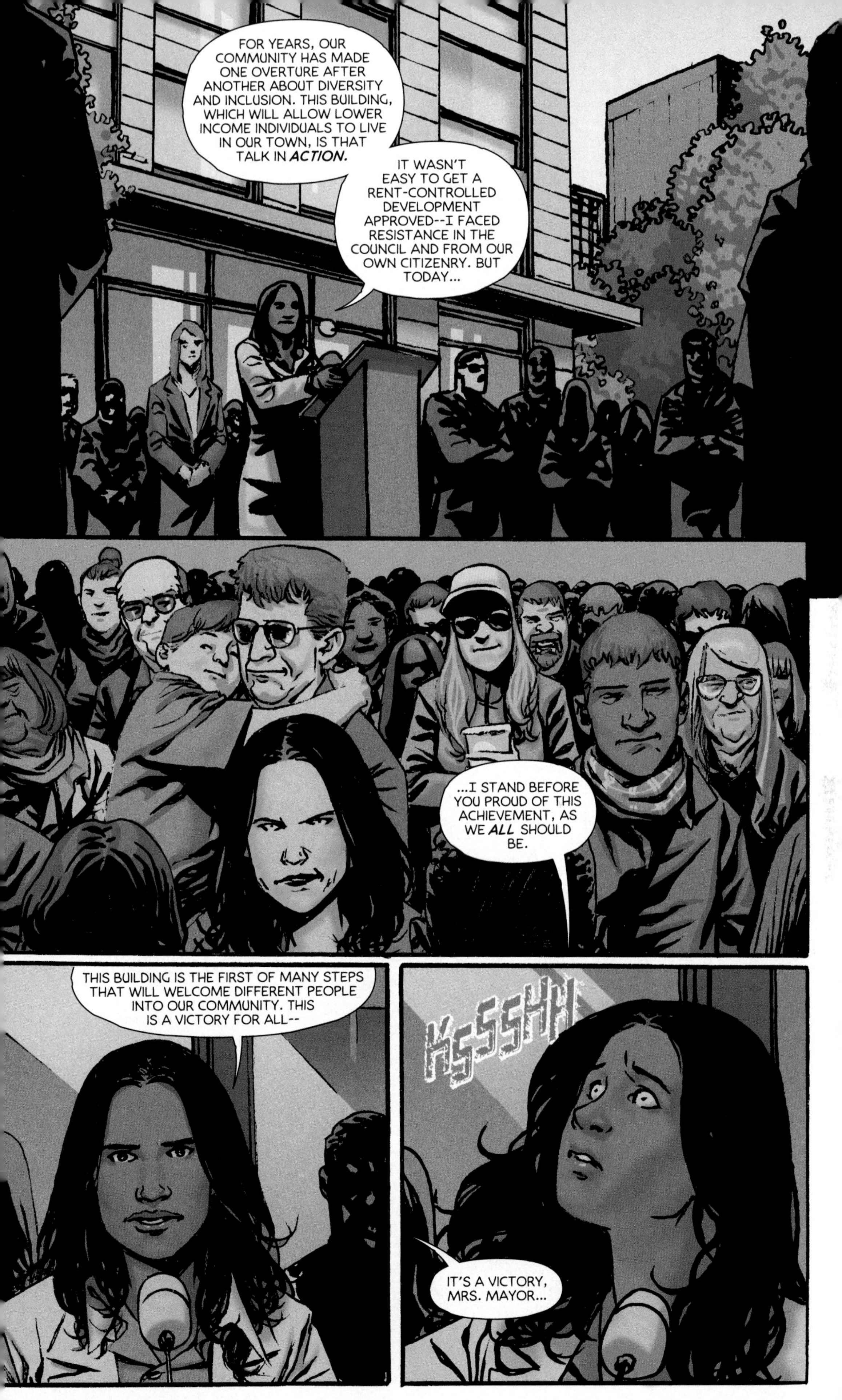
FOR YEARS, OUR COMMUNITY HAS MADE ONE OVERTURE AFTER ANOTHER ABOUT DIVERSITY AND INCLUSION. THIS BUILDING, WHICH WILL ALLOW LOWER INCOME INDIVIDUALS TO LIVE IN OUR TOWN, IS THAT TALK IN *ACTION.*
IT WASN'T EASY TO GET A RENT-CONTROLLED DEVELOPMENT APPROVED--I FACED RESISTANCE IN THE COUNCIL AND FROM OUR OWN CITIZENRY. BUT TODAY...
...I STAND BEFORE YOU PROUD OF THIS ACHIEVEMENT, AS WE *ALL* SHOULD BE.
THIS BUILDING IS THE FIRST OF MANY STEPS THAT WILL WELCOME DIFFERENT PEOPLE INTO OUR COMMUNITY. THIS IS A VICTORY FOR ALL--
KSSSHH
IT'S A VICTORY, MRS. MAYOR...

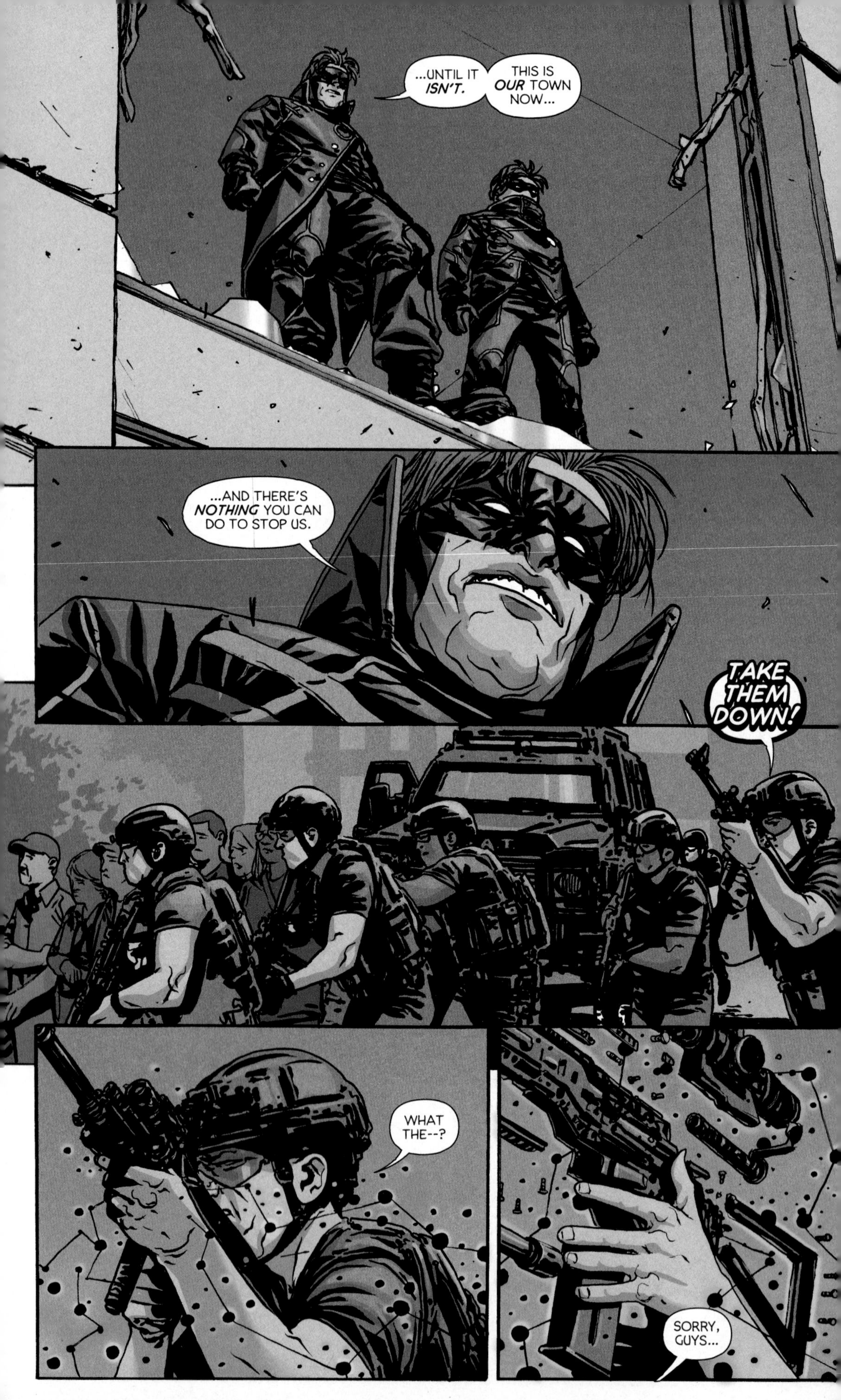
...UNTIL IT ISN'T.
THIS IS OUR TOWN NOW...
...AND THERE'S NOTHING YOU CAN DO TO STOP US.
TAKE THEM DOWN!
WHAT THE--?
SORRY, GUYS...

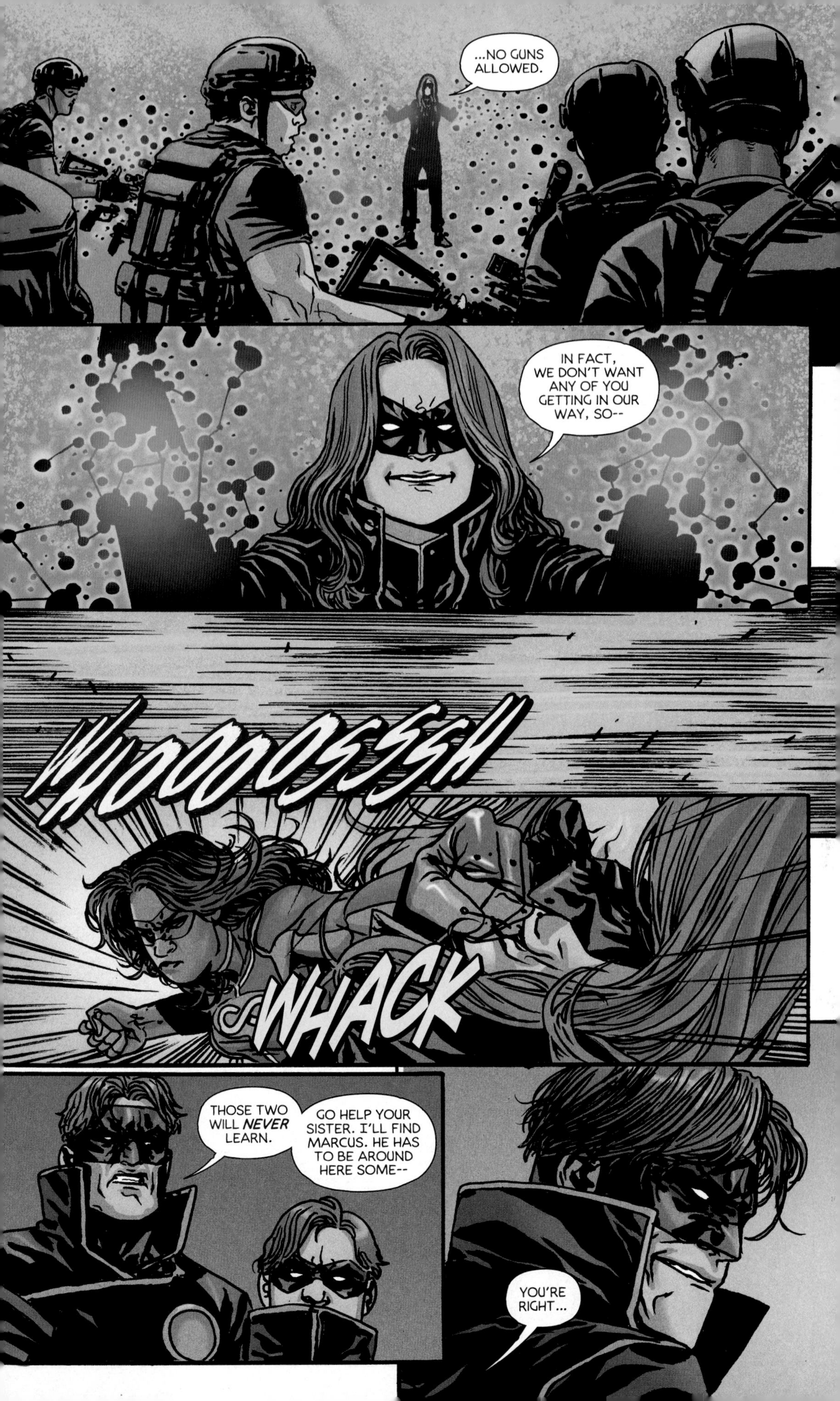
...NO GUNS ALLOWED.
IN FACT, WE DON'T WANT ANY OF YOU GETTING IN OUR WAY, SO--
WHOOOOSSSH
WHACK
THOSE TWO WILL *NEVER* LEARN.
GO HELP YOUR SISTER. I'LL FIND MARCUS. HE HAS TO BE AROUND HERE SOME--
YOU'RE RIGHT...

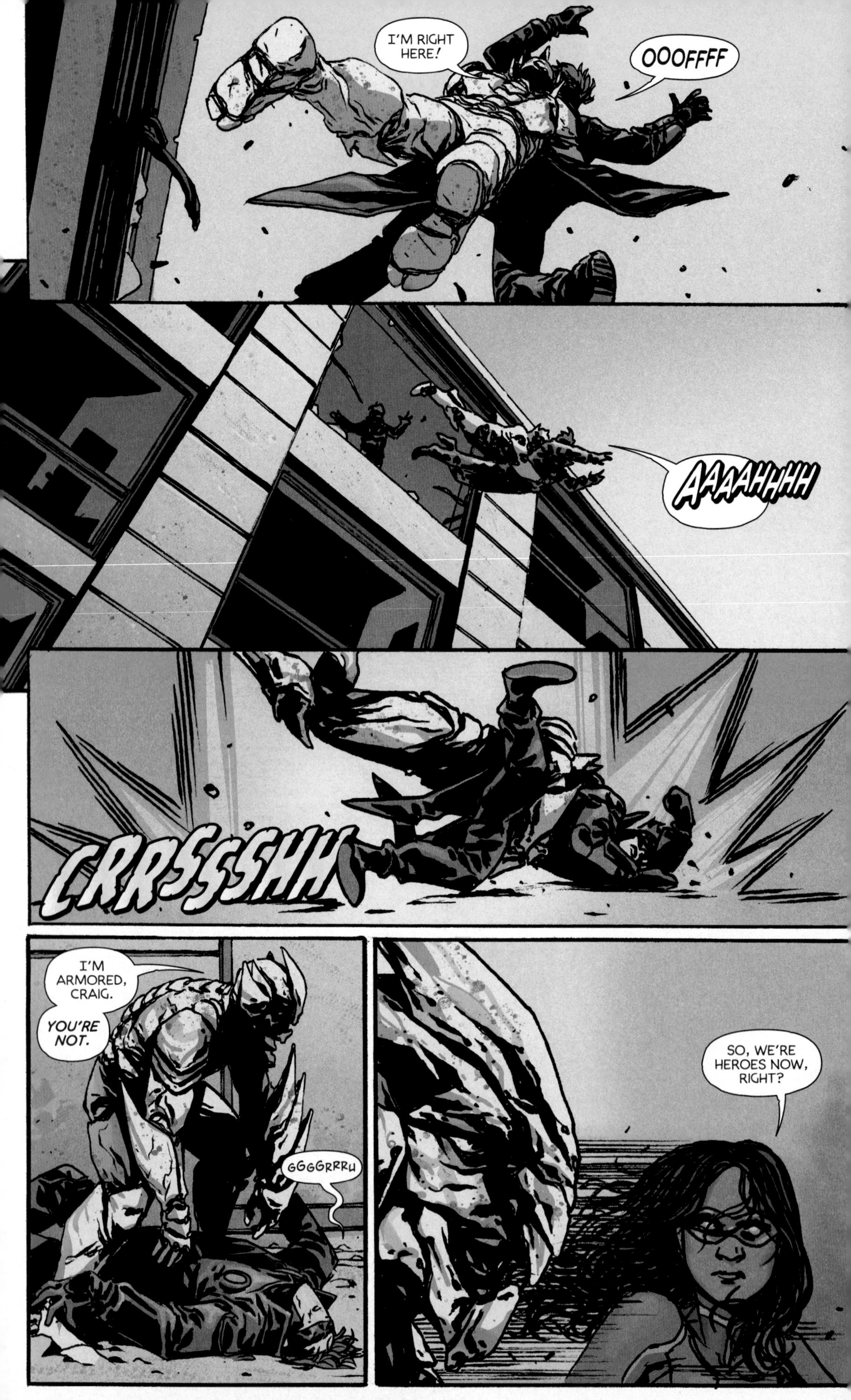
I'M RIGHT HERE!
OOOFFFF
AAAAHHHH
CRRSSSHH
I'M ARMORED, CRAIG.
YOU'RE NOT.
GGGGRRRU
SO, WE'RE HEROES NOW, RIGHT?

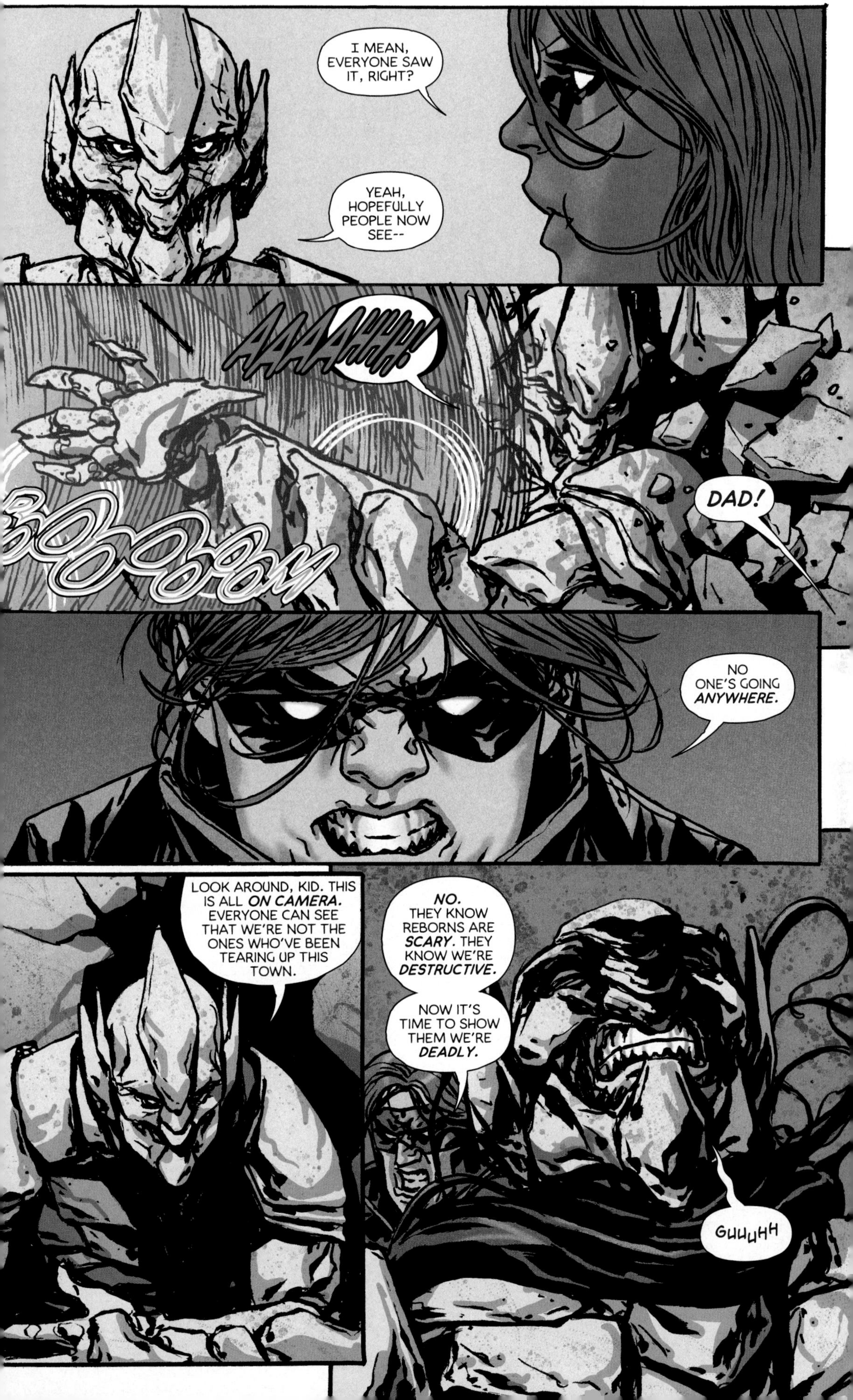
I MEAN, EVERYONE SAW IT, RIGHT?
YEAH, HOPEFULLY PEOPLE NOW SEE--
AAAAHHH!!
DAD!
NO ONE'S GOING *ANYWHERE.*
LOOK AROUND, KID. THIS IS ALL *ON CAMERA.* EVERYONE CAN SEE THAT WE'RE NOT THE ONES WHO'VE BEEN TEARING UP THIS TOWN.
NO. THEY KNOW REBORNS ARE *SCARY.* THEY KNOW WE'RE *DESTRUCTIVE.*
NOW IT'S TIME TO SHOW THEM WE'RE *DEADLY.*
GUUUHH

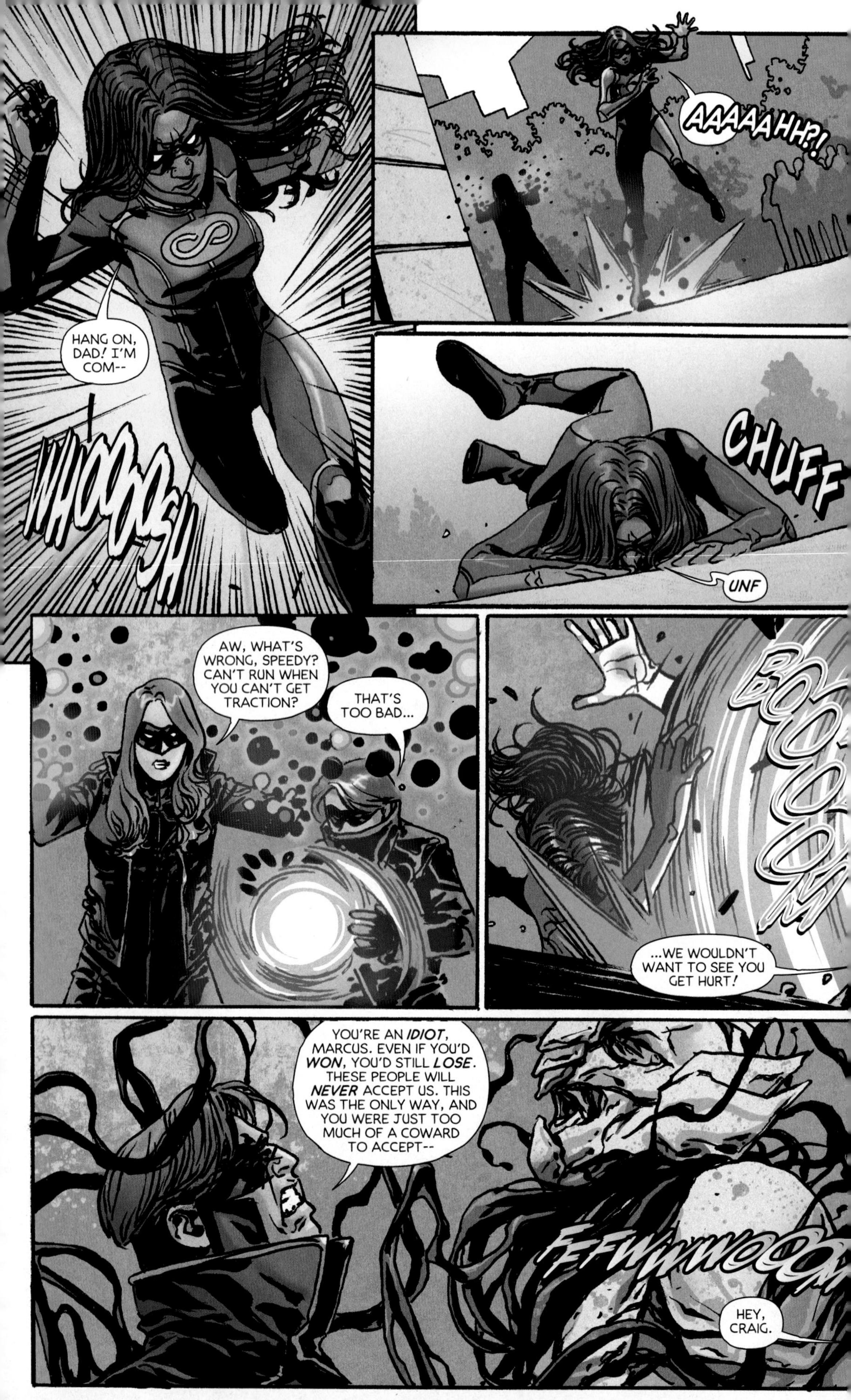
HANG ON, DAD! I'M COM--
WHOOOOSH
AAAAAHH?!
CHUFF
UNF
AW, WHAT'S WRONG, SPEEDY? CAN'T RUN WHEN YOU CAN'T GET TRACTION?
THAT'S TOO BAD...
BOOOOOM
...WE WOULDN'T WANT TO SEE YOU GET HURT!
YOU'RE AN IDIOT, MARCUS. EVEN IF YOU'D WON, YOU'D STILL LOSE. THESE PEOPLE WILL NEVER ACCEPT US. THIS WAS THE ONLY WAY, AND YOU WERE JUST TOO MUCH OF A COWARD TO ACCEPT--
FFWWWOOOM
HEY, CRAIG.

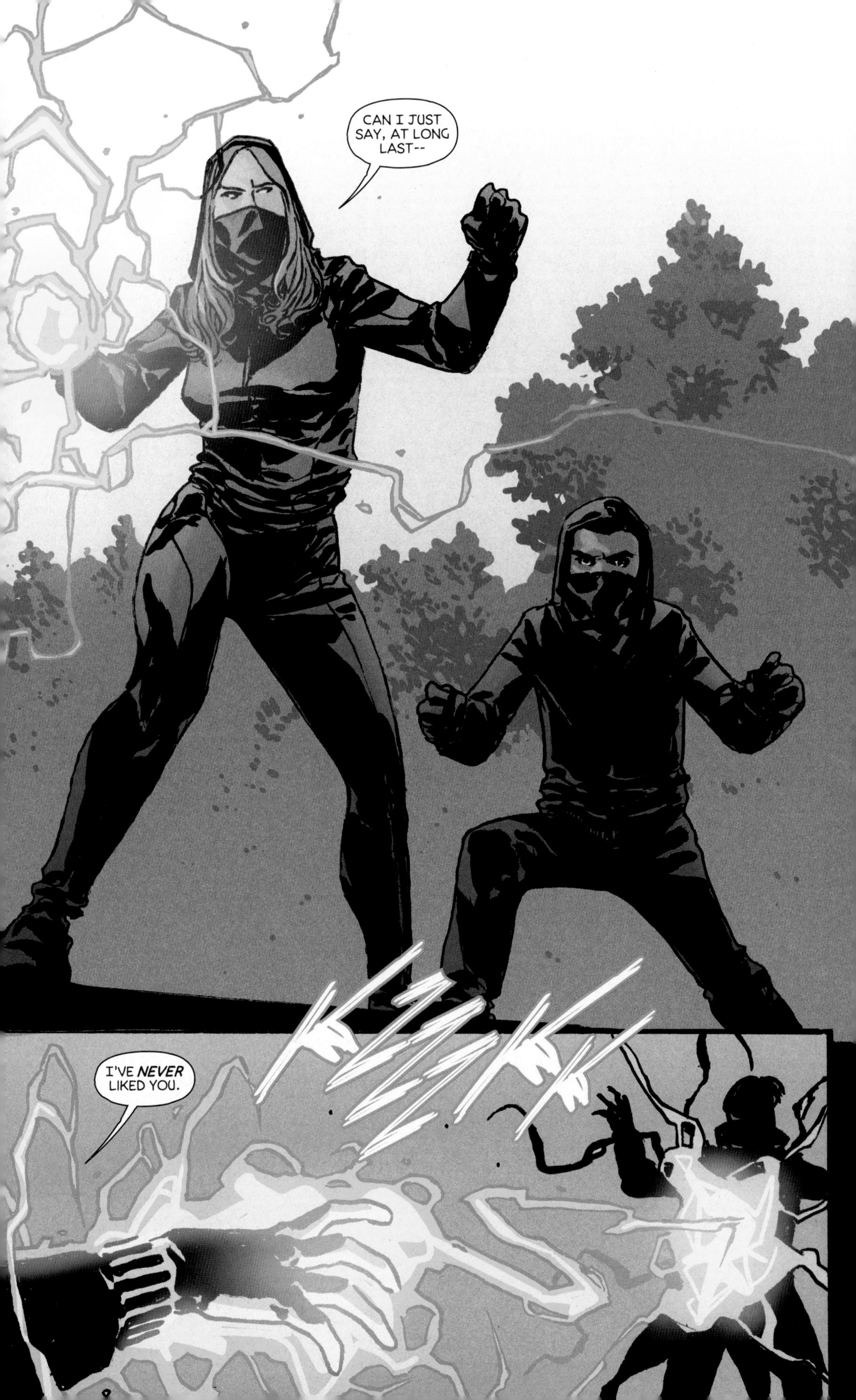
CAN I JUST SAY, AT LONG LAST--
I'VE NEVER LIKED YOU.
KZZKKK

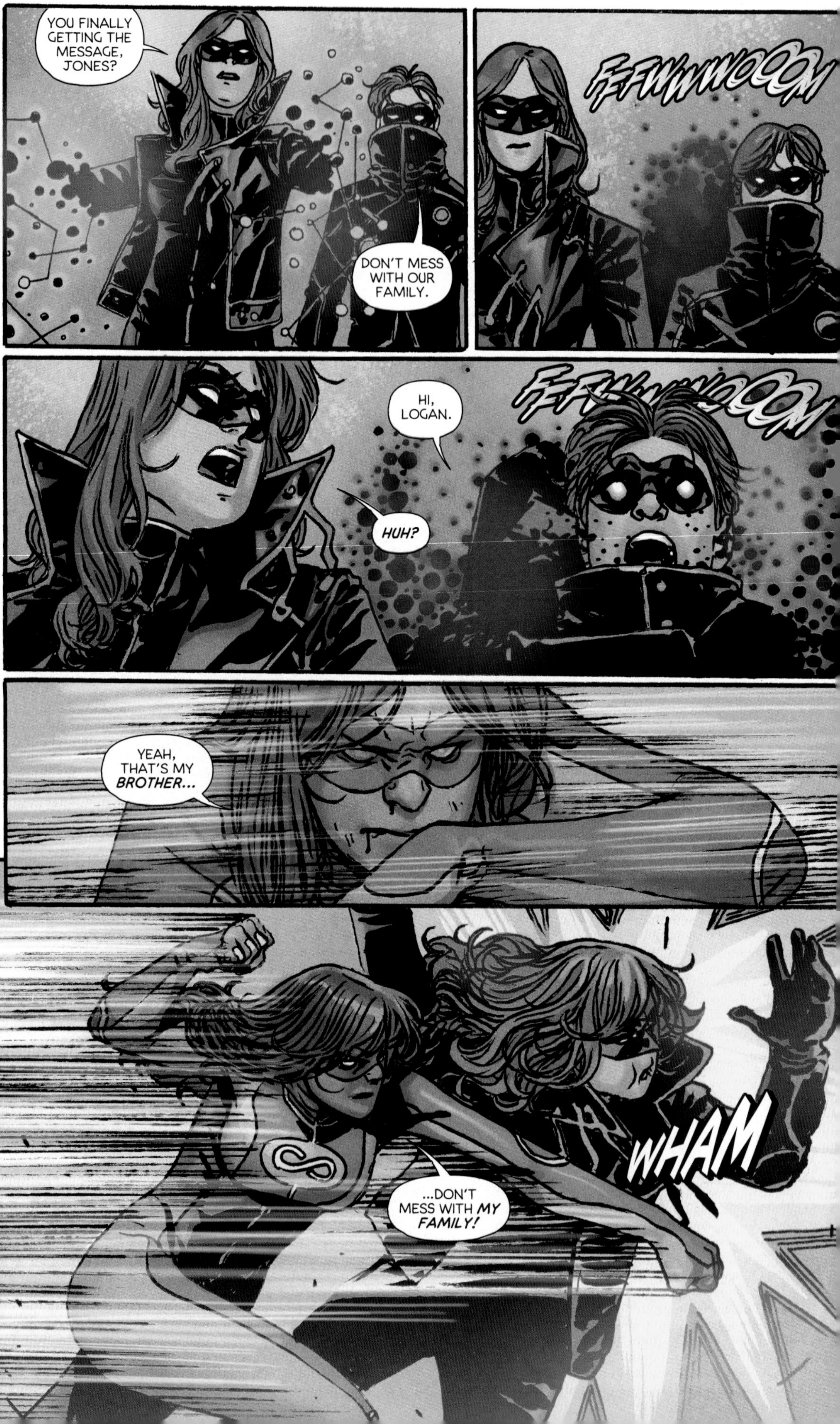
YOU FINALLY GETTING THE MESSAGE, JONES?
DON'T MESS WITH OUR FAMILY.
FFFWWWOOOOM
FFFWWWOOOOM
HI, LOGAN.
HUH?
YEAH, THAT'S MY BROTHER...
WHAM
...DON'T MESS WITH MY FAMILY!

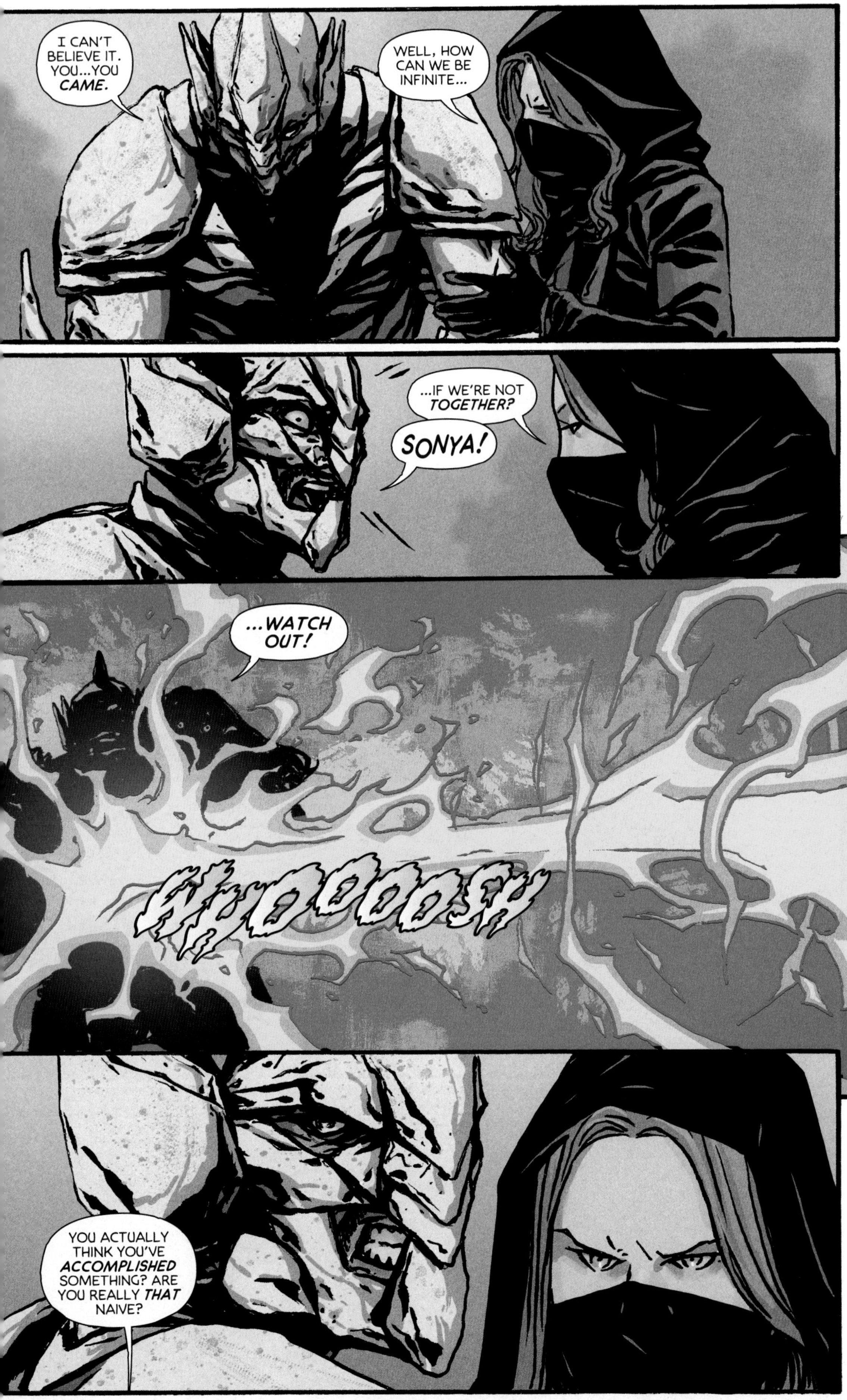
I CAN'T BELIEVE IT. YOU...YOU CAME.
WELL, HOW CAN WE BE INFINITE...
...IF WE'RE NOT TOGETHER?
SONYA!
...WATCH OUT!
WHOOOOSH
YOU ACTUALLY THINK YOU'VE ACCOMPLISHED SOMETHING? ARE YOU REALLY THAT NAIVE?

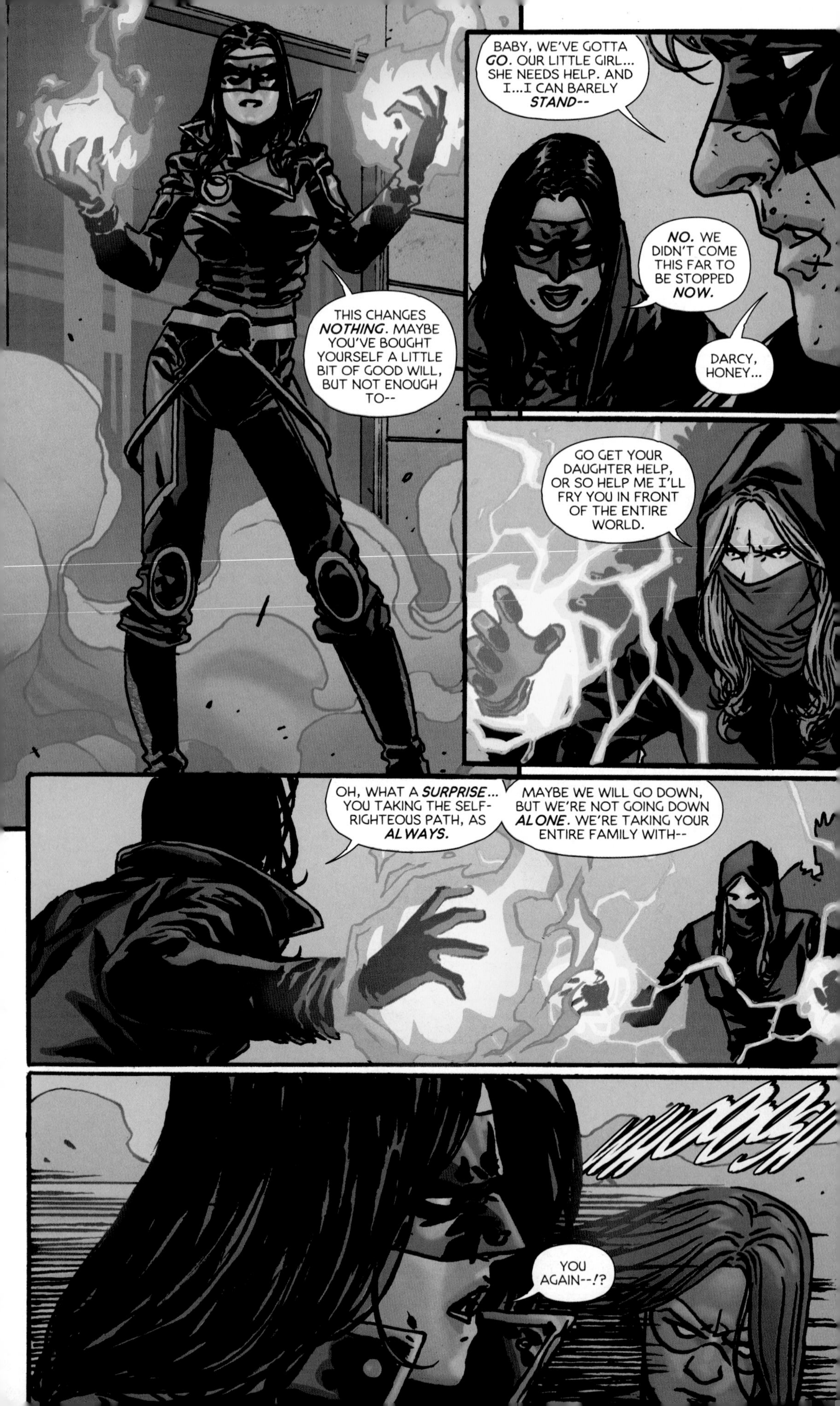
THIS CHANGES NOTHING. MAYBE YOU'VE BOUGHT YOURSELF A LITTLE BIT OF GOOD WILL, BUT NOT ENOUGH TO--
BABY, WE'VE GOTTA GO. OUR LITTLE GIRL... SHE NEEDS HELP. AND I...I CAN BARELY STAND--
NO. WE DIDN'T COME THIS FAR TO BE STOPPED NOW.
DARCY, HONEY...
GO GET YOUR DAUGHTER HELP, OR SO HELP ME I'LL FRY YOU IN FRONT OF THE ENTIRE WORLD.
OH, WHAT A SURPRISE... YOU TAKING THE SELF-RIGHTEOUS PATH, AS ALWAYS.
MAYBE WE WILL GO DOWN, BUT WE'RE NOT GOING DOWN ALONE. WE'RE TAKING YOUR ENTIRE FAMILY WITH--
YOU AGAIN--!?

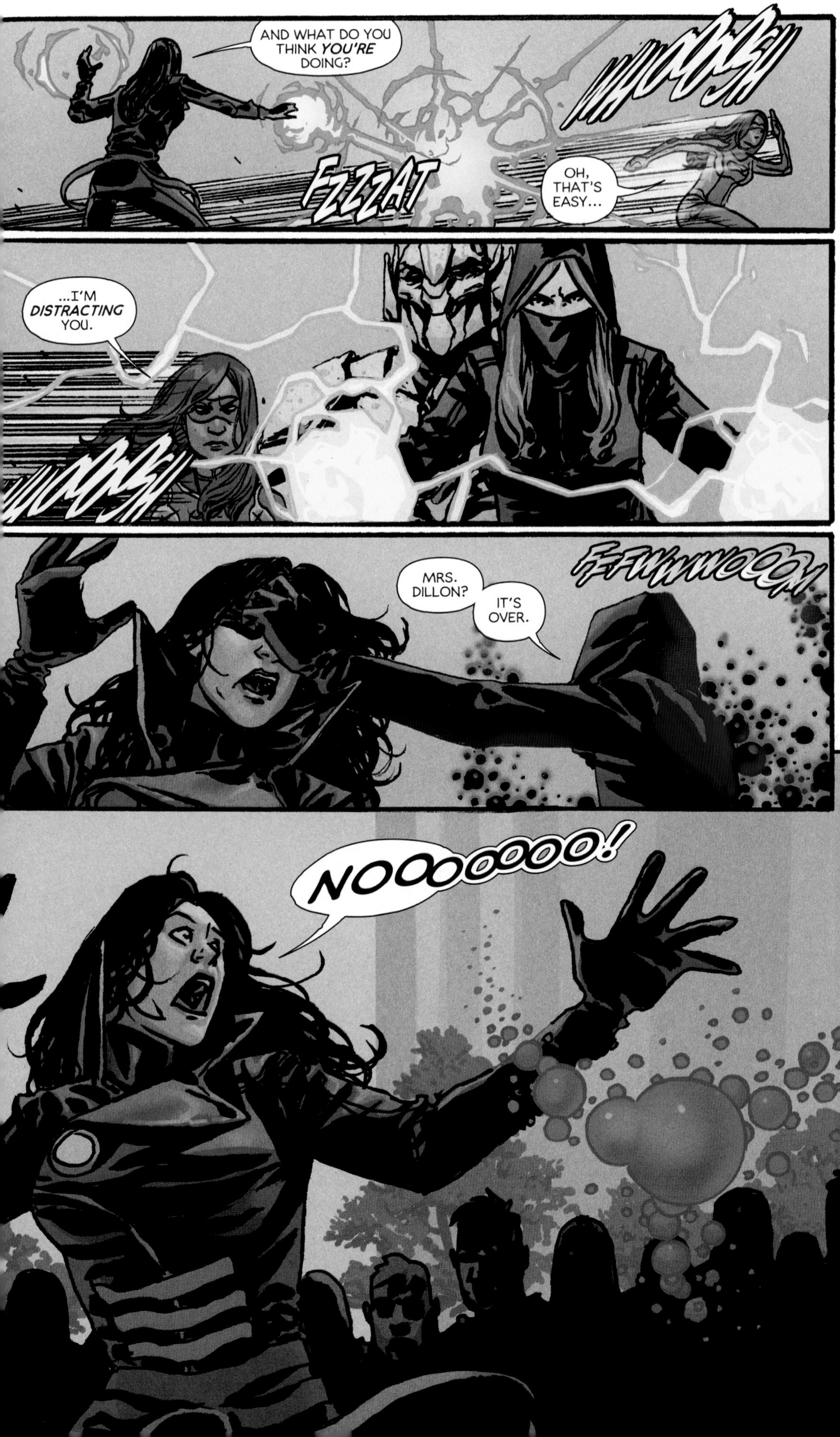
AND WHAT DO YOU THINK YOU'RE DOING?
FZZZAT
WHOOSH
OH, THAT'S EASY...
...I'M DISTRACTING YOU.
WHOOSH
FFWWWOOOM
MRS. DILLON?
IT'S OVER.
NOOOOOOO!

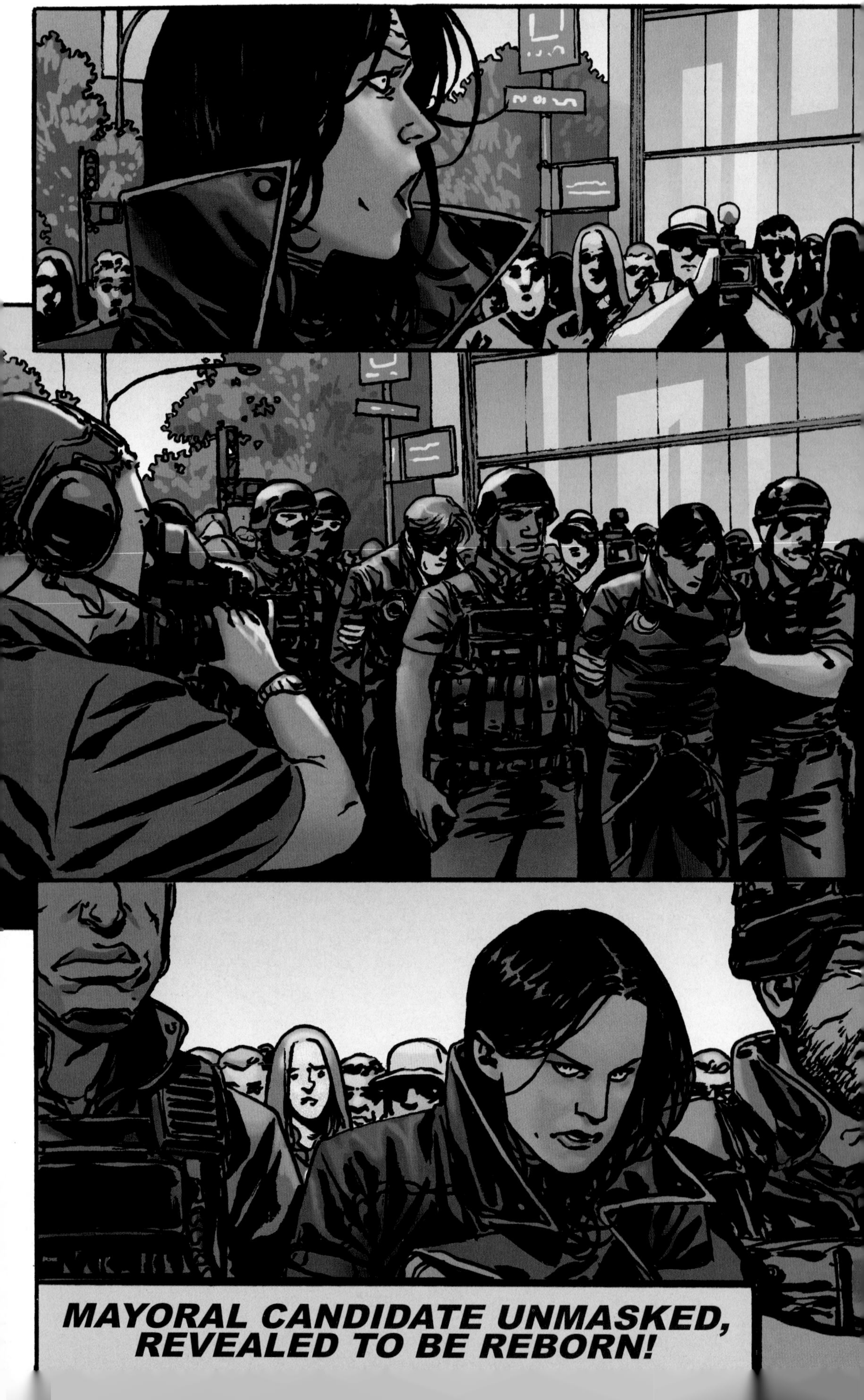
MAYORAL CANDIDATE UNMASKED,
REVEALED TO BE REBORN!

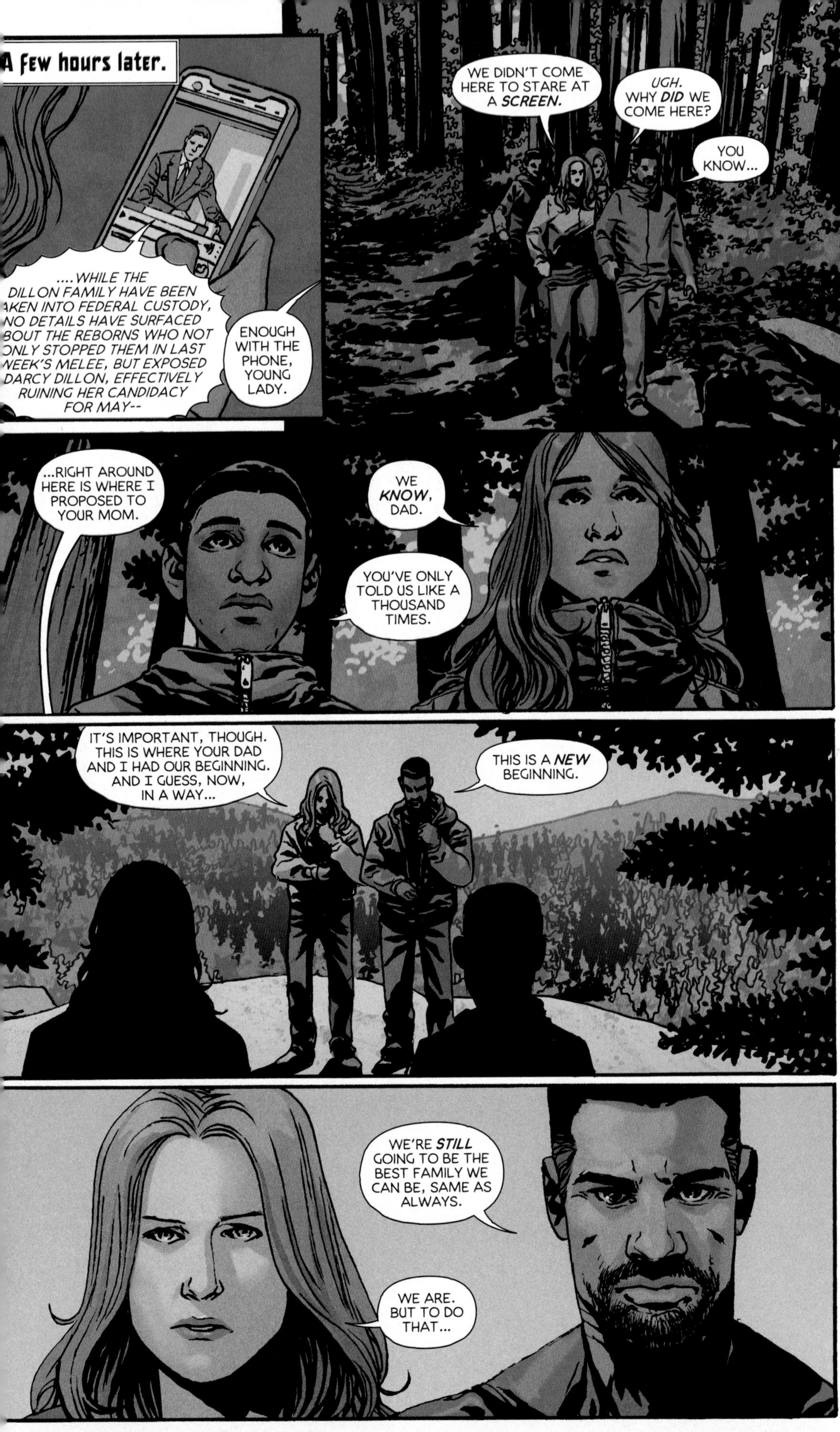

A few hours later.
....WHILE THE DILLON FAMILY HAVE BEEN AKEN INTO FEDERAL CUSTODY, NO DETAILS HAVE SURFACED BOUT THE REBORNS WHO NOT ONLY STOPPED THEM IN LAST WEEK'S MELEE, BUT EXPOSED DARCY DILLON, EFFECTIVELY RUINING HER CANDIDACY FOR MAY--
ENOUGH WITH THE PHONE, YOUNG LADY.
WE DIDN'T COME HERE TO STARE AT A SCREEN.
UGH. WHY DID WE COME HERE?
YOU KNOW...
...RIGHT AROUND HERE IS WHERE I PROPOSED TO YOUR MOM.
WE KNOW, DAD.
YOU'VE ONLY TOLD US LIKE A THOUSAND TIMES.
IT'S IMPORTANT, THOUGH. THIS IS WHERE YOUR DAD AND I HAD OUR BEGINNING. AND I GUESS, NOW, IN A WAY...
THIS IS A NEW BEGINNING.
WE'RE STILL GOING TO BE THE BEST FAMILY WE CAN BE, SAME AS ALWAYS.
WE ARE. BUT TO DO THAT...

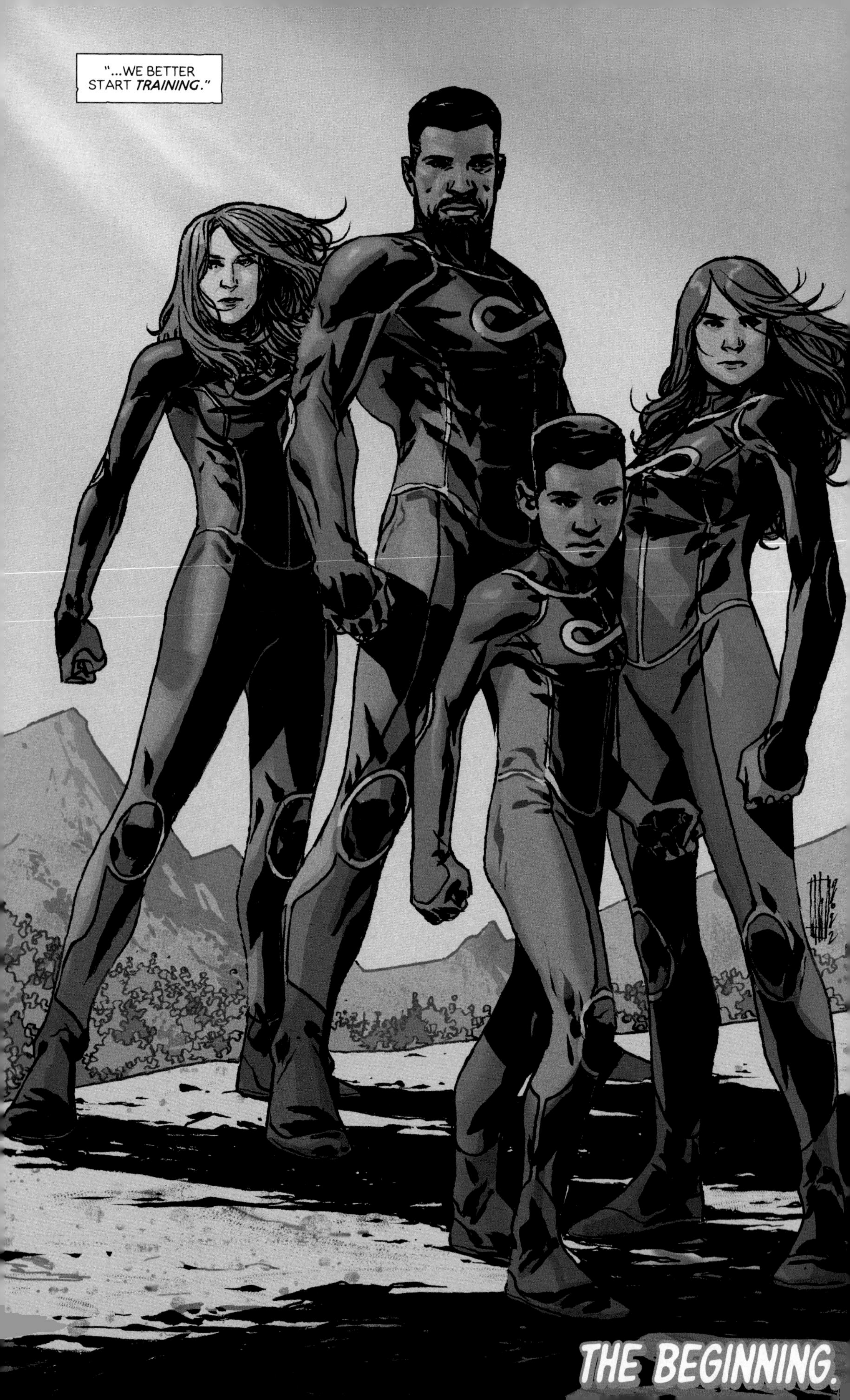
"...WE BETTER START *TRAINING*."
THE BEGINNING.

Issue #1 variant by
Mike Deodato Jr.
and Lee Loughridge

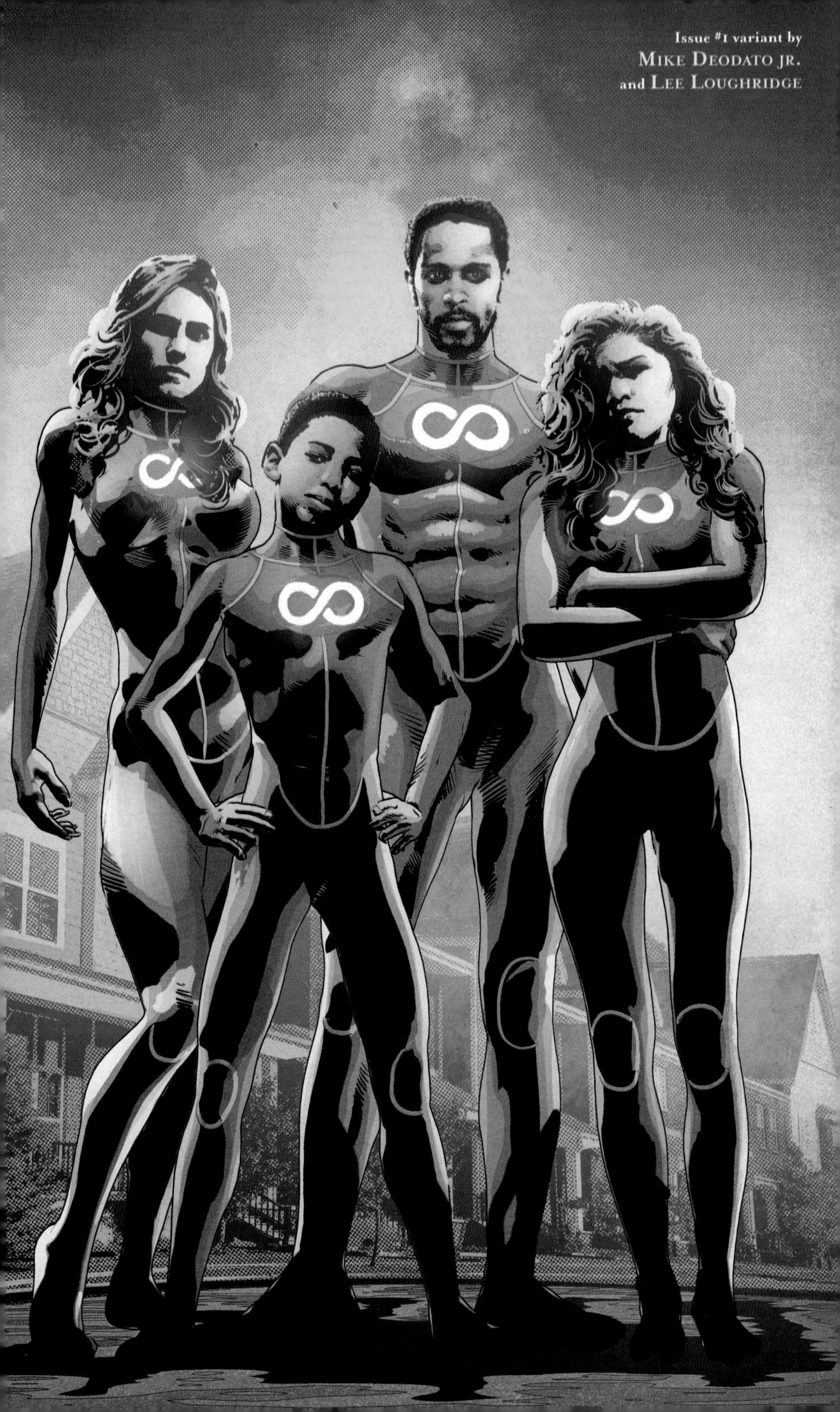

Don't even try to keep up with the creators of...

the Joneses

BY MICHAEL MORECI

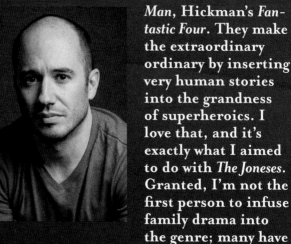

I don't write superhero comics. I know—it's a weird thing for me to say. We are, after all, in the backmatter of a superhero comic that I both wrote and co-created. Not only that, but this is the comics medium—a medium, by and large, dominated by superhero mythos—and I've been a comics writer for many years. Now, there are many reasons why I haven't journeyed into the capes genre, but paramount amongst them is, creatively, I haven't felt compelled …

…until I conceived *The Joneses*.

All my life, I've been drawn to superhero comics that intellectually and emotionally deal with life as we know it: *Astro City, Miracle*

Man, Hickman's *Fantastic Four*. They make the extraordinary ordinary by inserting very human stories into the grandness of superheroics. I love that, and it's exactly what I aimed to do with *The Joneses*. Granted, I'm not the first person to infuse family drama into the genre; many have done it before, though I'd argue *The Joneses* is different.

The Joneses is about being a family—a mother, father, son, daughter, husband, wife—right here, right now. We're living in distressing times, to say the least. No matter where you stand politically, our country, our world, is overwhelmed with strife everywhere you look. We're dealing with a pandemic we're dealing with social media, we're dealing with so many things, and it's becoming harder and harder for a family—a simple unit of people, bound together by blood and by love—to keep their hold on one another.

I used the word "extraordinary" above to describe what superheroes are. In this comic, what's extraordinary is the world they're living in—and not, necessarily, in a good way. The people—the Jones family at the heart of this story—are ordinary, despite their powers. They're me, they're you, they're all of us.

This is their story. Ordinary people in an extraordinary world, trying to keep their lives, and their love, strong despite the obstacles that come their way. ∞

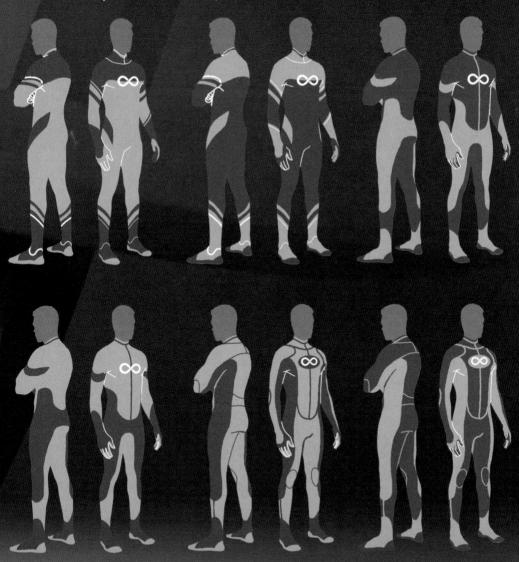

The Joneses suit designs by ALESSANDRO VITTI

Character Designs

BY ALESSANDRO VITTI

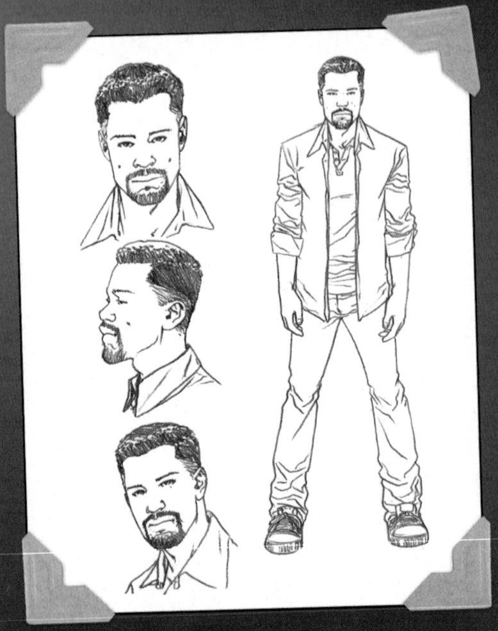

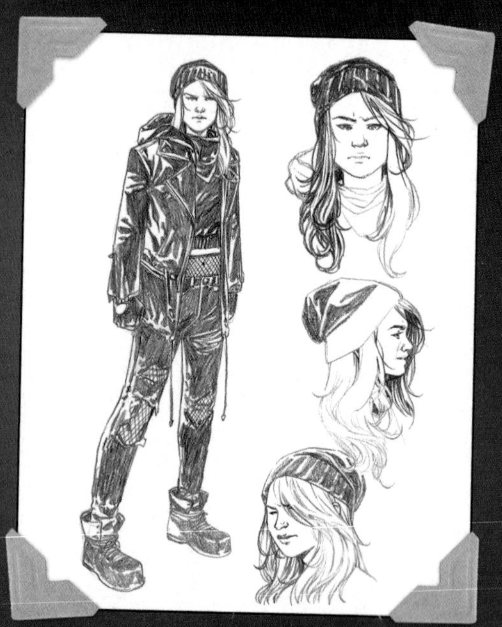

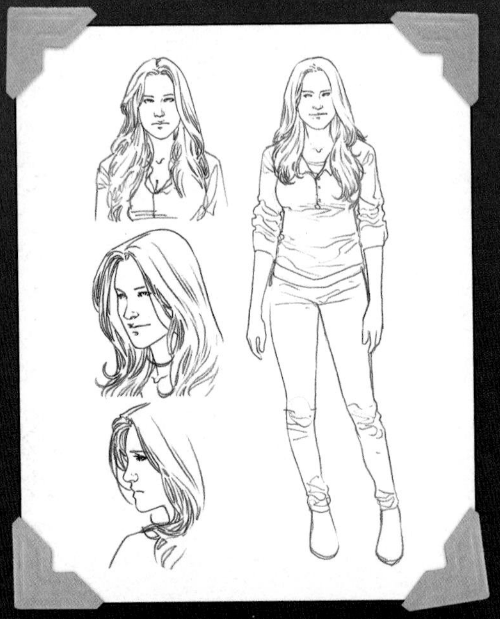

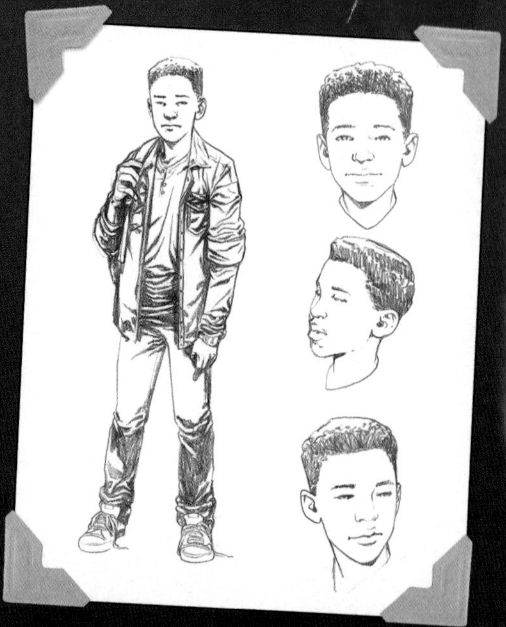

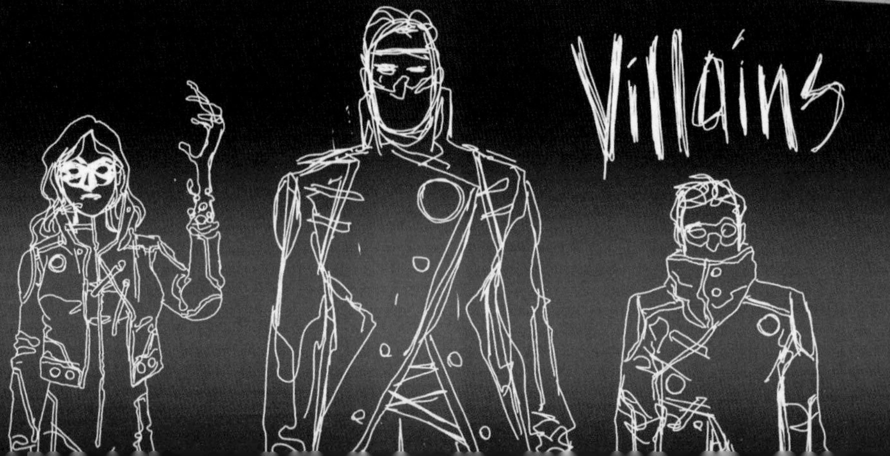
Villains